APPLIED PROBLEMS
IN MEMORY

APPLIED PROBLEMS IN MEMORY

Edited by

M. M. GRUNEBERG

Department of Psychology,
University College of Swansea,
University of Wales,
Swansea, UK

AND

P. E. MORRIS

Department of Psychology,
Fylde College,
University of Lancaster
Lancaster, UK

1979

ACADEMIC PRESS
London   New York   San Francisco
A Subsidiary of Harcourt Brace Jovanovich, Publishers

ACADEMIC PRESS INC. (LONDON) LTD.
24/28 Oval Road
London NW1

United States Edition published by
ACADEMIC PRESS INC.
111 Fifth Avenue
New York, New York 10003

Copyright © 1979 by
ACADEMIC PRESS INC. (LONDON) LTD.

British Library Cataloguing in Publication Data

Applied problems in memory.
  1. Memory
  I. Gruneberg, Michael M
  II. Morris, Peter E
  153.1'2   BF371   79–50522

  ISBN 0–12–305150–9

Printed and bound in Great Britain
by W & J Mackay Limited, Chatham

Contributors

J. ANNETT *Department of Psychology, University of Warwick, Coventry CV4 7AL, UK*

R. BULL *Department of Psychology, North East London Polytechnic, The Mills, Abbey Lane, London E15 2RP, UK*

S. J. CECI *Department of Psychology, University of North Dakota, Grand Falls, North Dakota 58201, USA*

B. CLIFFORD *Department of Psychology, North East London Polytechnic, The Mills, Abbey Lane, London E15 2RP, UK*

M. J. A. HOWE *Department of Psychology, University of Exeter, Washington Singer Laboratories, Prince of Wales Road, Exeter EX4 4QG, UK*

I. M. L. HUNTER *Department of Psychology, University of Keele, Keele ST5 5BG, UK*

D. M. JONES *Department of Applied Psychology, University of Wales Institute of Science and Technology, Llwyn-y-Grant, Penylan, Cardiff CF3 7UX, UK*

J. C. MARSHALL *Interfakultaire Werkgroep, Taal-en Spraakgedrag, Erasmuslaan 40, Nijmegen, The Netherlands*

E. MILLER *Department of Clinical Psychology, Addenbrooke's Hospital, 2 Bene't Place, Lensfield Road, Cambridge CB2 1EL, UK*

P. E. MORRIS *Department of Psychology, University of Lancaster, Fylde College, Lancaster LA1 4YF, UK*

G. UNDERWOOD *Department of Psychology, University of Nottingham, Nottingham NG7 2RD, UK*

Preface

The last twenty years have seen a considerable increase in investigations into theoretical aspects of memory, and many advances in our understanding of memory processes have undoubtedly resulted (see, e.g. Gruneberg and Morris, 1978). It can be reasonably claimed, however, that fewer workers have examined ways in which problems of practical significance in the field of memory can be resolved. Recently there have been signs that this state of affairs is about to change, as evidenced, for example, by the large number of psychologists who presented papers at the International Conference on Practical Aspects of Memory, held in Cardiff, last year (see Gruneberg *et al.* 1978). The conference demonstrated clearly the vast array of practical problems of memory to which the psychologist could usefully address himself, from the more obvious improvements in techniques for better remembering (mnemonic aids) to less "obvious" areas such as those of reading, memory in the aged, stress and so on.

This book seeks to examine applications of memory research in greater depth, by bringing together contributions from eminent workers in a number of important areas. An understanding of how memory is impaired under stress, for example, is of critical importance in training divers or airline pilots. An understanding of how memory deteriorates with age may enable an elderly person to be taught to cope with his home environment rather than having to be moved to an institution. An understanding of the memory accuracy of eyewitnesses may help to improve the probability of the guilty being convicted and the innocent going free. These and other important topics of practical application are considered in this volume.

That the book is focused on practical applications, should not, of course, be taken to indicate that a division can conveniently be made between the practical and the applied. Whilst it is undoubtedly true that some problems can usefully be investigated in an atheoretical context, it is also self-evident that a theoretical context is useful as a means of furthering understanding of practical problems. Indeed the hope is not only that theoretical understanding will further applied research, but that real life problems will provide insights of theoretical relevance.

In Chapter 1, Ian Hunter considers the role memory plays in the real world. He examines a wide range of situations where memory is important and illustrates the interdependence of memory devices and the everyday pursuits which they serve. Professor Hunter examines not only memory in the Western World, but also the importance of memory in primitive cultures.

Chapter 2, by Peter Morris reviews strategies that are known to aid learning and recall and highlights those aspects of memory for which few, if any, strategies have yet been developed. Their application in an educational setting is considered. In Chapter 3, Michael Howe and Stephen Ceci also discuss the educational implications of memory research. In particular they examine children's memory, illustrating the extent to which children's recall depends upon their knowledge, and their use of appropriate strategies. The extent to which such strategies may be taught is also considered. Another topic relevant to education is discussed in Chapter 4 by Geoffrey Underwood when he reviews memory and the reading processes. Memory research here is of practical significance in, for example, an evaluation of teaching schemes and in overcoming problems of slow readers.

In Chapter 5, Edgar Miller discusses the evidence for decline in memory with ageing and considers ways of minimizing any loss. One suggestion of major practical significance is that by utilizing cues familiar to the older person, and retraining basic skills, it might sometimes be possible to leave older people in their own homes, rather than place them in strange institutional environments, where the difficulties experienced in learning new materials may result in a rapid decline in social activity.

Factors influencing the reliability of eyewitnesses are reviewed by Ray Bull and Brian Clifford in Chapter 6. Often juries have to make judgements about the reliability of witnesses' memories, over and above that of judgements of honesty, and research in this area is considered. While research continues to show the frequent inaccuracy of witnesses, Bull and Clifford suggest ways, such as a change in the identification parade procedure, which may improve performance. Chapter 7, by Dylan Jones is concerned with memory in stressful conditions, which include not only disasters and battles but also noisy, overheated factories. His review indicates that under stress even memory for well-rehearsed procedures can fail, and suggests utilizing past habits of behaviour in procedures which take place under stress. In Chapter 8 John Annett considers the extent to which skills will be lost if they are not employed for some time. Findings tend to confirm that skills involving perceptual-motor tasks are easily retrieved after long periods, whereas tasks requiring memory for procedures of facts are less well retained. The chapter reviews the types of training which can affect the efficiency of a skill. Chapter 9 by John Marshall, deals with an aspect of memory disorder, language and memory.

Given the relative lack of focus on applications of memory, we feel that this book covers an impressive range of problems in which psychologists have recently been successfully engaged. Of course many problems remain unanswered and many areas deserve the cliché "more research is needed". It is our hope, however, that many of those reading this book will be struck by the intrinsic interest and importance of the topics covered, and will feel drawn to make their own contribution to the field.

May, 1979   *Michael M. Gruneberg*
                                                                        Peter E. Morris

Contents

Contents

Contents

1. Memory in Everyday Life

I. M. L. HUNTER

Department of Psychology,
University of Keele, UK

In his television series "The Ascent of Man", Bronowski (1973) includes a short length of film about making a Japanese sword. We see a master-craftsman working in the precincts of a Temple and fashioning a sword by a sequence of operations, every one of which is accompanied by ceremonial ritual. The ritual is governing the process of manufacture, ensuring that each stage is carried out correctly and at the right time. The ritual is, furthermore, the means by which the process has been handed down from generation to generation for more than a thousand years.

> The making of the sword, like all ancient metallurgy, is surrounded with ritual, and that is for a clear reason. When you have no written language, when you have nothing that can be called a chemical formula, then you must have a precise ceremonial which fixes the sequence of operations so that they are exact and memorable. (Bronowski, 1973, p. 131.)

However, there is more. As we watch the film, we realize that the film itself is also a record of the process of manufacture. Film, written language, ritual ceremony—each is, in its own way, a means of preserving and making accessible information about the manufacture of a Japanese sword.

The film raises two important aspects of memory and illustrates a working hypothesis which is central to this chapter. The first aspect concerns memory, the storage and appropriate retrieval of information, viewed as a goal in its own right. The point here is that this goal may be served by a great diversity of means or, as I shall call them, "memory-aiding devices". Some devices reside entirely in the head while others involve, to a greater or lesser extent, external supports such as social ritual or the written or taped or computerized records which loom so large in contemporary societies.

The second aspect concerns memory viewed as a resource which serves everyday pursuits. The sword-maker who is equipped with his memory-aiding ritual is a better craftsman than one without. For the same reason, a calculating machine with a "memory" is a more powerful problem-solving instrument than one without; and experienced surgeons are better operators than novices because of the greater armoury of knowledge and skill at their disposal. The point here is that memory serves an adaptive function which lies in the present.

The working hypothesis is that memory-aiding devices and everyday pursuits are interdependent. The manufacture of Japanese swords depends for its survival on the ritual, and the ritual depends for its survival on its usefulness in making swords. In brief, accomplishments of memory have their uses, and their uses serve to sustain and shape them. This hypothesis takes a stance which is broadly biological, evolutionary, historical and developmental: it is concerned with means and ends: it considers individual people and also communities of people. It generates four main deductions as follows. Given the prevalence of certain memory-aiding devices, there will exist everyday pursuits which they adaptively serve. Given the prevalence of certain everyday pursuits, there will exist memory-aiding devices which adaptively sustain them. When new pursuits arise, their development and survival will depend on the corresponding development of new memory-aiding devices. Lastly, when new memory-aiding devices arise, they will survive and develop only if uses are found for them; likewise, old memory-aiding devices will drop out when they cease to be useful.

The aim of this chapter will be, quite simply, to put some flesh on the working hypothesis which has just been sketched. In pursuing this aim, I shall not attempt the impossible task of treating exhaustively all the myriad interdependences which hold between memory and the great variety of everyday lives which people lead. Nor shall I attempt to cite all the contemporary psychological literature which illumines such interdependences. Indeed, I shall try to widen the scope of the literature by deliberately following lines of inquiry in which most present-day psychologists are not actively interested. In the first section, I shall pursue three questions. (1) By what means do people, in different parts of the world, hold in their head the number of days in each month of the year? (2) What are the broad implications of the widespread use of written, and related, records as memory-aiding devices? (3) What does numerical calculation require of memory, and by what means do people meet these requirements? In the second section, I shall consider the interplay between memory and life in non-literate cultures.

I. Memory and Its Uses

The Days of the Month

If I am asked how many days are in any particular month, say August, I can give the answer by looking up a printed calendar. Alternatively, I can subvocally recite part of a verse which, in full, runs as follows:

> Thirty days hath September,
> April, June, and November.
> All the rest have thirty-one
> Excepting February alone,
> Which has twenty-eight days clear
> And twenty-nine in each leap year.

I acquired this jingle in early childhood, and often call upon its help. My own experience with it is shared by many other people. A few people can say instantly how many days are in a particular month. A few cannot say at all without consulting a calendar. However, most people seem to follow my own procedure, although there are minor variations in the verse used.

Why should the verse be so widely known? Most of us find it useful to have available, in our head, the number of days in each month. The difficulty is that the information is unruly: the number of days varies irregularly from month to month. What the verse does is to regroup the information, invest it with rhyme and rhythm, and thereby cast the whole into a more easily rememberable form. In the light of our working hypothesis, we can say that the verse is widely current because it is a memory-aid of practical value. To draw the parallel between the evolution of organic forms and of mental forms, the verse is a mental form which has adaptive value and is thereby fit for survival. According to our hypothesis, we should further expect to find that, in any part of the world where everyday life makes it useful to have calendar information readily available, then that information should be organized into a rememberable form of some kind. Is this the case? I have, as opportunity allowed, asked people of various nationalities how they hold calendar information in their head. My inquiries do not constitute a systematic survey, but they reveal some relevant facts.

In Italy, France and the Netherlands there is indeed a rhyme which is closely similar in form and function to the English verse. However in many parts of the world such a verse is unknown and, in its place, there is a memory-aid involving knuckle counting. The knuckle device is used in Greece, Greek Cyprus, Finland, Russia, China, Tibet and most of South America. Clench your fist and count off the months on the knuckles and hollows alternately. January falls on a knuckle, so it is a long month; February falls on a hollow, so it is short; March falls on a knuckle, and so on. When you have located July on a knuckle, you have run out of knuckles, so start again on any convenient knuckle to give August, a long month, then September, which is short, and so on. Here is a memory-aid which applies the tally principle to parts of the body that happen to be conveniently available and suitably arranged.

In other parts of the world, neither the verse nor the knuckle-tally is used. Iranians, for example, have no need of either because their calendar is more orderly than ours. Each of the first six months has 31 days; each of the next five has 30; and the last has 29 except on every fourth year when it has 30. Such a regular arrangement scarcely calls for additional memory-aiding devices. In Thailand, the calendar is the same as ours but the name of each month contains, in the stem, the appropriate sign of the zodiac; and the suffix varies systematically with the number of days. Here in sequence are the names of the months as transliterated into English. Magarakom, Kumpapan, Minakom, Mesayon, Pruspakom, Mitunayon, Karakadakom, Singhakom, Kanyayon, Tulakom, Prusjikayon and Tanvakom. The name of each month thus contains within itself information about its length in days. Extra memory-aids are not needed. My sampling of the international evidence, then, supports the empirical generalization that: whenever a community of people have common need to hold calendar information in their head, then there is, in the community, some commonly occurring way of casting that information into rememberable form.

Memory and Literacy

In literate cultures, the most common type of memory-aiding device is the written record. People use shopping lists and commit to writing things they want to remember, such as appointments, addresses and telephone numbers. Students write notes while listening to lectures or while reading books. Shopkeepers, accountants and medical practitioners engage daily in making and arranging written records with a view to retrieving, by their help, information which will be needed for some future purpose. Busy professional people keep appointments diaries and filing cabinets, and accept that their colleagues are, like themselves, able to retrieve lots of information which they do not carry in their heads. Furthermore, what is true of written records is also true of more recently developed recording devices such as film, audiotape, videotape and computer records.

The use of written records as memory-aids is so commonplace that it is easy to overlook its implications for the kind of life we lead. Yet the repercussions are immense, and for four main reasons. First, on the individual level, the memos we write for our future use increase vastly the amount of stored information which we can retrieve with accuracy; we can thus deal with a wider and more complex range of present problems than we could readily face in the absence of our memos. Secondly, and still on the individual level, our written records, because they are fixed, can be inspected back and forth. We can cross-refer at leisure among different parts of the records and so draw out subtle implications and detect fine inconsistencies. When we try to work in a similar manner on information which we hold entirely in our head, especially if it is detailed and none too securely held, such selective retrieval and cross-comparisons are more of a strain and we are likely to lose track of what we are about. Thirdly, on an interpersonal level, the use of written records vastly augments what might be called the communal memory store. Such a store, as exemplified by a library or by the files of an office, can be added to and drawn from by more than one person, and by more than one generation of people.

The implications of these three kinds of memory augmentation could be elaborated at length. However, most people who live in a literate culture will readily appreciate some of their practical consequences for the everyday life of, for example, the scholar, committee person, lawyer and insurance claimant. For an extended discussion of some of the less obvious, but nevertheless far-reaching effects of literacy, see Goody (1977) who argues convincingly that modern scientific knowledge is essentially reliant on the memory-aids provided by literacy.

The fourth repercussion of written records is that they require, as a prerequisite, skills of literacy. We need to be able to read and write, classify records, arrange them and index them for retrieval purposes, and so on. In short, we need skill in dealing with information which is coded into written notation, and the acquisition of such "decontextualized" skills raises, in its turn, a host of educational problems (see Atkinson *et al.*, 1977; Bruner, 1972; Donaldson, 1978). Skills of literacy are, of course, multi-purpose, and memory is not the only function they serve. Nevertheless, throughout history, the advantages of augmented memory have been a main driving force in the development of literacy. In any community, the widespread incidence of literacy makes it possible for the community to extend enormously the amount of detailed information which it can register, store and retrieve by means of written records. This, in turn, increases the scope, complexity and precision of the enterprises that can be successfully coordinated by the community. And in turn, the continuing feasability of these enterprises requires the community to maintain an appropriate level of literacy.

To be specific, it is only in literate culture that it is possible to buy a packet of frozen vegetables from a supermarket. The availability of such a commodity depends on many things including a vast network of invoicing, stock control, transport arrangements, science-based technology, allocation of financial resources; in short, on a large number of activities which necessarily involve the use of written records. Without literacy, and the record-keeping it makes possible, the pack of frozen vegetables would cease to be available in the local supermarket. This nicely illustrates, at the social level, the interdependence between memory and everyday life. The mode of life makes demands on the kind of information which must be stored and retrieved; conversely, what the society is able to store and retrieve affects the mode of life that the society can sustain. By the same token, the large-scale, interlocking administrative structure of the modern state would be impossible without written records, and if widespread literacy were to disappear, so too would the modern state.

Numerical Calculation

Ask a wide cross-section of people to multiply 123 by 456, and watch how they get the answer. They may vary greatly in how they work, e.g. mentally, by paper and pencil, by abacus, logarithms, slide rule, calculating machine; and within each way, there may be various detailed routes. However, all people go through a sequence of inspecting the problem, deciding a method of calculation, and implementing the method step-by-step until the answer is reached. All people, also, rely heavily on memory, which contributes in three distinguishable ways. First, long-term memory (LTM) is used to furnish the chosen method of calculation. Secondly, LTM is used to provide a fund of numerical equivalents, e.g. that $6 \times 3 = 18$, that $6 \times 2 = 12$, that $5 + 3 = 8$. These equivalents are the basic building blocks, or constituent steps, of the calculation.

Thirdly, people use what might be called working or temporary or track-keeping memory. They must keep track of their calculative route and not miss a step or lose direction. They must also carry out a shifting succession of operations concerned with short-term registration, retention and retrieval of numerical data. At any moment, they may be working out the answer to a sub-problem while holding in temporary store the answer to a preceding sub-problem; at the next moment, they are retrieving that earlier answer to combine it with the newly-got answer. It is this track-keeping aspect which is the greatest burden in mental calculation, and which leads people to seek help from external memory-aiding devices. It is the aspect which compels people, who know the product of 6 and 6, to reach for paper and pencil when asked to multiply 666 by 666.

Calculation, then requires massive contributions from memory, both long-term and short-term. The history of calculation throughout the centuries (see Menninger, 1969) shows persisting efforts to meet these memory requirements by inventing forms of externalized memory. An early memory-aid was the counting-board or counting-frame on which pebbles or beads were placed and physically moved around: the word "calculate" comes from the Latin *calculus*, meaning "a small stone". A later aid was the invention of a written notation for numbers, the one we use today, which makes it possible to calculate by writing. These two devices help mainly with the track-keeping aspect. Other forms of external memory help mainly by providing an augmented store of equivalents, e.g. ready-reckoners and multiplication tables. Yet other devices help mainly by providing short-cut methods, e.g. logarithms. And present-day electric calculating machines enable people to relegate most, but not all, calculative effort to a device which provides an externalized store of equivalents and short-cuts and an externalized means of keeping track of the calculation in progress. It is, then, no exaggeration to say that advances in the history of calculation have, to a very large extent, been advances in ways of externalizing the heavy memory requirements of the process.

Mental calculation

Mental calculators clearly do not use external memory-aids. So how do they contrive to work so well and so rapidly? Broadly, the answer again concerns memory. They shift the burden of effort away from calculation as such onto LTM. Virtuoso mental calculators vary greatly, one from another, but their calculative feats always rest on their knowledge of numerical equivalents, calculative procedures and shortcut methods. Their fund of knowledge is vastly greater than normal; it is the product of years of experience, and is drawn upon with speed and accuracy.

Consider, for example, that you can multiply by 25 by dividing by 4 and multiplying by 100. What is 25 times 16? The answer, 400, comes so rapidly as to seem miraculous to anyone unfamiliar with the short-cut. Now there is literally no end to the numerical equivalents, inter-relationships and shortcuts which may be discovered. When a sizeable repertoire of these is held in memory and deployed in calculation, the resulting feats can be astonishing. Mental calculators of high calibre skilfully deploy extensive, recondite knowledge which is largely unknown to, and unsuspected by, most people, and which has usually been discovered by the calculators themselves.

In shifting the burden of calculation onto LTM, mental calculators vividly exemplify the trade-off relationship between LTM and the processing of data (see Lindsay and Norman, 1977, pp. 595–599). To illustrate, A. C. Aitken (Hunter, 1962) was asked to multiply 123 by 456. He gave the answer after a pause of two seconds, then commented.

> I see at once that 123 times 45 is 5535, and that 123 times 6 is 738. I hardly have to think. Then 55 350 plus 738 gives 56 088. Even at the moment of registering 56 088 I have checked it by dividing by 8, so 7011, and this by 9 gives 779. I recognize 779 as 41 by 19. And 41 by 3 is 123, while 19 by 24 is 456. A check you see, and it passes by in about one second.

This example shows how an exceptionally skilled mental calculator, as compared with the rest of us, needs to do less actual calculation, thanks to his resources of LTM. The efforts which have gone into building these resources now save calculative effort, just as memorizing a multiplication table saves later calculative labour.

The use of LTM to lighten the task of calculation is nicely illustrated by Devi (1977). Shakuntala Devi is an Indian with considerable skill in mental calculation and her book aims to show readers how to accomplish various kinds of mental calculation. One chapter, for example, shows how to calculate the day of the week on which any given date fell or will fall. The chapter starts by saying that, to do this mentally, you first need to commit to memory four short tables of data. Most other chapters start likewise: memorize some set of data and it will serve as a resource to lighten the labour of calculation.

Leaving aside fine details, which are discussed by Hunter (1962, 1977c), the key point about skilled mental calculators is that they use a fund of numerical and calculative knowledge which is both vast and readily accessible. It is this fund which enables them: to inspect a problem and select an appropriately useable method of calculation; to implement their chosen method in a succession of large steps, each of which is taken automatically although it would put us to some difficulty; to progress from one step to the next with a speed and an ease that does not disrupt track-keeping; and to deploy various unconventional methods which minimize the amount of numerical detail that needs to be held temporarily in mind at any one time, i.e. in the words of G. P. Bidder, a notable mental calculator, "to bring all calculations, as far as may be practicable, into one result, and to have that one result alone, at a time, registered upon the mind".

The acquisition of this serviceable fund involves, of course, extensive experience and practice. However, the biographies of mental calculators make clear that this does not greatly involve a bleak process of memorization for its own sake. Rather, the fund is built up, piece by piece, as a byproduct of the individual's intense interest in numbers and in calculation. The fund grows because of its usefulness in pursuits which interest the individual. This point is important throughout the study of memory at large and is much emphasized by Soviet students of memory (see Smirnov, 1973 and Yendovitskaya, 1971) although often lost sight of by Western psychologists.

The above point is illustrated by a comment of A. C. Aitken concerning his long-standing interest in numbers:

> It is a good exercise to ask oneself the question: what can be said about this number? Where does it occur in mathematics, and in what context? What properties has it? For instance, is it a prime of the form 4n + 1, and so expressible as the sum of two squares in one way only? Is it the numerator of a Bernoullian number, or one occurring in some continued fraction? And so on. Sometimes a number has almost no properties at all, like 811, and sometimes a number, like 41, is deeply involved in many theorems that you know.

The outcome of such persistent questioning and experience with calculation is a fund of knowledge which enables Aitken to calculate with economy of effort. For example, after calculating the decimal equivalent of the fraction 1/851, he remarks:

> The instant observation was that 851 is 23 times 37. I use this fact as follows. 1/37 is 0·027027027 and so on repeated. This I divide mentally by 23. 23 into 0·027 is 0·001 with remainder 4. In a flash I can get that 23 into 4027 is 175 with remainder 2. And into 2027 is 88 with remainder 3. And into 3027 is 131 with remainder 14. And even into 14027 is 609 with remainder 20. And so on like that. Also, before I even start this, I know that there is a recurring period of sixty-six places.

Calculating by Japanese abacus

The Japanese abacus or *soroban* is basically an oblong wooden frame holding a number of parallel rods on which wooden beads slide up and down (see Kojima, 1954, for details). It enables people to calculate at astonishing speed. In modern Japan, its use is commercially important, like typewriting or shorthand. Most children learn its use from the age of about eight years, and more than two million Japanese take proficiency tests in abacus skill. There are qualifying exams for ten grades of skill and, after that, for ten levels of master grade up to grand master.

Top-grade abacus operators compete well with the best operators of electric calculating machines. In adding or subtracting numbers, no matter how many, the abacus gets the answer in about half the time needed by the machine. (If devotees of computers are sceptical, let them note that, with the abacus, "entry" and "operate" are done simultaneously by a single, albeit intricate, movement of the fingers.) In multiplying or dividing, the abacus is faster when the given problem contains not more than about ten digits in all, e.g. multiply a five-digit number by another five-digit number. With larger multiplications and divisions the machine is faster, and the larger the problem the greater its lead over the abacus.

As compared with the machine, one of the chief disadvantages of the abacus is that its mastery needs more time and practice. To become top-grade, you need to put in something like one hour of daily practice for two years. As with any complex accomplishment, such as chess or violin playing, it also seems that you are best to start young and have a good teacher: examiners claim that abacus operators never pass the top-grade exam if they take up their studies after they are out of their teens. Long practice is needed because speed of operation comes, as in mental calculation, through building up in LTM a large repertoire of readily available numerical equivalents which, in this case, involve progressively more complex and intricate patterns of finger movements.

Hatano *et al.* (1977) investigated experimentally the calculative performances of ten young women, aged 16 to 18 years, who were reasonably expert abacus operators. The investigations were suggested by two everyday observations. The first is that experts may dispense with the abacus and work by means of a merely imagined abacus, sometimes moving their fingers as though moving actual beads. These finger movements seem analagous to lip movements during silent reading and, like them, they drop out as the operator becomes more skilled. Grand masters of the abacus usually work mentally without any finger movements and their speed of working seems actually to improve as a consequence. Accordingly subjects were asked to calculate using only a mental representation of an abacus. The subjects complied without loss of speed, and only the less proficient operators showed finger movements. All subjects were then asked to keep their fingers motionless and, in other tests, to tap rhythmically on the table with one hand. The more expert operators were unaffected by these restrictions, but the mental working of the less expert was impaired.

The second everyday observation is that abacus experts may converse during calculation. This suggests that, as in driving a car, abacus calculation makes little demand on attention and, in particular, deploys little in the way of linguistic processes. Accordingly, while using the actual abacus, subjects were asked to deal, in mid-calculation, with an extra task, i.e. a simple question which was presented orally and had to be answered orally. Subjects dealt with these questions, without impairment of calculation, provided they were non-numerical, e.g. "What is your name?", "What is the highest mountain in Japan?", "What is the capital of England?" However, numerical questions interfered with calculation, e.g. "What is 3 plus 8?", "What is 72 divided by 6?".

To conclude this section on calculation, let us highlight four general points. First, there is more than one way of calculating, each with its own distinctive strengths and weaknesses. Secondly, the ways in which people calculate depend partly on the historical and cultural context in which they live: consider that most Westerners have never even seen the skilful use of the abacus. Thirdly, the way in which people organize and develop calculative skill depends partly on the human constitution, which seems to be much the same the world over. Fourthly, calculation, by whatever means, requires heavy contributions from memory, both long-term and short-term; and different calculative systems are distinctive, one from another, largely because of the ways in which they meet these memory requirements.

II. Memory in Non-Literate Cultures

Cultural Transmission

In non-literate cultures, there are, of course, no written records to function as memory-aiding devices. Practical knowledge is used "in context", is not translated into decontextualized written form, and is passed from one individual to another in a context of shared activities and oral communication. Thus, children acquire practical knowledge of, say, cookery by being in the company of adults who are preparing and cooking food, and by gradually playing a more active role in the process. Likewise with hunting, farming, boating and social customs. When children grow up, their offspring acquire practical knowledge in the same way. In this fashion, practical knowledge is transmitted through the generations. So long as the context in which the knowledge is applied remains stable, the knowledge itself can remain stable across generations. However, if the context alters, the knowledge undergoes adaptive changes.

Verbal knowledge concerning myths and legends is transmitted orally through, as it were, a long chain of conversations between members of the culture. Much of this verbal knowledge might strike outsiders as merely quaint. However, it has, no less than practical knowledge, adaptive significance for everyday life. Myths and legends serve to make the world intelligible, and to explain and to prescribe the conduct of life and social relations; they act, in part, as a means whereby people hold customs and beliefs in memory. As with practical knowledge, the real-life significance of oral tradition introduces, into its transmission, pressures towards both stability and change.

Stability in oral tradition

The stable transmission of oral tradition is helped by various memory-aiding devices. Perhaps the most common of these is verse, that is, speech which is cast into a metrical pattern of syllables, long or short, stressed or unstressed. Verse, which may involve rhyme or may not, is often sung and is often accompanied by musical instruments. Verse is an effective memory-aid because the rhythmic pattern guides and constrains the moment-by-moment choice of words. Thus, in listening to well-constructed verse, we are able to form, at each moment, fairly strong expectations about the kind of thing we will hear next; this makes it easier to comprehend what comes. Likewise in recalling such verse, the framework provides strong retrieval cues for what should come next; this helps recall performance. In brief, well-structured verse provides a context, or frame of reference, which supports and facilitates both our comprehension and our remembering of the verse's constituent parts. No wonder that non-literate people seem, without exception, to cast their most important legends, myths and rituals into the form of songs and verses.

Verse is not, however, the only device which helps the stable transmission of oral culture. Consider four other commonly occurring types of memory aid. First, drum rhythms,

> Throughout Africa drum rhythms are used as a mnemonic aid. Words and phrases can be transposed into the drum code in all languages in which the height of the tone plays a phonological role. It is easier to remember these rhythms than the phrases themselves from which the tonal melody derives. In West Africa, the history of the royal house of

Dagomba, as well as that of the Akan States, is partially preserved by means of the drum code. (Vansina, 1973, p. 39.)

Secondly, formalized recital. Recital of the tradition may be done under ceremonial circumstances which are, in various ways, conducive to accurate rendering. Often the recital is performed by a group of people in unison. This effectively controls the frequency with which the tradition is repeated or rehearsed. For the less experienced performers, it also provides feedback on the correctness of their recital, and therefore a learning opportunity. Over the generations, group recital sustains stable transmission despite the gradual replacement of older by younger performers.

Thirdly, geographical locations. Legends and myths are often attached to particular localities, natural or man-made. To illustrate, present-day Aborigines, who live in the Western Desert region of Australia, still retain myths, "Dreamings", which relate to the terrain. The landscape is criss-crossed with the meandering tracks of ancestral beings. Thus, the geography is a supporting frame of reference for the myths. Reciprocally, the myths furnish the geography with human significance and, furthermore, are useful as a framework for route finding and spatial orientation. There are attested cases of Aborigines who have moved to parts of the country where they have never been before and have been able to keep their bearings, and even know the location of waterholes, because they know the stories told about the country (see Lewis, 1976).

Fourthly, specialized remembrancers. Certain individuals have special responsibility for remembering particular parts of the oral tradition, and for teaching their knowledge to their eventual successors.

In Rwanda, genealogists, memorialists, rhapsodists, and *abiiru* were each responsible for the faithful preservation of a certain category of traditions. The task of the genealogists, *abacurabwenge*, was to remember the lists of kings and queenmothers; that of the memorialists, *abateekerezi*, to remember the most important events of the various reigns; the rhapsodists, *abasizi*, preserved the panegyrics on the kings; and lastly the *abiiru* preserved the secrets of the dynasty. (Vansina, 1973, p. 32.)

Change in oral tradition

Pressures towards alteration are illustrated by two examples given by Goody and Watt (1968). First, the state of Gonja in northern Ghana is divided into several chiefdoms, and the custom is that certain of these provide in turn the ruler of the whole state. When asked to explain the custom, the Gonja refer to a legend which tells how a certain man arrived and founded the state, establishing himself as chief and his sons as divisional rulers, and how, when he died, his sons succeeded to the paramountcy in turn. The legend was first written down at the turn of this century and, at that time, the founder was said to have had seven sons. This number corresponded to the number of territorial rulers who were eligible for the paramountcy. However, at about that time, the number of such territories was reduced, for political reasons, to five. When the legend was recorded again, sixty years later, the founder was said to have had five sons, and no mention was made of the two divisions which had now vanished from the political map.

  The second example concerns the Tiv people of Nigeria. They give genealogies of their forebears, going back some twelve generations to a founding ancestor. The everyday significance of these genealogies is that they govern certain rights and obligations between one man and another. They are cited whenever such rights and duties come into dispute. And because of their social significance, these genealogies were written down by the early British administrators in Nigeria. Forty years later, these written pedigrees were the source of disagreement. The administrators regarded them as records of historical fact. The Tiv now claimed that they were incorrect. What neither party fully appreciated was that time inevitably brings about changes which require readjustments in the genealogies if they are to continue to carry out their function as memory-aids for present-day social relationships.

  Goody and Watt (1968) comment as follows.

> In drawing attention to the importance of these assimilating mechanisms in non-literate societies, we are denying neither the occurrence of social change nor yet the "survivals" which it leaves in its wake. Nor do we overlook the existence of mnemonic devices in oral cultures which offer some resistance to the interpretative process. Formalized patterns of speech, recital under ritual conditions, the use of drums and other musical instruments, the employment of professional remembrancers—all such factors may shield at least part of the content of memory from the transmuting influence of the immediate pressures of the present . . . (However) what the individual remembers tends to be what is of critical importance in his experience of the main social relationships. In each generation, therefore, the individual memory will mediate the cultural heritage in such a way that its new constituents will adjust to the old by the process of interpretation that Bartlett (1932) calls 'rationalizing' or the 'effort after meaning'; and whatever parts of it have ceased to be of contemporary relevance are likely to be eliminated by the process of forgetting. (pp. 30–31.)

Let us now pursue further two memory-aiding devices used in non-literate cultures. The first is verse, as exemplified in the singing of epic poetry. The second is the tally, as exemplified in the message sticks of Australian Aborigines.

The Singing of Epic Poetry

Homeric oral poetry

The use of verse as a memory-aiding device reaches its height in Homeric oral poetry. The "Iliad" and the "Odyssey" which the Greeks attributed to Homer, are the most grand and most widely known examples of oral epic poetry. The poems are in unrhymed hexameters and have existed in written form for two thousand years. However, they were not originally *written* for any audience of readers; rather, they were sung for an audience of listeners. They were first composed and sung, to the musical accompaniment of a stringed instrument, by a bard who lived around the eighth century B.C. in a non-literate culture. The poems owe nothing to literacy and their tight, intricate architecture is a direct consequence of their origins.

Scholarly analyses of Homeric poetry are provided by Bowra (1972), Kirk (1965), Lord (1960) and Parry (1971). Here, consider the barest outline of the poems' evolutionary background. The poems were composed within the context of a tradition of epic poetry which had been evolving for centuries and had built up, and refined, a great repertoire of ingredients, e.g. a cast of heroes and gods, a stock of phrases, a corpus of episodes and adventures, a store of themes, and a metre (the Greek hexameter) into which these ingredients could be fitted. This repertoire was extensive because for generation after generation individual singers had added a fresh ingredient here and another there; and it was suited to its expressive purpose because, over the generations, needless alternatives and clumsy components had been systematically if gradually discarded.

Such, then, was the tradition which a young singer encountered and assimilated, and in which he learned to work with greater or lesser fluency and skill. Such were the ingredients which a Homer had available and from which he synthesized supreme songs. In composing his epic, the skilful singer drew upon his fund of resources according to a firm but flexible set of guidelines. He worked, as Homeric scholars say, to a formulaic system, that is, a system of rules which govern the assembly of ingredients which are, themselves, finely tailored to the needs of the rule-system. Once mastered, such a system provides the poet with the means of remembering verses easily and of composing fresh lines with minimum effort. To illustrate, Homeric poetry makes extensive use of the "formula" which, in its technical sense, refers to a word or phrase which expresses a particular meaning in a set form for a particular metrical length. The standardized epithet is an example of a "formula".

> Epithets are standardized not only for people but also for many familiar objects, and once again they vary according to the portion of verse that it is desired to fill. If the idea "of a ship" has to be expressed in the latter part of a verse, the ship will be described as "equal", "curved around" or "dark prowed" simply according as the final 2, $2\frac{1}{2}$ or $3\frac{1}{4}$ feet have to be filled. If the case is changed then the epithet may have to be changed too, and νηὸς ἐίσης becomes νηὶ μελαίνη. That is not because ships in the dative are any blacker and less equal than those in the genitive, nor is it because a ship in a particular context is envisaged as black rather than equal: it is black simply and solely because after the word νηί and to fill the measure ◡–◡̲ we require an epithet of that value beginning with a consonant—since νηί ends in a vowel. The Greek for "equal" will not do; the Greek for "black" will. (Kirk, 1965, p. 8.)

Yugoslavian singers

Oral epic poetry is not confined to the Homeric songs and has existed in various languages at various times in various cultures, always as part of a tradition and always involving some formulaic system (see Chadwick and Chadwick, 1932, 1936, 1940 and also Bowra, 1952). Most of these traditions have now become extinct with the rise of literacy and the way of life it brings. However, in the 1930s, Milman Parry, the "Darwin of Homeric studies", made extensive investigations in Yugoslavia where the tradition was, at that time, still very much alive. He studied this living tradition both for its own sake and for the light it might cast on that older, but now dead, tradition from which the Homeric songs had sprung. Details of Parry's meticulous studies are given by Lord (1960) and Parry (1971) and tell us much about the role of memory in the singing of epic poetry. These details are the basis of the following brief account which is, for convenience, expressed in the present tense.

Epic poetry in Yugoslavia is oral and does not involve the use of written records in any way. It is the chief entertainment of the adult male population in the villages and small towns. It is sung on various occasions in private houses, coffee houses, taverns and at festivals. The singer accompanies himself on a stringed instrument and uses a metrical line of ten syllables. The song is typically a few hundred lines long but sometimes much longer, e.g. one of the longest fills 97 12-inch phonograph records, consists of 13 331 lines, and occupies a total singing time of between 16 and 17 hours. The singing of such songs is a formidable feat of memory but, significantly, not in the way we might at first suppose. If we were to witness such a singer, we might assume that he is engaged in an act of reproductive memory, that he has previously studied the poem and learned it by heart. We might compare his performance with that of a concert pianist who is playing a score which he has committed to memory. However, this is not at all what is going on.

To grasp what the singer is doing, we must firmly lay aside our familiar notion of a poem as something which exists in one definitively correct version and in a humanly decontextualized form. Such a notion comes from our literary background, and is entirely alien to the Yugo-slavian singer and his audience. Rather, we must focus on the singer who is, here and now, deploying his talent to tell a tale which will capture the interest of his listening audience, and do so against the background of various distractions and interruptions. What matters is the perfor-mance at this moment in time and in this place. What the singer is doing is improvising, albeit within the framework of a highly complex tradition.

The singer is drawing on his acquired fund of ingredients, and selecting and sequencing them according to intricate conventions. In this way he is singing the "true" tale, that is, the one which gives the essentials of the story; which remains within the tradition; which can, within limits, be expanded and contracted; and which requires no adherence to any notion of word-by-word "accuracy". In these respects, he resembles a skilled performer of jazz. Thus, from one singing to the next, the "same" song may vary considerably in length and detail; yet large parts may be nearly identical, not for the sake of "accuracy", but because the conventions which operate at correspond-ing moments in the tale can be met only by selecting one particular phrase.

The feat of memory lies, then, in the singer's having acquired a vast fund of ingredients and having mastered this fund to the point where he can draw flexibly upon it for the purposes of extempore composition. The most impressive aspect of his performance is his speed of composi-tion. He sings at the rate of from ten to twenty ten-syllable lines a minute. This speed is possible only because it involves a special techni-que of composition based on a fluently useable fund of knowledge which has been built up over a period of years. It is this fund which enables the skilful singer to please his listeners, who partly share the fund, and to listen to a new song and take it easily into his own repertoire. It is this fund which enables the singer to remember an especially finely-wrought song and repeat it almost verbatim.

In describing how a singer learns his art, Lord (1960) divides the process into three periods. First, the young boy listens while others sing. He thus becomes familiar with the heroes and their names, with faraway places, the customs of long ago, the rhythm of the singing, and the rhythm of the thoughts as they are expressed in song. The second period begins when the youth himself attempts to sing. He imitates some song he has heard and faces the problems of fitting the thoughts and their expression into a fairly rigid form. This requires long practice, sometimes in private and sometimes in the presence of an indulgent family or group of friends. The third period begins when the singer is competent to sing one song all the way through for a critical audience. This third period continues with the singer increasing the repertoire of songs he can sing, improving his singing of the songs he already knows, and acquiring greater competence in the artistry and technique of composition. In time and with experience and if circumstances are favourable, he may develop into an exceptionally able singer who stands, in relation to the tradition in which he works, as Homer stood in relation to that tradition of which he was both the product and the supreme exponent.

Australian Message Sticks

The word "tally" comes from the Latin *talea*, meaning "a rod, or stick, or cutting", and refers to the practice of notching a stick to keep track of events. In various forms, the tally has been used extensively as a memory-aiding device. For centuries the English treasury used notched sticks to keep official records of state finances. Ancient Peruvians achieved a similar purpose with their *quipu*, pieces of string in which knots were tied. The prayer bead of Mohammedans and the rosary beads of Roman Catholics use the tally principle. Further examples are given by Menninger (1969). Perhaps the most interesting use of the tally principle is the Australian message stick.

In 1889, A. W. Howitt reported how Australian Aborigines used, as a memory-aid, a piece of wood with incised markings. The Aborigines studied by Howitt lived in Eastern Australia and had no written language and very few material possessions. They lived in small nomadic groups which met occasionally to exchange news and to hold ceremonies which marked the main stages of their lives. From time to time, the older members of one group sent messages to the older members of another group, but the messages were carried by one of the young men, and this is where the message stick came in. The following account has been lightly edited for brevity from Howitt (1889, pp. 318–320).

This example comes from the Wotjoballuk tribe of the Wimmera River in Victoria. The particulars are obtained by enquiry from the old men of that tribe. Messages were sent by the old men by messengers whom they instructed, and to whom message sticks were given. Having consulted together, and having arrived at a determination, as for instance that some other part of the tribe should be summoned to meet with their part of it on some festive occasion, or for some other purpose, the principal man among them prepares a message stick by making certain notches upon it with a knife. In old times the marks were made with a mussel shell. The man who is to be charged with the message looks on while the headman makes the message stick (*galk*), and he thus learns the connection between the marks upon the stick and his message. A notch is made at one end to indicate the sender, and possibly notches also for those who join him in sending the message. A large notch is made on one edge for each tribal group which is invited to attend. If all the people are invited, the stick is notched on the edge from end to end. If part only are invited, then a portion only of the stick is notched. If very few are invited to meet, then a notch is made for each individual as he is named to the messenger.

The oldest man (Headman) having made such a message stick hands it to the old man nearest to him, who inspects it and, if necessary, adds further marks and gives corresponding instructions. Finally, the stick having passed from one to other of the old men present is handed to the messenger who has received his verbal message in connection with it. The messenger carried the stick in a net bag, and on arriving at the camp to which he was sent, he handed it to the headman at some place apart from the others, saying "So-and-so sends you this", and he then gives his message, referring as he does so to the marks on the stick. The headman having examined the stick hands it to the old men, and having satisfied himself how many people are wanted and how many local divisions of the tribe are to be present, and having made such other enquiries as may be necessary, calls all the people together and announces the message to them. The stick is retained by the recipient, who carries it back when he goes to attend the meeting it calls together. The messenger meanwhile lives in the camp until they all depart, when he accompanies them.

Much of the message is carried in the messenger's head, or as the Aborigines say "in his mouth". And the stick provides a durable, external frame of reference which guides and prompts his recall: each mark represents some key point and helps to bring it to mind. A less conspicuous function of the stick is that it influences the way the message is presented to the messenger. The use of the stick constrains the elders to compose their message in an orderly way, extract key points and group these together, and arrange these groupings in some sequence. The message is thereby cast into a form which relates, point by point, to the markings which, in their turn, provide retrieval cues.

How far do the markings resemble written language? Does one kind of mark consistently represent one kind of information, and another kind of mark another kind of information? By and large, not. Howitt reports many local variations in the detailed use of message sticks but found that they could not usually be "read" by anyone who did not have the particular message explained orally. It sometimes happened that people, who had been in frequent communication with each other by means of message sticks and were generally acquainted with each other's concerns, could guess, with some degree of certainty, at the meaning of a marked stick, but this was rare. Typically the stick could be interpreted only by individuals to whom the message had been given by word of mouth. So, while the stick could be seen as pre-figuring written language, it actually works on the tally principle, i.e. each mark corresponds to some item of information but no individual mark suggests what that information might be. Given the absence of written language and the importance of conveying the message exactly, this ingenious use of the tally principle provides an eminently serviceable memory-aiding device.

III. Overview

This chapter has been concerned with the working hypothesis that: there is a necessary interdependence between, on the one hand, the memory-aiding devices which sustain accomplishments of memory and, on the other hand, the role which these accomplishments serve in the pursuits of everyday life. The chapter has, in effect, used this hypothesis in order to survey a succession of memory-involving pursuits, each relatively self-contained and each of some interest in its own right. Let us now look at this survey as it relates to the four main deductions mentioned at the start of the chapter.

The first deduction was: given the prevalence, in an individual or in a community, of certain memory-aiding devices, there will exist everyday pursuits which they adaptively serve. I have provided illustrations of this deduction in several memory-aiding practices. For example, knuckle counting in relation to the months of the year; the making and filing and indexing of written records; the use of written notation and of sliding beads in numerical calculation; the recital by a group of an oral tradition; the formulaic structure of Homeric poetry; the notching of sticks by Aborigines. Each of these practices would, when viewed in isolation, puzzle the proverbial visitor from another planet. Yet each makes sense when viewed as a memory-aiding device which plays a useful role in the everyday life of the people concerned.

The second main deduction was: given the prevalence of certain everyday pursuits, there will exist memory-aiding devices which adaptively sustain them. The pursuits, which the above memory-aiding devices help to support, illustrated this second deduction. Further illustration is found in the case of S. V. Shereshevskii (Luria, 1968) who had an extraordinary ability to memorize strings of items, and who eventually made his livelihood by exhibiting this ability. He used a system of memory-aiding devices which he had, over the years, refined and adapted so as to be progressively more and more serviceable in his memorizing pursuits. Yet another illustration is the case of A. C. Aitken (Hunter, 1977a) who also had extraordinary abilities of memory which also played important roles in his everyday life. He too used a system of memory-aiding devices which he had developed and refined over the years, but his system was radically different from that of Shereshevskii, and much better adapted to the accomplishments of memory and of thinking, which were of value to Aitken.

The third deduction was: when new pursuits arise, their development and survival will depend on the corresponding development of new memory-aiding devices. This deduction was illustrated in the historical development of numerical calculation, the formulaic structure of oral epic poetry, and the use of written, and related, external recording devices (see also Schmandt-Besserat, 1978). It could also be illustrated by the history of science which has relied so much on the development of recording devices for storing and retrieving precise details, and also on ways of assembling masses of detail into compact patterns such as theoretical principles and laws: such principles serve the function of data reduction and of making the data easier to grasp, remember and use.

The third deduction was also illustrated by the biographical development of individual mental calculators who progressively build up their repertoire of LTM resources. It is noteworthy that these developments are paralleled in the biography of any skilful practitioner in any field. For example, in classical Rome, Cicero completed his book "De Oratore" ("The making of an orator") in 55 B.C. and Quintilian completed his book on the same theme in A.D. 95. Both men were highly accomplished legal advocates and their books were concerned to pass on to others the practical skills of legal advocacy. The books make clear that the education of an expert advocate is many sided, beginning in childhood, progressing into adult life, and is never fully perfected. It involves the acquisition of a vast fund of learned resources which is supported by a host of memory-aiding devices and which is so organized that items from the fund can be retrieved intuitively, that is, flexibly, appropriately to present circumstances, and with minimum effort.

The same point is made by Yehudi Menuhin, the virtuoso violinist, with regard to the education of a violinist:

> Our reason is geared to taking one problem on its own, analysing it, and reaching a conclusion about how we shall proceed. But when we are faced with ten different factors, all acting upon each other and among them creating some astronomical total of variables, reason is defeated and only intuition can cope. Thus it is in violin playing—too much going on for direction by the conscious mind. In teaching, therefore, one can only go so far: one can prepare the ground, loosen the muscles, strengthen the fingers, point out all the elements to be coordinated so that any combination of movements can be made at any time. Then the player's vision takes over, intuitively selecting from these billions of possibilities the thousands it needs. (Menuhin, 1976, pp. 371–372.)

The fourth deduction was: when new memory-aiding devices arise, they will survive and develop only if uses are found for them and, likewise, old memory-aiding devices will drop out if they cease to be useful. This deduction could have been illustrated nicely by reference to recent work on the development, in children, of voluntary memorizing abilities (see Kail and Hagen, 1977; and Hunter, 1976, 1977b). However, this chapter illustrated this deduction mainly by reference to the historical consequences of literacy and of science-based technology. Historically, the development of writing proved its worth as a memory-aiding device which served various everyday pursuits; this led to the rise of widespread literacy and the decline of many of the memory-aiding devices which non-literate cultures had used for so long. This history, and its significance for everyday life, need not be laboured; but it raises one intriguing question.

From Plato onwards, claims have been made that the use of writing leads to a decline in memory abilities. Is this claim correct? The answer must be both yes and no. Written records enable us to store and retrieve certain items of information without having to hold anything in our head except what computer scientists call the "address" of the information. To that extent, we can dispense with memory-aiding devices for holding these items of information in our head. Thus, people in literate cultures do not, like people in non-literate cultures, recite lengthy oral traditions and, in this respect, they have "poorer memories". However, if we view written records as an alternative means of holding information in memory, there is little doubt that literate cultures require more extensive and more detailed resources of memory than do non-literate cultures. In that sense, most of us who live in modern industrialized societies have "better memories" than our non-literate counterparts. Our way of life makes heavier demands on our memory-handling abilities, and also makes us sensitive to notions of literalness, reproductive accuracy and historical truth in a way which does not seem to hold in non-literate cultures, e.g. the idea of a poem as existing in only one authoritative version.

This chapter, then, has used a working hypothesis in order to view various interdependences between memory and everyday life. The hypothesis has served to interrelate a wide diversity of observations and psychological inquiries. It seems, furthermore, to have plenty of travel left in it.

References

Atkinson, R. C., Spiro, R. J. and Montague, W. E. (Eds) (1977). "Schooling and the Acquisition of Knowledge". Lawrence Erlbaum Associates, New Jersey.

Bartlett, F. C. (1932). "Remembering." Cambridge University Press, Cambridge.

Bowra, C. M. (1952). "Heroic Poetry." Macmillan, London.

Bowra, C. M. (1972). "Homer." Duckworth, London.

Bronowski, J. (1973). "The Ascent of Man." British Broadcasting Corporation, London.

Bruner, J. S. (1972). "The Relevance of Education." George Allen and Unwin, London.

Chadwick, H. M. and Chadwick, N. K. (1932, 1936, 1940). "The Growth of Literature." 3 Vols. Cambridge University Press, Cambridge.

Devi, S. (1977). "Figuring." Andre Deutsch, London.

Donaldson, M. (1978). "Children's Minds." Fontana, London.

Goody, J. (1977). "The Domestication of the Savage Mind." Cambridge University Press, Cambridge.

Goody, J. and Watt, I. (1968). The consequences of literacy. In "Literacy in Traditional Societies" (J. Goody, Ed.). Cambridge University Press, Cambridge.

Hatano, G., Miyake, Y. and Binks, M. G. (1977). Performance of expert abacus operators. Cognition 5, 47–55.

Howitt, A. W. (1889). Notes on Australian message sticks and messengers. J. Anthropol. Inst. 18, 314–332.

Hunter, I. M. L. (1962). An exceptional talent for calculative thinking. Br. J. Psychol. 53, 243–258.

Hunter, I. M. L. (1976). Memory: theory and application. In "Piaget, Psychology and Education" (V. P. Varma and P. Williams, Eds). Hodder and Stoughton, London.

Hunter, I. M. L. (1977a). An exceptional memory. *Br. J. Psychol.* **68**, 155–164.

Hunter, I. M. L. (1977b). Imagery, comprehension and mnemonics. *J. Mental Imagery* **1**, 65–72.

Hunter, I. M. L. (1977c). Mental calculation. *In* "Thinking" (P. N. Johnson-Laird and P. C. Wason, Eds). Cambridge University Press, Cambridge.

Kail, R. V. and Hagen, J. W. (Eds) (1977). "Perspectives in the Development of Memory and Cognition." Lawrence Erlbaum Associates, New Jersey.

Kirk, G. S. (1965). "Homer and the Epic." Cambridge University Press, Cambridge.

Kojima, T. (1954). "The Japanese Abacus." Tuttle, Tokyo.

Lewis, D. (1976). Observations on route finding and spatial orientation among the Aboriginal peoples of the Western Desert region of Central Australia. *Oceania* **46**, 249–282.

Lindsay, P. H. and Norman, D. A. (1977). "Human Information Processing." (second edn) Academic Press, London and New York.

Lord, A. B. (1960). "The Singer of Tales." Harvard University Press, Cambridge, Massachusetts.

Luria, A. R. (1968). "The Mind of a Mnemonist." Cape, London.

Menninger, K. (1969). "Number Words and Number Symbols." M.I.T. Press, Cambridge, Massachusetts.

Menuhin, Y. (1976). "Unfinished Journey." Macdonald and Jane's, London.

Parry, M. (1971). "The Making of Homeric Verse." Oxford University Press, Oxford.

Schmandt-Besserat, D. (1978). The earliest precursor of writing. *Scient. Am.* **238**, 6, 38–47.

Smirnov, A. A. (1973). "Problems of the Psychology of Memory." Plenum, New York.

Vansina, J. (1973). "Oral Tradition." Penguin University Books, Harmondsworth, England.

Yendovitskaya, T. V. (1971). Development of memory. *In* "The Psychology of Preschool Children" (A. V. Zaporozhets and D. B. Elkonin, Eds). M.I.T. Press, Cambridge, Massachusetts.

2. Strategies for Learning and Recall

P. E. MORRIS

Department of Psychology,
University of Lancaster, UK

I. Where Memory Fails

How often do you wish for a better memory? I doubt if a week goes by without most of us failing to remember something. With resignation or with anger we blame our memories. Research on memory improvement is an area of psychology which does not need justification to the man-in-the-street. He can see the point of such research, but he may, rightly, wonder if psychologists have much to offer him. I think that psychologists can offer some positive advice. Where they cannot help they may be able to explain. The positive advice that can be offered is, as we shall see, mainly concerned with learning apparently meaningless or disconnected facts. With some effort on the part of the learner he can be trained to perform apparently amazing feats of memory. He could for example, memorize in a few minutes the order of a shuffled pack of cards. There are many commercial memory improvement courses and books by memory experts that offer to develop a "superpower" memory. Few who try their methods complain of being deceived. However, equally few individuals acquainted with these memory improvement methods feel that their memory problems have been solved. I will describe the bases of these memory improvement techniques later in the chapter. First I want to consider what more we want from our memories.

If we are to tackle the problem of faulty memories we need to know what common faults occur. Failures in memory can be roughly divided into failure to remember facts and failure to perform actions. "Facts" is used very loosely here. The situation to which I refer is the one in which you probe your memory for some bit of information, but recall is not possible. Names, postal codes, telephone numbers, jokes, items on the shopping list are a few examples. Actions include appointments, taking pills, remembering to go shopping and so on. Both sorts of memory failure occur to us all. However, the solutions to the two types of problems may be quite different.

Considerable research has been directed at problems which can be roughly classified as the "storage of facts" type. From such research we can develop a view of the nature of the memory system which helps us understand why facts are remembered and forgotten and which suggests ways of improving the initial storage and subsequent retrieval of these facts. Before reviewing this knowledge, I must face the fact that psychologists have far less to say about how we remember or forget to perform actions. I suspect that the greatest embarrassments for which our memories take the blame come from failure to remember to do something. To give a recent, personal example, I arrived, in my football kit to play for the Departmental Five-a-Side team to find everyone else there in states of exhaustion. I had been told that the game was from twelve noon until one o'clock but remembered the arrangement as one o'clock. I will not dwell on the jibes about the memory of the Departmental "memory expert". I will just say it was embarrassing. Notice, incidentally, that in this particular example, a failure in the memory of a fact led to an apparent failure in the memory for an action. The two types of failure are interrelated. Further evidence of the importance of remembering future plans will be found in Harris' (1978) survey of memory aids. He found that by far the most commonly used memory aids are "external" aids such as shopping lists and writing on one's hand which are attempts to provide cues to recall actions that must be performed. Psychologists need to give an account of how we remember what we are to do or have already done. If they cannot, they will not be able to explain or aid an important aspect of memory failure.

Remembering Future Actions

We plan our lives. Over months, we know when we will have holidays, birthdays and other important events. In the shorter term we sketch out a scheme which determines what we do. Most of us, if asked, can give an outline of how we intend spending the next few hours.

Psychologists have had very little to say about such plans, but unless we understand them and have models rich enough to encompass them we will fail to explain much human activity including such non-activity as forgetting parts of our plans. The importance of plans and intentions has been championed by Miller *et al.* (1960) and by humanistic psychologists such as Shotter (1976). However, these individuals have got little farther than acknowledging the existence of planning. Most psychologists have been concerned with situations which can be examined in a brief laboratory experiment. Not surprisingly they have not tackled the problem of long term, directed human activity.

To understand why we forget or fail to carry out various actions we first need to understand how we normally remember to carry out prior planned actions. We do not know this. All that can be offered here are some observations about such plans.

Plans can be modified and updated. Some errors in remembering plans may recur when modification has not taken place for some reason, or because the old plan is followed rather than the new. How, why and when are all questions that demand a clearer model of plan formation and execution.

Plans for future actions run at a high cognitive level. That is, they are in terms of actions which can be analysed down considerably into many component actions which make up the general activity. For example, at 5.20 p.m., I intend to pick up my wife from work. That is what I would say if you asked me what I intended to do at 5.20. However, to do it I shall have to leave the room, find the car key, unlock the car and so on. Each of these actions could themselves be further analysed. Craik (1966) gives a wartime analogy.

> . . . the C-in-C Fighter Command presumably says: "we want a sweep carried out over such and such an area"; he does not have to add: "this means that Spitfire number so and so on such and such a station must have so many gallons of petrol in its tanks and care must be taken that its plugs are clean and guns are loaded". These latter details are delegated to subordinates. In just the same way, for rapidity and certainty in action, it is essential that certain units of activity, such as looking at an object, walking, grasping, using words, or balancing one's body, should be delegated to lower levels . . . (Craik, 1966, p.38.)

There is further discussion of such hierarchies by Broadbent (1977).

Each of the components of the hierarchy can have faults, and errors and forgetfulness can occur within sub-routines of the programme. Reason (1977) has analysed examples of such errors. His general approach comes from the study of skilled performance. He sees behaviour as the carrying out of plans which are composed of sub-routines of previously learned behaviour requiring varying degrees of feedback and supervision from higher intentional systems for their success. He suggests four categories of errors; storage, test, discrimination and selection. These are in turn subdividable into a total of eleven error types. Examples of a storage error are forgetting items in a plan, such as forgetting to post a letter, or forgetting preceding actions, such as boiling a second kettle after the tea has been made. Not all apparently "forgetful" errors are classified as failure of storage. Failures in testing during the operation of a plan can lead to errors like starting to get into a bath with one's clothes on. The system may make errors of discrimination, leading to actions which are appropriate in similar but not these circumstances, such as the discrimination error of taking out one's own front door key when approaching a friend's house. Selection errors occur when an inappropriate action is substituted for a correct one in the overall running of the plan. These may occur in many ways. Branching errors can occur when actions share common initial components, then diverge. So, for example, going out to the car, past the gardening clothes may lead to the clothes being put on. There may be inappropriate insertions or omissions in plans, so that for example, the light may be turned on when leaving the room in daylight. Reason has attempted to classify reports of memory failure by his system, and finds that the most common involve forgetting items in a plan, making branching errors, forgetting preceding actions and inserting or omitting actions in plans.

Possible reasons for forgetting our plans are implied in Reason's analysis. There may be failure to set up the appropriate plan in the first place, or failure to modify the prepared plan. Anecdotal evidence about memory errors can suggest other variables. We often forget an appointment if we are absorbed in the ongoing events at the time. It is as if a degree of cognitive capacity is required to review our present state in our day's plan. In less demanding periods during the day we may consciously review and update our plans, making use of the available capacity. Errors can occur through incorrect entries in our plan, as happened in my football fiasco.

In a recent study, Wilkins and Baddeley (1978) simulated a pill-taking schedule by having subjects press a button on a portable box at four set times per day for a week. The subjects virtually never forgot that they had pressed the button, although they did often miss a button press. Wilkins and Baddeley also found a negative relationship between subjects' scores on a free recall task and their performance in the button pressing, providing some empirical support for the separation of memory for intentions and for facts. Further, Herrmann and Neisser

(1978) in a factor analysis of subjects' reports of memory problems found separate factors for reports of the ability to remember intentions and other abilities such as memories for names.

We know so little about our plans, how they are constructed, modified, examined, deleted. For example, how are our plans organized so that we clear from memory the intention to do a job once it is done as in the Wilkins and Baddeley study? If the entry in memory is not cleared or modified we would be frequently starting to do things we had already done. Of course, such modifying of memory must take place, but it is not obvious that the current conceptualizations of the memory processes that are presented in textbooks on memory, can cope adequately with even such a simple thing as knowing that you have done what you intended to do.

Memory for Facts

From the severe limitations of our knowledge about memory for future actions we can turn with optimism to the problems of memory for facts. Much more research and thought has been directed to studying what determines the encoding, storage and retrieval of items of information. Elsewhere (e.g. Morris, 1978a), the properties of the encoding and retrieval systems have been reviewed. The central problem for a memory system is to lay down at the initial acquisition stage a record in a form which can be retrieved when retrieval is appropriate. When that will be is, of course, unpredictable at the encoding stage. The ideal is for a specific cue to be available at the encoding stage and again at the retrieval stage. In these circumstances, subjects can often recall words which they did not even recognize as having been presented earlier (e.g. Tulving and Thompson, 1973).

The amount that can be recalled is considerably influenced by the task which the learner is performing at the same time as initial acquisition. There is much better recall if the semantic properties of the items have been emphasized by, for example, getting the subject to judge whether the word is a member of a particular class of items (animals, living things, etc.) than if the structure or the sound of the word is emphasized by judgments about rhyming or the letters involved (e.g. Craik and Tulving, 1975). Conversely, where much processing capacity is committed to other activities, as in dichotic listening tasks, memory for even the shadowed message is poor.

It is easier to remember sense than nonsense. It is easier to remember a coherent story, the construction, elements and interconnections of which we understand than it is to learn apparently disconnected items (e.g. Bartlett, 1932; Gomulicki, 1956). In recent years there has been considerable effort towards modelling the nature of storage of meaningful material in long term memory (LTM) (cf. Morris, 1978b; Kintsch, 1977). All such models incorporate not just representations of the items remembered, but the relationships which, in most models, link the items together and provide the routes through which the memory is searched. In such models it is easy to enter a new instance of a well-known item, such as "dog", and all that is known about dogs is made available by linking this new entry to the defining entry for dogs. If a new word is encountered there is no existing defining entry, no network of prior occurrences.

In addition to the importance of the cues encoded and available at retrieval, the type of encoding in which the subject engages, and the meaningfulness of the material, other factors such as existing knowledge, interest and amount of time given to the learning are all important. All the factors which influence memory reflect the fact that the memory system is not the thing of central importance in the cognitive system. The main activities of the cognitive system are directed to making sense of and dealing with the ongoing interactions between the individual and the world. The memory system aids this central cognitive function by supplying the available information from past experience. It also receives from the cognitive central processor the results of the current activity and it is these that are stored. It is not the memory system which makes efforts after meaning. Meaning and understanding are terms more appropriately applied to the activities of the central cognitive function. It is here that a précis of what is going on is formed, here that verbatim information is discarded. The memory system stores the results of our making sense of our experiences rather than the experiences themselves. The memory system is not something which is switched on and off for long periods, it is continuously probed for information relevant to the current concerns of the central processor. What is retrieved depends in part on these concerns, in part on the original encoding. Some forgetting may result from the decay of the memory trace, but frequently we fail to remember because the initial encoding was inappropriate to the existing demands of the central processing. The existing demands may be directed towards recall, as in a memory experiment or an examination. They may be otherwise engaged. In either case recall will depend upon the nature of the ongoing processing.

II. Improving Memory

After this consideration of the nature of the memory system we can begin to ask how memory can be improved. The approach to improvement will depend upon the nature of the specific situation. An examination of the situation will suggest one of a variety of tactics. For our purposes we can ask several questions, which are summarized in Fig. 1.

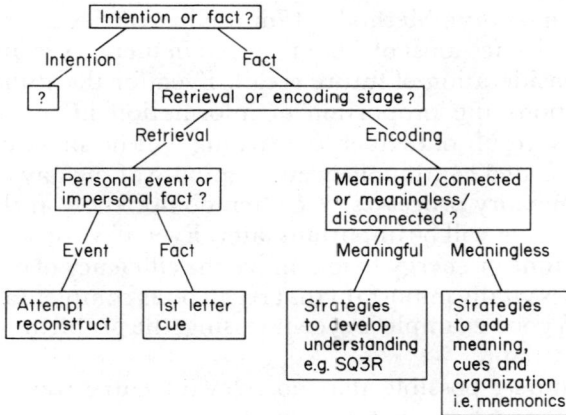

Fig. 1. *An analysis of memory problems and possible strategies to overcome them.*

First, is the problem one of remembering to do something (an intention) or remembering a fact? If an intention, as the discussion earlier showed, we know little about the underlying processes and have little advice. However, the frequency of use of external memory aids reported by Harris (1978) suggests that these are worth employing. If the problem is one of remembering facts, then the second question is: Is the problem at the acquisition or the recall stage? In other words, is the issue one of how to learn something to maximize the ease of later recall, or is the problem one of retrieving something already entered (one hopes) into memory? If it is the former then a whole range of techniques may be exploited. If the latter, then the situation is more difficult. If the problem is one of optimizing learning, then the third question is: Is the material to be learned connected and meaningful or disconnected and meaningless?

Whichever answer is given the next stage will be to maximize the known factors which influence memory. Where the material is connected and meaningful this task is relatively easy. If however, the material is disconnected and meaningless it will be necessary to find ways of imposing meaning, supplying interconnections and providing retrieval cues. For the former case various study skills can be recommended, for the later case, a range of mnemonic techniques exist which can supply what is missing. The next three sections tackle the answers to the questions.

Improving Retrieval

How can we improve our recall of information when it is already entered into memory? Methods of improving retrieval would be particularly useful since most of what is stored in memory is input without conscious consideration of future recall. Even for the student revising for examinations the proportion of information in memory that is entered as the result of deliberate learning will be small compared to that being encoded continuously every minute of the day as a result of the normal memory processes. We often do not know at the time that what is happening will be important later. Even if we do know, we may not have the time or energy to maximize the efficiency of our encoding. It is sometimes vitally important that recall be as complete and accurate as possible. A good example is eyewitnessing, the problems of which are discussed in Chapter 7.

It is, of course, possible that no relevant entry was made in the memory, or that whatever trace was laid down has decayed or been eroded through interference from similar entries so that no recall will be possible. Even so, there will be many situations where recall seems impossible and yet we feel fairly confident that the information is available in memory but not accessible at this instant. This "feeling of knowing" is often a guide to the availability of information in memory (see Gruneberg, 1978, for a recent review). For example, Hart (1965) found that 78% of items which subjects claimed they were certain they knew, but could not recall were later recognized while only 30% of items which subjects claimed they did not know were recognized. However, although the feeling of knowing is a guide to the contents of memory it may be unreliable.

For example, Gruneberg and Monks (1974), studied the recall, cued by their first letter, of capital cities which the subjects had been initially unable to recall. They found better cued recall for capitals which subjects reported feeling they knew. However, in a later analysis (Gruneberg et al., 1977) it was found that, for the same rated degree of feeling of knowing, those capitals which the group as a whole tended to know were better recalled than those which were not known to the majority of the group. This apparent variability in the prediction of subsequent recall from the same degree of rated feeling of knowing might reflect an insensitivity in the measure of feeling of knowing. However, it is likely that the subjects were partially ignorant of their own memories. A feeling of knowing may be a predictor of subsequent recall, but it is not necessarily an accurate estimate of the existence or non-existence of any given memory trace.

Faced with the need to recall something that is not immediately recallable there are two commonly adopted strategies. If what is to be recalled is an event which happened to the individual concerned, they may try to reconstruct the situation via memories that are accessible. So, when a car key is lost the searcher attempts to remember when he last had it, what he did, where he went and so on. If, on the other hand, what is to be recalled is a name or a word then people attempt to cue themselves by, for example, running through the alphabet hoping that the appropriate first letter may trigger recall.

To my knowledge, the effectiveness of the reconstruction-of-context method has not been tested experimentally, but there is anecdotal evidence that it can be surprisingly powerful. Lindsay and Norman (1972) describe the common stages through which people pass when asked, for example, "What were you doing on Monday afternoon in the third week of October two years ago"? Realizing that the memory search will be difficult they try to avoid starting. If persuaded to have a go, they replace the immediate question by one that is likely to lead to an answer, for example, "Where was I two years ago?". From the answer to this question more specific questions can be devised. If, for example, the subject was a student they may try to recall their time-table for the first term of the appropriate year. Eventually, quite vivid memories may be elicited.

The first letter strategy has been studied by Gruneberg and Monks (1976). Subjects attempted to name the capitals of countries. After two attempts at the given list they were told, during their third trial to go through the alphabet to see if the letters cued recall. Recall did improve both compared to earlier recall and to a control group. While this is clearly a valuable strategy since it improves recall, why it does so is still in doubt. Gruneberg and Monks (1976) found that subjects using the first letter strategy took longer in their recall attempt than did controls. When Gruneberg, (personal communication), persuaded subjects to take a similar amount of time over recall, the difference disappeared. Thus the strategy may succeed, not because it supplies appropriate cues but rather because it maintains the task while other factors bring about the better retrieval.

The problem of retrieval is the problem of finding an appropriate retrieval cue. What is an appropriate cue will depend on the conditions at the initial encoding. Events and items which occurred at the time of encoding may both determine the way in which the information was initially encoded and themselves act as retrieval cues. The work of Tulving and his associates (e.g. Tulving and Osler, 1968; Tulving and Thomson, 1973) has demonstrated that weakly associated words (e.g. *village* for CITY) are particularly good cues for the to-be-remembered items if the cues are present at both encoding and the retrieval stage. Barclay *et al.* (1974) have illustrated how what is an appropriate cue will depend upon the encoding context. Thus, for example, where subjects had studied the sentence *The student spilled the ink*, the cue *Something messy* was effective in retrieving "ink", but where they had studied *The student picked up the ink, something in a bottle* was a more effective cue, although it was not effective for the first sentence.

The problem for the person attempting retrieval is therefore to find a cue which is relevant to the situation in which encoding initially took place. It is, therefore, not surprising if the strategy of attempting to recall the original learning context is a good method of overcoming a memory block.

It is interesting that while there are a considerable number of strategies which improve learning there are relatively few for improving retrieval. Presumably, this reflects the basic problem at the retrieval stage that recall is dependent upon the original encoding. Much can be done to direct that initial encoding, but once it has been completed the opportunities for improving recall are limited. Even so, there are probably a number of ways in which retrieval can be maximized awaiting discovery.

Learning Organized, Meaningful Material

When you know that you will need to recall some information it is possible to manipulate and exploit your memory system much more efficiently than when you have control merely of the retrieval strategies. Normally, there are few problems in remembering organized, meaningful material. Such material is ideally suited to the functioning of the memory system. This is almost a truism since to say that something is meaningful and organized is to say that it fits easily with past experience and it can be analysed without difficulty by the cognitive system. However, problems in memorizing meaningful material do arise for students who are required to remember accurately vast quantities of such information, and for actors and others who need to learn not just the basic message of the material but its verbatim contents.

There has been much research and even more proffering of good advice on ways to study. One commonly advocated study technique will be described at the end of this section.

I doubt if more than a tiny proportion of students actually put this advice on study skills into practice. Unfortunately, we are all lazy, and most techniques which improve learning require more initial effort than passively reading and hoping that something is "going in". As with all skills, the skill of good memory requires considerable investment of effort while it is being acquired. Even when we know of efficient methods of learning, we may not feel like the extra mental effort which they often require. However, students who are equipped with a knowledge of efficient study techniques can put them into practice so far as they wish.

Active Learning

It is possible to repeat the material to be memorized over and over again and not increase the likelihood of it being remembered. For example, Craik and Watkins (1973) had subjects rehearse aloud the last four words in free recall lists for twenty seconds. In a later test the recall of these words was no better for this group than for a control group who had not received this extra rehearsal time. The extra rehearsal maintained the words in memory over a short period but did not increase the long-term probability of recall. What does increase long-term recall is active examination of the material. Where the learning material is apparently unconnected words, classifying the words and thinking of associations to them greatly improves LTM (Craik and Tulving, 1975).

Even more valuable is a search for the meaningful relationships between the words. This is even more important for the sort of learning which a student must undertake. When the underlying logic and structure of what is to be learned is understood, recall is far easier. The material is no longer disconnected, but can be recalled in "chunks" with one part cueing the recall of another. Overall understanding of the logic of what is being learned provides a framework for recall, with what is known cueing what has yet to be recalled. As was discussed earlier, current models of LTM stress the importance of the relations between the items stored in the initial encoding and subsequent retrieval. Actively searching out such interconnections will maximize the efficiency of the encoding with the fullest interconnection, and retrieval pathways will also be encoded.

Several examples of the value of comprehension for memory are given by Bransford and Johnson (1973). In one study, the following is part of a passage given to subjects.

If the balloons popped the sound would not be able to carry since everything would be too far away from the correct floor. A closed window would also prevent the sound from carrying, since most buildings tend to be well insulated. Since the whole operation depends on a steady flow of electricity, a break in the middle of the wire would also cause problems. Of course, the fellow could shout, but the human voice is not loud enough to carry that far. . . .

Some subjects were supplied with the context which makes the passage intelligible. They were shown a picture of a girl at the window of the top floor of a high building, listening to a loudspeaker floating outside the window, suspended by balloons and attached to a microphone on the ground into which a guitarist is singing.

Subjects shown the picture prior to reading the passage recalled over twice that of subjects given no context, or of those who saw the picture after attempting to learn the passage.

Self-testing

Part of an active approach to learning should involve frequent self-testing. Apart from the salutory realization of how little has been acquired, there is considerable evidence that the act of recall improves the probability of recall in the future.

A test immediately after learning improves LTM. (La Porte and Voss, 1975). Cooper and Monk (1976) review the research which has manipulated the number of study and test trials during learning. They conclude that the general finding is that subjects who are tested during the original learning session have better LTM of the material than those who have only studied it without being tested.

Part or Whole Learning

One of the longest running issues in the experimental study of memory has been whether what is to be learned should be tackled as a whole or divided into parts (cf. Higbee, 1977). For example, when learning a poem should you concentrate on one verse at a time or keep reading through the whole poem? The natural inclination is towards part learning, but since Steffens (1900) there have been frequent demonstrations that whole learning can be more efficient.

The whole method benefits by placing each part in context so that not only is the full meaning of the whole of the material better appreciated but one part can prompt the recall of another. The difficulty with the part method is putting the parts together (Breen and Jurek, 1975).

Higbee claims that continued practice with the whole method improves its efficiency and that its efficiency is greater the more mature and intelligent the learner.

The parts method encourages the learner since several parts may be mastered in the time that would be required to show any improvement in the whole method. The more material there is to be learned and the more distinctive the parts, the more efficient the parts method will be.

It would be wrong to maintain that there is a right and wrong way or that either technique will always be better. Rather, an examination of the material to be learned is called for so that the more appropriate approach can be adopted.

Other Factors

If there is no general conclusion concerning part-whole learning, there is a general consensus on the value of spaced versus massed practice and on overlearning. Spreading out the learning sessions with breaks in between usually improves acquisition (e.g. Crowder, 1976). Breaks help because they relieve boredom and fatigue. Efficient strategies for memorizing require effort and concentration and cannot be maintained for very long without a change. Of course, the benefits of spaced practice should not be overemphasized. It is better to be studying than not to be studying, and it takes time to "get into" a topic.

Overlearning is simply the continuation of study beyond the stage at which it is just possible to correctly recall the information. A demonstration of how learning continues beyond this stage was given by Kruger (1929). He had subjects learn lists of 12 nouns until they correctly recalled the list, or for half as long, or as long again, as it took to learn the list to one correct recall. When tested a day later, those subjects who had been trained until they could just recall the list correctly recalled less than 30% of the words. However, those who had overlearned for half as long again recalled almost 40% and those who had overlearned for twice the time recalled almost 50% of the nouns. Also, after a month both the overlearning groups were quicker than they had been originally in relearning the list but the group that had not overlearned showed almost no benefit from the original learning.

The SQ3R Method

The SQ3R is a widely recommended method of study (see e.g. Morgan and Deese, 1969; Rowntree, 1970). The abbreviation stands for Survey, Question, Read, Recite, Review.

The Survey stage involves skimming through what is to be studied, reading any summary, noting the headings and examining any pictures or graphs. The purpose of the survey is to obtain an overview of the material to come, to provide a framework to help comprehension and to activate appropriate knowledge that you already possess. As the Bransford and Johnson (1973) demonstration described earlier illustrates, a knowledge of the theme and context of what is read can greatly improve comprehension and recall.

The Question stage involves a second skimming, this time asking questions based on the headings. These questions give you a purpose and interest in the reading as you look for their answers. Asking such questions can improve your learning (Frase and Schwartz, 1975).

At the Read stage the material is read thoroughly, keeping the questions already asked in mind.

The Recite stage is a re-reading stage, but now questions should be asked about the headings and other key sections and after each section the student tries to describe to himself the central contents of the section.

In the Review stage the material is surveyed again noting what could and could not be recited and questioning oneself again. Further reviews at a later time help to refresh and consolidate the learning.

It can be seen that the SQ3R method attempts to maximize the known properties of the memory system. Its Survey stage activates what knowledge is already possessed and provides understanding of the context and approach of the material. The Question stage leads the learner to actively process what is read. The Recite stage keeps active involvement, supplies feedback on what has been acquired and develops retrieval skills.

Techniques such as SQ3R will make the most of study where a lot of meaningful material must be learned.

Not everything is meaningful or well organized. Sometimes we need to learn apparently unconnected facts. To do so we can turn to mnemonic techniques.

III. Mnemonics

There are many situations in which there is little inherent logical structure to aid understanding and memory. There is no special connection between an individual and his/her telephone number. Nor is there any inherent relationship between a person's name and his/her appearance. Words in a foreign language may bear no similarity to their English equivalent. The order of the colours of the rainbow, the colour coding of electrical resistors, the number of days in each month, these and many other examples could be quoted, of unrelated information which it is valuable to know. Over the last 2500 years a variety of techniques have been developed to help such learning. Two common mnemonics are the rhyme "Thirty days hath September . . ." to recall the lengths of the months and "ROY G BIV" and "Richard of York Gave Battle In Vain" to cue the order of the colours of the rainbow. However, several more mnemonics with a wider usefulness will be discussed below.

The memory system is most efficient when dealing with meaningful, integrated material where clear retrieval cues are available. Consequently the mnemonic devices supply meaning, integration and cues where none naturally exist. Successful mnemonics can be seen as making use of the properties of the memory system. Looked at in this way they seem sensible solutions to memory problems. However, they have not always been seen in this light. The highly desirable emphasis on the importance of children understanding what they are learning rather than parroting facts was easily carried to the point of assuming that everything that needed to be learned could be acquired "in a meaningful fashion". Thus, for example, Howe (1970) stated that "If something is worth learning there is almost always a meaningful way of learning it". It is certainly worth trying to find a meaningful way of learning any given material. However, where meaning cannot be found it seems sensible to find a way of supplying meaning, organization and cues. That is what mnemonics do. They have often been regarded as tricks. They certainly can be used as tricks. Just as a champion snooker player can put on a display of his skills so an expert in mnemonics can earn his living by artificial stage demonstrations. Yet the snooker player can use his skill to win championships and the expert in mnemonics can apply his skills to real life memory problems. Mnemonics can appear odd, even bizarre if their underlying functions are not understood. They supply meaning and order to inherently meaningless, disordered material. To do so they must embellish what is being learned. They cannot draw out properties of the material, they have to add to it in ways that will aid later recall. Mnemonics have been developed through practical trial and error. As will be seen later, not everything that is advocated by proponents of mnemonics is necessarily an aid to memory.

Phonetic Translation System

The phonetic translation system is an example of a mnemonic which provides meaning and order. Since it also contributes to the Peg Mnemonic, which is the basis of most memory improvement systems, it is convenient to describe it first.

The translation system links a particular consonant sound with each of the digits from 0–9. The most commonly used translations are shown in Table 1. The sounds are not randomly chosen, but are related to the digits in some way, so that acquisition and retention of the translations is simplified. The main letters representing the sounds for 1, 2, 3, 6, 7, 8 and 9 have some structural similarity to the digit, while the remainder have phonetic or semantic associations. Thus, t (1) has one down-stroke, n (2) has two and m (3) has three; S (0) represents the Z, S sound of zero and 1 (5) links with the Roman numeral L for 50. The translation involves sounds, not specific letters. All the sounds in the system are consonant sounds.

Table 1. The phonetic translation system.

Digit	1	2	3	4	5	6	7	8	9	0
Sounds	t	n	m	r	l	j	k	f	b	s
	d					sh	g	v	p	z
						ch				

Once the translation system has been memorized it becomes possible to translate numbers into meaningful words and phrases by first converting the digits into their appropriate sounds and then inserting vowel sounds to make meaningful words. Ideally these words should be concrete and appropriate to the material being memorized. To give a recent personal example, following another of my football games the opposition wanted to arrange a re-match and their captain told us his extension number (4180) while both teams were in the showers. Paper and pencils are not provided in our showers and while most of our team went off muttering 4180 . . . 4180 . . . I offered the phonetic translation "RighT FarCe". This is not a perfect use of the system, since the "r" sound in "farce" could be translated as representing 4. However, since we have only four digit extensions this was unlikely and the translation enables me to remember the number many days later. With more consideration "ReD FaCe" would have been equally appropriate and more accurate. This example indicates how a random set of numbers can be made meaningful and appropriate by the mnemonic, and the order of the numbers retained by the structure of the phrase.

The phonetic translation system was first introduced by Winckelman in 1648. He used letters to represent numbers. The use of consonants that were similar to the digits they represented was introduced by Gregor von Feinaigle in 1813. Loisette (1896) prepared the particular set of consonant sound substitutions that are used in most memory courses and systems today. The translation system is useful in its own right for remembering numbers but it is particularly valuable in supplying pegs for the Peg or Hook system.

Peg or Hook Mnemonic

Distinct, preferably unique retrieval cues, integratively associated with the information to be recalled are the ideal for efficient retrieval. The Peg mnemonic provides these conditions. The mnemonic allows unrelated concrete items such as a shopping list to be recalled in any order. Where abstract information is to be retained a concrete substitute must be found. It is usually possible to find a concrete term that is associated with an abstract concept and will serve in the mnemonic. The need for concrete items arise because the method links the items to be remembered to an already known list of peg words by means of mental images. The items must therefore be imageable.

The most easily acquired set of peg words is given by the rhyme "one is a bun, two is a shoe, three is a tree, four is a door, five is a hive, six is sticks, seven is heaven, eight is a gate, nine is a mine, ten is a hen". The words "bun", "shoe", etc. form the pegs which stand for the numbers. Thus, if ten items have to be retained, beginning with car, pen and book then a mental picture linking a car and a bun (e.g. a bun inside a car) is formed to retain the first item, an image incorporating a shoe and a pen for the second, a book and a tree for the third, and so on. Traditionally, it has been taught that the images formed should be as bizarre as possible. However, as we will see later, bizarreness is of little importance. What is important is that the image involves an integration of the peg item and the to-be-remembered item. At the recall stage the memorizer recalls the appropriate peg, which cues the image, which elicits recall. Recall can be in any order.

Obviously, if only ten pegs were available the mnemonic would be severely limited. However, the phonetic translation system allows a virtually unlimited number of pegs to be constructed. For each number a peg word can be composed. If this is done in advance the words can be

easily memorized because of their construction via the phonetic translation system and they will be available to the memorizer when
required. Books on memory improvement such as Higbee (1977) and
Lorayne (1957) list suitable peg words. Example peg words for 20, 21
and 22 are nose, net and nun.

The mnemonic has been demonstrated to lead to considerable
improvement in recall (e.g. Bugelski *et al.*, 1968; Hunter, 1964, Paivio,
1971). For example, Morris and Reid (1970) taught the "one is a bun"
rhyme to a group of subjects who then memorized a list of ten digit-
noun pairs. Their recall was twice that of a control group who had not
been taught the method.

The peg method can be used to memorize long lists. It can, however,
be modified to suit specific tasks or demonstrations. Much of "The
Memory Book" by Lorayne and Lucas (1976) is an account of ways of
applying the technique. The memory feat of recounting the order of a
pack of cards is a special use of the peg system. Pegs for the order from
1–52 are learned and also pegs to represent the individual cards in the
pack. Then, for each card an image is formed linking the particular
card with its appropriate position peg word.

Several factors may influence the efficiency of the mnemonic. First,
subjects need sufficient time to undertake all the activities involved. It
takes time to recall the peg word and compose an image. At recall it
takes time to recall the image and translate back. Bugelski *et al.* (1968)
found that their mnemonic subjects did no better than control subjects
when only two seconds was allowed per item. The difference between
the groups was most pronounced at an eight second per item rate. At
faster rates subjects had problems using the mnemonic. Morris and
Reid (1973) have shown that on average subjects take just over two
seconds to report forming an image linking two concrete nouns. Recalling the peg adds more time.

A second factor is the extent to which the same peg words can be
repeatedly used. Clearly, the more frequently they are used the less
original they will be as retrieval cues. Since the strength of the peg system
is that it supplies distinctive cues that are available at both acquisition
and retrieval the repeated use of these cues should weaken the efficiency
of the mnemonic. However, while interference no doubt does occur, the
overall power of the mnemonic means that it still remains a very good
learning technique. Thus, Morris and Reid (1970) found subjects had no
problems from interference when learning six consecutive reorderings of
the same nouns by the "one is a bun" mnemonic, and Lorayne (1957) who
uses the method repeatedly in his stage demonstrations reports no real
interference problems. Probably methods of avoiding interference are

unnecessary unless the same pegs are to be used to store many different lists of items for long periods. Then it may be necessary to mark each image from each list in a distinctive way, for example including in the image for each item a feature to distinguish that particular list. Other solutions, such as progressively elaborating each image by incorporating the features of both the new list and all previous lists has been found to improve recall (Bower and Reitman, 1972).

A final factor to be considered here is the concreteness of the peg words. In general, concrete words are better cues for recall than abstract words (e.g. Paivio, 1971; Morris and Reid, 1975). However, Paivio (1971) reported an experiment in which abstract peg words (e.g. "one is fun, two is true . . .") led to as good recall as the one is a bun rhyme. While Santa *et al.* (1973) supported Paivio (1971) and Delprato and Baker (1974) found better recall with concrete peg words and Di Vesta and Sunshine (1974) discovered differences depending on the imagery ability of the subject. As a practical strategy therefore, it would seem wise to use concrete peg words when possible.

There are other factors which may influence the power of the mnemonic, but these are general to the use of imagery as a memory aid and will be discussed after a description of the next two mnemonics which both rely upon imagery.

The Place or Loci Method

The major disadvantage with the peg method is the need to memorize a long list of pegs. The place method avoids this by making use of well-known, ordered retrieval cues. The pegs of the peg method are replaced by locations in the physical world. So, for example, a familiar street or room or set of rooms can be used. Suppose that a street is chosen. Then an image of the first item to be remembered is formed in conjunction with the first distinctive feature in the street, perhaps the first house. The next item is linked imaginally with the second feature, say the telephone box, and so on down the street. To recall the items one takes an imaginary walk down the road, examining each place and "reading off" the images formed.

The place method is much older than the peg method, traditionally having been devised by a Greek poet, Simonides about 500 B.C. (Yates, 1966). The place method was used by Greek and Roman orators and this is the source of the alternative name for the method, *loci*, which is Latin for places. Classical links can be found in the very word Mnemonic which derives from the ancient Greek goddess of memory, Mnemosyne, who was the mother of the nine Muses.

The place method shares with the peg method the provision of specific, concrete retrieval cues that are linked with the items to be recalled, and are available in the same form at acquisition and retrieval (Tulving and Osler, 1968). Its disadvantages include the need for a large number of well-known places, the possibility of overlooking some places and lack of the flexibility of recall order which the peg mnemonic provides.

There have been several experimental demonstrations of the effectiveness of the mnemonic. For example, Bower (1973) describes how subjects using the place mnemonic to learn five lists of 20 nouns presented at a rate of five seconds per word could recall, on average 72% of the nouns on a test after learning all the lists, while control subjects given no specific technique recalled only 28%. Groniger (1971) found that his subjects took less time to learn two lists of 25 nouns by the method of loci than did control subjects, and when tested after five weeks could still remember 20 of the words in their correct order compared to the ten recalled by the control subjects.

The Link Method

Both the Place and the Peg mnemonics involve linking the items to be remembered to cues which are already known. Where all that is required is the recall of a list of items in a specific order a simpler method is the Link mnemonic. Instead of associating each item with an independent cue, each item is linked with the preceding and subsequent item. If the first four words to be remembered are *car*, *table*, *tower*, *window* then an image is formed of, say, a car standing on a table, then an image of a tower on a table, then an image of a large window in a tower, and so on. No pegs or loci are required, but recall can proceed only through the list, the recall of car cueing the image of a car on a table, the recall of table cueing the image of a tower on the table and so on. There is always the danger of the chain being broken by failure to recall. Even so, the Link method has been shown to be an excellent technique for serial learning, (e.g. Delin, 1969). Bugelski (1974) reported an average of 15 items recalled from a 20 word serial list by subjects using the method, while control subjects averaged only five items.

Remembering Names to Faces

Many people complain of being unable to remember names. They are introduced and told the name but in a few minutes they find that it has been forgotten. Part of the failure to retain the name comes from the lack of attention which it receives. It is heard, but since it plays no part in the conversation, which is probably demanding a good deal of attention, the name is not associated with anything to further its retention and is soon lost from memory. Lorayne who can remember the names of his audience after being introduced to each one briefly, emphasizes the importance of paying attention to the name, using it several times in the conversation and not letting it slip away unnoticed. To improve recall even more he advocates an imagery mnemonic to link the name with the face. The name is examined and some concrete, imageable substitute found. For example, Gorden converts to Garden. Then a prominent feature of the person's face is chosen and the image linked with that place. So, over Mr. Gorden's big chin you imagine a garden growing. Later the face will recall the image and the image the name. Morris *et al.* (1978) tested the effectiveness of this mnemonic. Subjects learned names, randomly chosen from the telephone directory to faces also randomly chosen. After being given a brief training in the method subjects improved by almost 80% in their recall of names while control subjects made no improvement. Many people fear that the mnemonic will lead to embarrassing mistakes but there is no evidence that such errors occur, and if in doubt you can keep quiet. The advantage of the mnemonic is that the number of times when you are in doubt is considerably reduced.

Imagery in Mnemonics

The Peg, Place and Link methods all employ mental images. Why images? There is probably nothing uniquely valuable about images as such. Enormous improvements in memory can be produced by techniques which link the items together via sentences and stories rather than images (see the next section). The important element seems to be the provision of some situation or context which links the items either to their cues or to one another. Imagery provides many opportunities for such linking because it makes available all the visual–spatial relationships that one object can hold to another. Thus, there may not appear to be much in common to link a car and a table, but a car can be imagined on a table and the two are involved together. The importance of the integration of the items to be remembered in the image are emphasized by the experiments of Bower (1970) and Morris and Stevens (1974). Bower had subjects learn pairs of words either by forming an image linking them together, or by forming separate images of the items on either side of the "imaginal field". These latter subjects had no better recall than control subjects but those forming linking images were far superior in their recall. Morris and Stevens showed that forming images to single words does not improve free recall. It is only when the words are linked together, in this case in triplets, through images that recall was improved. Thus, although imagining single items will increase recognition (Morris and Reid, 1973, 1974) it does not affect recall. Images when used with the mnemonic must link together the items and cues.

Should images be bizarre to maximize their effectiveness? From the time of the Romans onwards the value of bizarre images has been emphasized (e.g. the "Ad Herennium" cited by Yates, 1966). A bizarre image should be a more distinctive entry in memory than an image of a conventional scene and there presumed to be more memorable. However, evidence of the benefits of bizarre imagery has been scanty. Many studies which have deliberately manipulated the instructions on the type of image to be generated have found no benefits through instructions emphasizing bizarreness. (Delin, 1969; Bower, 1970; Wortman and Sparling, 1974).

In an earlier review of mnemonic techniques (Morris, 1977) I suggested that the failure of bizarre images might result from either insufficient time being allowed for the formation of the bizarre image or from the novelty of the method for experimental subjects. While the memory expert who recommends bizarre imagery is repeatedly using the same pegs and imagery as a method, the usual experimental subject may have rarely if ever used the mnemonic. The memory expert will have more problems with interference than the laboratory subject and bizarre images may help avoid confusion. In a study by myself and Alison Prentice at Lancaster University, (Morris, 1978c), we attempted to test these two possibilities. In the first experiment we confirmed that subjects requested to form bizarre images took longer to report an image than subjects forming conventional images. The mean time, for conventional images, was two seconds but for bizarre images it was four seconds. We then tried to maximize interference by having subjects learn a list of 75 paired-associates in which the same word served as stimuli five times spread randomly throughout the list. The pairs were presented at a rate (ten seconds per pair) which we believed would allow bizarre images to be formed. The recall test required subjects to write next to the stimulus words the five items which had been paired with that word. Even with the situation designed to favour bizarre images the subjects forming conventional images recalled as well as the bizarre imagery group, with, in fact, a higher mean recall, but the differences not being significant (mean recall for bizarre imagers 33·8 for conventional imagers, 37·2). Nappe and Wollen (1973) also found that allowing extra time for bizarre images to be formed did not lead to better recall with such images. Hauck *et al*. (1976) had subjects use an imagery mnemonic for several days but again bizarre images did not produce better recall.

Lesgold and Goldman (1973) did find better recall if different objects were used when repeatedly imaging the same stimulus word with new response words. If the word was "window" the use of a new window each time led to better retention. Perhaps the degree of interference from repeated use of images has not yet been experimentally matched to that of the frequent mnemonic user. Perhaps the emphasis on bizarreness developed through other features which accompany bizarre images but are usually achieved by ordinary images in experimental studies. Requiring bizarreness would have encouraged the formation of an image in which the items interacted. It may also encourage the recall of many of the properties of the items in the search for a bizarre situation, and as such improve encoding. It may keep interest in the mnemonic task. Whatever is the case it seems that it is the formation of images that link items together, not their bizarreness that is important.

Stories and Associations

The forming of images is only one way of providing a meaningful link between the items to be learned. Another alternative is to compose stories or sentences linking them together. Again, it is the linking that is important. The most dramatic demonstration of the story mnemonic was by Bower and Clark (1969) who had subjects learn 12 lists of ten nouns by making up a story linking them together. They were allowed as long as they required and control subjects were given the same time but no mnemonic instructions. After each list both groups had almost perfect recall, but when tested on all 12 lists at the end, given the first words and told to recall them in order, the story group remembered about 93% and the control subjects about 13%. There have been several other demonstrations of the effectiveness of the linking of items by stories or sentences (e.g. Murray, 1974; Bower and Winzenz, 1970).

First Letter Mnemonics

These, perhaps the most popular forms of mnemonics, come in two types, the acronym, in which the first letters of the words to be remembered spell out a meaningful word, and the acrostic in which the first letters of the words to be remembered are used as the first letters of other words which form an easily retained sentence. So, of the two common mnemonics for the spaces and lines of the treble clef, FACE is an acronym while Every Good Boy Deserves Favour is an acrostic.

First letter mnemonics are popular among students as a means of learning for examinations (Gruneberg, 1973) and as a way of tackling list learning in psychological experiments (Blick *et al.*, 1972). However, while some tests of the power of the mnemonic have shown improvements through its use (e.g. Manning and Bruning, 1975) many more studies have found no effect of the mnemonic (e.g. Boltwood and Blick, 1970; Waite *et al.*, 1971) and Nelson and Archer (1972) obtained no improvement in overall recall but only in retention of order.

Morris and Cook (1978) tried to locate the conditions under which the mnemonic improves recall. In our first experiment we manipulated the concreteness and abstractness of the mnemonic words and compared subject- and experimenter-generated words. The subjects learned six lists of five unrelated words. When recall was tested there was no sign of the mnemonic improving recall in any of the conditions. If anything it made things worse, though not significantly.

We then argued that perhaps the mnemonic does not help retrieval of the words where the items are all new and unconnected. The strength of the mnemonic may be in retaining the correct order of items which are already well known but where the ordering of them is both apparently random and important to know. For example, the acronym CLOD retains the information that *C*ambridge University colour is *L*ight blue and *O*xford is *D*ark blue. Remembering that the colour is blue is not the problem. It is knowing which shade of blue goes with which University.

In our second experiment we therefore provided subjects with lists in which the items were well known but the order was random. Subjects learned three orderings of the days of the week. One group was also supplied with first letter mnemonics such as SMiTe ThiS WiFe where the capital letters represented the days of the week. There was far better recall in the correct positions by subjects given the mnemonics (80% correct vs 54%). Where the mnemonic was correctly recalled 92% of the errors were reversals in which Tuesday was given for Thursday, Saturday for Sunday, or vice versa.

Gruneberg *et al.* (1977) found that subject-generated acrostics helped the retention of lists which were selected from categories such as birds and trees. It appears, therefore, that first letter mnemonics can aid the learning of related words. However, since the initial acquisition of the lists was matched by training to one correct recall there is the possibility that the mnemonic group who took longer over this initial learning may have received more opportunity for overlearning some of the items (Underwood, 1964). The general conclusion on first letter mnemonics would seem to be that they are not a good technique for learning lists of new items, especially when other very effective methods exist. However, they do provide a way of retaining order in items that are either known or can be learned relatively easily, as in the Gruneberg *et al.* study. They will still lead to errors when more than one item shares the first letter. This is an obvious point, perhaps, but one of the best known acrostics for the cranial nerves, "On Old Olympus Towering Top, A Finn and German Viewed Some Hops" contains three Os, two Ts and two As!

Rhymes

Perhaps the most commonly used mnemonic in Britain and the USA is the "Thirty days hath September" verse. Composing rhymes is probably not a common mnemonic technique. Where rhymes exist however, they are adopted. Poetry is easier to learn than prose (McGeoch, 1942). This appears to be at least partly through the limitations that the rhyme and rhythm impose. Only certain words will fit, and the structure of the poem can be seen as providing a continuous retrieval cue. Bower and Bolton (1969) were able to demonstrate that rhymes limit possibilities and so aid recall. This has implications for the type of rhyme to be used when composing a mnemonic verse. However, as Hunter shows (Chapter 1) there is far more involved in the remembering of sagas and the long poems that record the traditions of non-literate societies than the mere advantages to memory of rhythm and rhyme.

IV. Recent Applications of the Mnemonics

Images and Advertising

Many companies use a standard picture to advertise their product. How valuable are these pictures? How easily is the name of the company or brand associated with the picture? Does seeing the picture remind one of the name? Lutz and Lutz (1977) developed predictions about the efficacy of such pictures from research on imagery. They hypothesized that pictures which incorporated and linked the product and the company in the picture should form better cues to the recall of the brand name. This turned out to be the case. In the experiment subjects had to learn to associate the given company or brand names with particular products or services. Recall was tested by providing the list of products and subjects recalled the brand name. All the materials were taken from the yellow pages, avoiding names that were known to the subjects or were artifactually easy to learn. Supplying the brand pictures at the learning stage improved later recall only when the picture integrated the brand and the product together. It was not sufficient for the name, as a word, to be partly incorporated in the picture, both brand and product needed to be visually represented in an interactive way.

The Keyword Method for Second Language Learning

Atkinson and Raugh have developed a mnemonic which they call the keyword method to help the initial acquisition of vocabulary when learning a second language (Atkinson and Raugh, 1975; Raugh and Atkinson, 1975). One of the problems in language learning is to master a sufficient vocabulary. The keyword method involves two links. The foreign word is linked to the keyword by similarity in sound and the keyword is linked to the English translation by a mental image. For example, the Spanish word *caballo* is pronounced "cob-eye-o" and means horse. The sound of the word includes the sound of the English word *eye*. With *eye* as the keyword one might imagine a horse kicking a giant eye. Similarly, the Spanish word for duck is *pato*, pronounced "pot-o". With *pot* as the keyword one could imagine a duck with a large pot on its head. Via the acoustic similarity and the linking images the keywords connect the English and the foreign words.

Atkinson and Raugh examined the effectiveness of this mnemonic in several experiments. In one experiment 120 Russian words were taught in three sub-vocabularies of 40 words. The sub-vocabularies were taught by running through the list three times. On each occasion the Russian word was heard through headphones three times while the English word was displayed. For the keyword group the keyword was also shown. After every run through the list the subjects were tested by hearing the Russian word and typing the English equivalent. In the fourth day all 120 items were tested, and they were tested again six weeks later when subjects were called back without warning. In the first full test of all the items, subjects using the keyword method recalled 72% of the English equivalents to 46% recalled by the control subjects. At the late test after six weeks the keyword subjects could still remember 43% of the words, compared with 28% recalled by the control subjects. Atkinson and Raugh found that performance was better when keywords were provided than when subjects made up their own. Indeed, when given a choice, subjects requested prepared keywords on 89% of occasions. However, they did find that recall was better when subjects generated their own images rather than being given cartoons or sentences linking keyword and English word.

Atkinson (1975) has put into practice the keyword method in a course on Russian at Stanford University. The method illustrates a modern, computer controlled application of an ancient technique that would have been approved by Simonides and Cicero.

V. Problem of Measuring the Effectiveness of a Memory Strategy

Atkinson and Raugh (1975) found that when subjects learning a Spanish vocabulary were told to rote rehearse the words as the method of learning, only 28% of the words were recalled compared to 88% by the keyword group. This difference is much larger than when no strategy was suggested to the control subjects and illustrates both the importance of the choice of strategy and the problem of the appropriate control group in measuring the power of mnemonics. If the control subjects receive no instructions on how to tackle the learning they may adopt many and various methods, changing them through experience (Morris and Reid, 1970). Alternatively, they may be instructed to follow some strategy. There is the problem of knowing the extent to which they obey the instructions. This will vary with the personality of the subjects and experimenter, the nature of the instructions, the ease of the technique and its naturalness and success for the subject. Assuming, as the massive differences between or even within subjects under different instructions suggest, that at least a high proportion of subjects can usually be induced to follow the given strategy, which strategy should be chosen? Often rote rehearsal has been selected. However, we now know that for long term retention reheasal which incorporates no further analysis of the items but simply keeps them "echoing" in the mind is a very poor strategy (e.g. Craik and Watkins, 1973). Any report of the power of a mnemonic can only be in relative terms, in comparison to a specified control condition. For practical purposes this may be a group given no specific mnemonic instructions since then the degree of improvement is relative to what would have occurred without advice on a method of learning; it is a measure of the practical result of the experimenter's intervention. Even so, it will be relative to the prior knowledge of the control group. Subjects drafted in from Psychology courses probably know much more about mnemonic techniques than they did ten years ago, and consequently this baseline will have been raised.

VI. Conclusions

Is a good memory really necessary? Means of storing and retrieving information are improving all the time. We can all keep a diary, look up a reference book and before long we may be able to call up data on our own private computer terminal. Certainly, we now have access to stored information with a freedom that places a different demand upon memory than was appropriate two hundred years ago. Even so, we must not confuse the possession of information in a book or a computer with the accessibility of this information. The value of information depends on its being available when required. It is no use my owning a book on accounting if I do not understand it when I open it, if I do not remember that I own it when I am faced with an accounting problem, if I cannot find the solution without reading the entire book or if the book is packed in a trunk in the attic when I need it in my office. Even a diary becomes a burden if it has to be consulted too frequently, if the entries need to be very long, or if the user is mobile rather than desk bound. Our memories are used in conjunction with diaries and books rather than replaced by them. Those involved in teaching do need to consider the interrelationship of what they teach and the information sources available to the student. However, many facts as well as procedures for retrieving facts need to be stored and retrievable from memory.

A good memory is essential for intelligence and creativity. To solve a problem requires the recall of the appropriate components and strategies. Just as there is no point in having books on some subjects if they are never available when required, there is no point in knowing about something if that knowledge is not retrieved at the appropriate time. Much of everyday life is a form of problem solving, involving comprehension in the light of past experience.

One possible danger of reliance upon mnemonics is that the information will be encapsulated in the mnemonic and not integrated into the general development of knowledge in semantic memory. For example, many English people who use the "thirty days" rhyme to remember the lengths of the months are probably not aware of the regular pattern in the lengths of the month. With the exception of July and August, when two 31 day months occur together, and February with its exceptionally short and variable length, the long and short months alternate. This makes possible the knuckle mnemonic described by Hunter (Chapter 1). Knowledge of this pattern is probably unnecessary, but it illustrates the inherent danger which complete reliance upon a mnemonic can carry. The danger is difficult to evaluate, any disadvantages have to be weighed against the advantages of being able to recall in the first place! Such evidence as there is suggests that mnemonics become unnecessary as knowledge of the information they convey increases. They are useful to aid the initial acquisition of the information but with its continued use they drop out and are no longer relied upon (Atkinson, 1975; Barnes and Underwood, 1959).

Psychologists can give advice on memory improvement where what is to be learned are facts or disconnected items. We have little to say about memory for future actions or on ways of aiding retrieval. We are largely ignorant about memory in everyday life. This is only partially the result of the associationist, Ebbinghaus tradition (Ebbinghaus, 1885). It also reflects the difficulty of studying long term, realistic, intentional activities and their consequent failures. However, more efforts toward such studies need to be made.

References

Atkinson, R. C. (1975). Mnemotechnics in second-language learning. *Am. Psychol.* **30**, 821–828.

Atkinson, R. C. and Raugh, M. R. (1975). An application of the mnemonic key word method to the acquisition of a Russian vocabulary. *J. exp. Psychol.: Human Learning and Memory* **104**, 126–133.

Barclay, J. R., Bransford, J. D., Franks, J. J., McCarrell, N. S. and Nitsch, K. (1974). Comprehension and semantic flexibility. *J. Verb. Learn. Verb. Behav.* **13**, 471–481.

Barnes, J. M. and Underwood, B. J. (1959). "Fate" of first-list associations in transfer-theory. *J. exp. Psychol.* **58**, 97–105.

Bartlett, F. C. (1932). "Remembering". Cambridge University Press, Cambridge.

Blick, K. A., Buonassissi, J. V. and Boltwood, C. S. (1972). Mnemonic techniques used by college students in serial learning. *Psychol. Reports* **31**, 983–986.

Boltwood, C. E. and Blick, K. A. (1970). The delineation and application of three mnemonic techniques. *Psychonomic Sc.* **20**, 339–341.

Bower, G. H. (1970). Imagery as a relational organiser in associative learning. *J. Verb. Learn. Verb. Behav.* **9**, 529–533.

Bower, G. H. (1973). "How to . . . uh . . . Remember!" *Psychol. Today* **7**, 63–70.

Bower, G. H. and Bolton, L. S. (1969). Why are rhymes easy to learn. *J. exp. Psychol.* **82**, 453–461.

Bower, G. H. and Clark, M. C. (1969). Narrative stories as mediators for serial learning. *Psychonomic Sc.* **14**, 181–182.

Bower, G. H. and Reitman, J. S. (1972). Mnemonic elaboration in multilist learning. *J. Verb. Learn. Verb. Behav.* **11**, 478–485.

Bower, G. H. and Winzenz, D. (1970). Comparison of associative learning strategies. *Psychonomic Sc.* **20**, 119–120.

Bransford, J. D. and Johnson, M. K. (1973). Consideration of some problems of comprehension. In "Visual Information Processing" (W. G. Chase, Ed.). Academic Press, New York and London.

Breen, M. J. and Jurek, J. M. (1975). Serial learning as a function of age and part versus whole learning procedures. *Psychol. Reports* **36**, 767–773.

Broadbent, D. E. (1977). Levels, hierarchies and the locus of control. *Q. Jl exp. Psychol.* **29**, 181–201.

Bugelski, B. R. (1974). The image as mediator in one-trial paired-associate learning. III Sequential functions in serial lists. *J. exp. Psychol.* **103**, 298–303.

Bugelski, B. R., Kidd, E. and Segmen, J. (1968). Image as a mediator in one-trial paired-associate learning. *J. exp. Psychol.* **76**, 69–73.

Cooper, A. J. R. and Monk, A. (1976). Learning for recall and learning for recognition. *In* "Recall and Recognition" (J. Brown, Ed.). Wiley, London.

Craik, F. I. M. and Tulving, E. (1975). Depth of processing and the retention of words in episodic memory. *J. exp. Psychol.: General* **104** 268–294.

Craik, F. I. M. and Watkins, M. J. (1973). The role of rehearsal in short-term memory. *J. Verb. Learn. Verb. Behav.* **12**, 599–607.

Craik, K. J. W. (1966). "The Nature of Psychology". Cambridge University Press, Cambridge.

Crowder, R. G. (1976). "Principles of Learning and Memory". Lawrence Erlbaum Associates, Hillsdale, New Jersey.

Delin, P. S. (1969). The learning to criterion of a serial list with and without mnemonic instructions. *Psychonomic Sc.* **16**, 169–170.

Delprato, D. J. and Baker, E. J. (1974). Concreteness of pegwords in two mnemonic systems. *J. exp. Psychol.* **102**, 520–522.

DiVesta, F. J. and Sunshine, P. M. (1974). The retrieval of abstract and concrete materials as functions of imagery, mediation and mnemonic aids. *Memory and Cognition* **2**, 340–344.

Ebbinghaus, H. (1885). "Über das Gedächtnis". Duncker, Leipzig. (Translation by H. Ruyer and C. E. Busserius (1913)). "Memory". Teachers College, Columbia University, New York.

Frase, L. T. and Schwartz, B. J. (1975). Effect of question production and answering on prose recall. *J. educ. Psychol.* **67**, 628–635.

Gomulicki, B. G. (1956). Recall as an abstractive process. *Acta Psychol.* **12**, 77–94.

Groninger, L. D. (1971). Mnemonic imagery and forgetting. *Psychonomic Sci.* **23**, 161–163.

Gruneberg, M. M. (1973). The role of memorisation techniques in finals examination preparation—a study of Psychology students. *Educ. Res.* **15**, 134–139.

Gruneberg, M. M. (1978). The feeling of knowing, memory blocks and memory aids. *In* "Aspects of Memory" (M. M. Gruneberg and P. E. Morris, Eds). Methuen and Co., London.

Gruneberg, M. M. and Monks, J. (1974). Feeling of knowing and cued recall. *Acta Psychol.* **38**, 257–265.

Gruneberg, M. M. and Monks, J. (1976b). The feeling of knowing, memory aids and memory blocks. Proceedings of the Annual Conference of the BPS. *Bull. Br. Psychol. Soc.* **29**, 203.

Gruneberg, M. M. and Monks, J. (1976a). The first letter search strategy. *IRCS Med. Sci: Psychology and Psychiatry* **4**, 307.

Gruneberg, M. M., Monks, J. and Sykes, R. N. (1977). The first letter mnemonic aid. *IRCS Med. Sci: Psychology and Psychiatry* **5**, 304.

Gruneberg, M. M., Monks, J. and Sykes, R. N. (1977). Some methodological problems with feeling of knowing studies. *Acta Psychol.* **41**, 365–371.

Harris, J. E. (1978). External memory aids. *In* "Practical Aspects of Memory" (M. M. Gruneberg, P. E. Morris and R. N. Sykes, Eds). Academic Press, London and New York.

Hart, J. T. (1965). Memory and the feeling of knowing experience. *J. educ. Psychol.* **56**, 208–216.

Hauck, P. D., Walsh, C. C. and Kroll, N. E. A. (1976). Visual imagery mnemonics: Common vs. bizarre mental images. *Bull. Psychonomic Soc.* **7**, 160–162.

Herrmann, D. J. and Neisser, U. (1978). An inventory of everyday memory experiences. *In* "Practical Aspects of Memory" (M. M. Gruneberg, P. E. Morris and R. N. Sykes, Eds). Academic Press, London and New York.

Higbee, K. L. (1977). "Your Memory: How It Works and How to Improve It". Prentice-Hall, New Jersey.

Howe, M. J. A. (1970). "Introduction to Human Memory". Harper and Row, New York.

Hunter, I. M. L. (1964). "Memory". Penguin, Harmondsworth.

Kintsch, W. (1977). "Memory and Cognition". Wiley, London.

Kruger, W. V. F. (1929). The effect of overlearning on retention. *J. exp. Psychol.* **12**, 71–78.

La Porte, R. E. and Voss, J. F. (1975). Retention of prose materials as a function of postacquisition testing. *J. educ. Psychol.* **67**, 259–266.

Lesgold, A. M. and Goldman, A. R. (1973). Encoding uniqueness and the imagery mnemonic in associative learning. *J. Verb. Learn. Verb. Behav.* **12**, 193–202.

Lindsay, P. H. and Norman, D. A. (1972). "Human Information Processing". Academic Press, New York and London.

Loisette, A. (1896). "Assimilative Memory, or How to Attend and Never Forget". Funk and Wagnalls, New York.

Lorayne, H. (1957). "How to Develop a Super-Power Memory". Frederick Fell, New Tork.

Lorayne, H. and Lucas, J. (1976). "The Memory Book". Allen, London.

Lutz, K. A. and Lutz, R. J. (1977). Effects of interactive imagery on learning: application to advertising. *J. appl. Psychol.* **62**, 493–498.

Manning, B. A. and Bruning, R. H. (1975). Interactive effects of mnemonic techniques and word list characteristics. *Psychol. Rep.* **36**, 727–736.

McGeoch, J. A. (1942). "The Psychology of Human Learning". Longmans, Green, New York.

Miller, G. A., Galanter, E. and Primbram, K. H. (1960). "Plans and the Structure of Behavior". Holt, New York.

Morgan, C. T. and Deese, J. (1969). "How to Study". McGraw-Hill, New York.

Morris, P. E. (1977). Practical strategies for human learning and remembering. *In* "Adult Learning: Psychological Research and Applications (M. Howe, Ed.). Wiley, London.

Morris, P. E. (1978a). Encoding and retrieval. *In* "Aspects of Memory". (M. M. Gruneberg and P. E. Morris, Eds). Methuen and Co., London.

Morris, P. E. (1978b). Models of long term memory. *In* "Aspects of Memory" (M. M. Gruneberg and P. E. Morris, Eds). Methuen and Co., London.

Morris, P. E. (1978c). Sense and Nonsense in Traditional Mnemonics. *In* (M. M. Gruneberg, P. E. Morris and R. N. Sykes, Eds). "Practical Aspects of Memory" Academic Press, London and New York.

Morris, P. E. and Cook, N. (1978). When do first letter mnemonics aid recall? *Br. J. educ. Psychol.* **48**, 22–28.

Morris, P. E., Jones, S. and Hampson, P. J. (1978). An imagery mnemonic for the learning of people's names. *Br. J. Psychol.* **69**, 335–336.

Morris, P. E. and Reid, R. L. (1970). Repeated use of mnemonic imagery. *Psychonomic Sci.* **20**, 337–338.

Morris, P. E. and Reid, R. L. (1973). Recognition and recall: Latency and recurrence of images. *Br. J. Psychol.* **64**, 161–167.

Morris, P. E. and Reid, R. L. (1974). Imagery and recognition. *Br. J. Psychol.* **65**, 7–12.

Morris, P. E. and Reid, R. L. (1975). The role of stimulus and pair imagery in paired-associate learning. *Br. J. Psychol.* **66**, 153–156.

Morris, P. E. and Stevens, R. (1974). Linking images and free recall. *J. Verb. Learn. Verb. Behav.* **13**, 310–315.

Murray, F. S. (1974). Effects of narrative stories on recall. *Bull. Psychonomic Soc.* **4**, 577–579.

Nappe, G. W. and Wollen, K. A. (1973). Effects of instructions to form common and bizarre mental images on retention. *J. exp. Psychol.* **100**, 6–8.

Nelson, D. L. and Archer, C. S. (1972). The first letter mnemonic. *J. educ. Psychol.* **63**, 482–486.

Paivio, A. (1971). "Imagery and Verbal Processes". Holt, Rinehart and Winston, New York.

Raugh, M. R. and Atkinson, R. C. (1975). A mnemonic method for learning a second-language vocabulary. *J. educ. Psychol.* **67**, 1–16.

Reason, J. (1977). Skill and error in everyday life. *In* "Adult Learning: Psychological Research and Applications" (M. J. A. Howe, Ed.). Wiley, London.

Rowntree, D. (1970). "Learn How to Study". MacDonald, London.

Santa, J. L., Ruskin, A. B. and Yio, A. J. H. (1973). Mnemonic systems in free recall. *Psychol. Reports* **32** 1163–1170.

Shotter, J. (1976). "Images of Man". Methuen and Co., London.

Steffens, L. (1900). *Zeitschrift Psychology* **22**, 241–382. (Quoted by Wordworth, R. S. (1938) in "Experimental Psychology". Holt, New York.

Tulving, E. and Osler, S. (1968). Effectiveness of retrieval cues in memory for words. *J. exp. Psychol.* **77**, 593–601.

Tulving, E. and Thompson, D. M. (1973). Encoding specificity and retrieval processes in episodic memory. *Psychol. Rev.* **80**, 352–373.

Underwood, B. J. (1964). Degree of learning and the measurement of forgetting. *J. Verb. Learn. Verb. Behav.* **3** 112–129.

Waite, C. J., Blick, K. A. and Boltwood, C. E. (1971). Prior use of the first letter technique. *Psychol. Reports* **29**, 630.

Wilkins, A. J. and Baddeley, A. D. (1978). Remembering to recall in everyday life: an approach to absentmindedness. *In* "Practical Aspects of Memory" (M. M. Gruneberg, P. E. Morris and R. N. Sykes, Eds). Academic Press, London and New York.

Wortman, P. M. and Sparling, P. B. (1974). Acquisition and retention of mnemonic information in long term memory. *J. exp. Psychol.* **102**, 22–26.

Yates, F. A. (1966). "The Art of Memory". Routledge and Kegan Paul, London.

3. Educational Implications of Memory Research

M. J. A. HOWE AND S. J. CECI

Department of Psychology,
University of Exeter, UK
and
Department of Psychology,
University of North Dakota, USA

I. Introduction

It is hard to think of any educational goal for which the ability to retain information is unimportant; human memory is crucial for acquiring the knowledge and skills we learn at school. This chapter starts by illustrating some of the ways in which memory contributes to competence at educational tasks. Comprehension, computation and reasoning depend upon memory, and the difficulty of such tasks is often related to the weight of the memory demands they impose. Furthermore, individual differences in task performance are related to differences between people in their ability to retain information in memory. If we can help children and adults to remember more effectively, widespread educational gains will follow.

The first step towards achieving the goal of increased remembering is to acquire a reasonably detailed understanding of the ways in which people who can perform successfully at various memory tasks differ from those individuals whose performance at the same tasks is less successful. Developmental research involving comparisons between children and adults, and between younger and older children, and research comparing memory task performance by normal and mentally retarded individuals has yielded a considerable amount of information about the detailed processes that lead to individual differences in memory.

When we have identified some of the component processes and strategies that underlie individual differences in memory, we will be able to use this knowledge in two ways. First, we can attempt to discover methods of adapting the requirements of educational tasks so that they do not exceed the memory limitations of the students concerned. The potential of such "cloth-cutting" exercises is not unlimited, but they can be productive. The second way to use knowledge about individual differences in memory in order to help students achieve educational goals is more exciting, and the possible gains are greater. This way is to provide teaching and instruction that will enable people to adopt the memory strategies of older or more successful individuals. There now exists a body of research evidence indicating that this approach can often be effective. A substantial part of the chapter is concerned with efforts to improve performance at memory skills that are basic to the acquisition of human knowledge and human abilities.

II. Functions of Memory in Human Performance

Memory Load and Task Difficulty

Memory has an obvious role in certain kinds of tasks, such as remembering a telephone number, memorizing a poem, remembering what one needs to buy at a shop, or learning the dates of presidents and kings, for example, but it is no less essential in other tasks that are not ostensibly ones of memorization. In fact, memory is an essential component of a wide variety of human abilities. Consider two instances. The first is a problem of mental arithmetic, to multiply 222 by itself. This is very difficult: many of us would find it impossible to multiply 222×222 "in our heads". Why is this so? The computational requirements are not particularly demanding; we simply have to know that $2 \times 2 = 4$, and we need to be able to add numbers, and that is about all we have to do apart from having to remember various combinations of numbers. It is this latter requirement that is the main source of difficulty. Humans have a strictly limited capacity to keep quantities of items in mind. This quickly becomes apparent if we ask ourselves how to make the task of multiplying 222 × 222 easier. The answer, of course, is to find a way of easing the memory load, for instance, by using paper and pencil to store, externally, the information that we find so difficult to retain in our heads while we undertake the multiplication and addition operations that are, ostensibly, the important requirements of the task. If it was not for the need to retain items in memory, multiplying 222 × 222, or even 2 222 222 × 2 222 222 for that matter, would only be a slightly more difficult problem of mental arithmetic than multiplying 22 × 22. We might note at this point that the human limitation that is important here is not one of total storage capacity; indeed people do retain vast amounts of information. The main limitation lies in the number of separate items we can hold for short periods, typically several seconds, in a temporary or "working" memory store where the items are kept available for mental processing and can be consciously attended. (See Chapter 1.)

Another task in which the centrality of memory is not immediately obvious is described by Trabasso (1977). He introduces this problem.

(1) Edith is fairer than Suzanne.
(2) Edith is darker than Lili.
(3) Who is the darkest?

Trabasso points out that problems of this kind are generally considered to measure logical reasoning abilities, in particular the capacity to make "transitive inferences". Alternatively, however, the task requirements can be described in the terms of the information processing required to perform them. In setting out what needs to be achieved in order to solve the above problem correctly, Trabasso notes that it is essential to interpret the premises appropriately and to represent them mentally as some kind of ordered list. The processes that make this possible are essentially ones of encoding, representing, recoding, transforming, ordering, listing, scanning, matching and retrieving; in short, the cognitive functions of a human memory system. Analysis of the task requirements in terms of component functions such as these is considerably more fruitful than simply labelling the problem as one that necessitates "logical reasoning" or "transitive inferences".

In this and other instances we find that when we start to consider the kinds of detailed human functions that are necessary in order to perform a reasoning task, the operations of human memory are prominent amongst the essential functions. Thus Atwood and Polson (1976) have demonstrated that correctly performing the water jar problem described by Luchins (1942), in which water has to be poured between jugs of different sizes in a sequence of moves in order to produce a specified distribution, depends upon both temporary and long term retention of various items of information. Atwood and Polson provide a detailed description of the task requirements, showing the ways in which problem solving in this kind of situation depends upon memory. Reed and Johnson (1977) investigated the role of memory in the "Missionaries and Cannibals" problem, in which one has to specify how a number of people can be transported across a river in a boat of limited capacity under the constraint that there are never more cannibals than missionaries in any single location. These authors noted that ability to solve new problems depends to a large extent upon memory for the solution of previous problems.

The mental processes necessary for solving reasoning problems are not *exclusively* those of memory, and linguistic as well as logical operations are involved, but memory skills are nevertheless crucial to human reasoning. Indeed, even the most simple kinds of comprehension depend upon effective memory. "The man kicked the dog" would form a meaningless word sequence to a reader who was unable to retain information pertaining to the first few words until he reached the final ones. The remembering that is necessary for comprehending a lengthy and complex sentence may be considerable. The degree of difficulty of many tasks is closely related to the memory demands they impose.

Individual Differences in Memory and Human Abilities

Individual differences in memory make major contributions to individual differences in performance at mental skills. Scores on tests of short-term memory (STM) are generally found to be highly correlated with scores of mental ability. Whimbey *et al.* (1969) observed that people who gain high scores on tests of STM tend to perform well at other tasks that require information to be stored in memory whilst other data is being received and processed.

Whimbey *et al.* found there was a correlation of $+ 0.76$ between digit span test scores and scores on a mental addition test containing items which took the form, "You have 8A, 3B, 2C and 5D and you add to them 2B and 5D. How many of each category do you now have?". The high correlation between scores on the two tests suggests that a specific memory component, and not simply general intelligence, is important in the addition task. This conclusion is supported by Whimbey *et al.* who observe that the correlations between addition and vocabulary test scores were very low. The correlations that are found between STM test scores and general measures of intelligence are, in general, as large as those between intelligence and any other specific abilities. Rohwer and Dempster (1977) report correlations of +0·67 between digit span and WISC IQ scores and + 0·93 between digit span and WAIS vocabulary sub-test. In addition, Labouvie *et al.* (1973) have established that LTM as well as STM performance is related to mental ability. These authors observed that subjects' performance on a delayed multi-trial free recall task was strongly correlated with performance on several tests of primary mental abilities. In an unpublished study by Ceci, a correlation of − 0·89 was found between memory test performance and severity of learning disabilities in school children of normal intelligence who were reported to be experiencing difficulty in acquiring basic skills.

Working Memory

Having established that memory processes are crucial in many educational tasks that are not ostensibly ones of memory, and that ability to remember influences performance in various skills that are important in education, we can begin to enquire into the ways in which memory skills are involved in broader capacities, such as learning, reasoning, calculation and comprehension. Most researchers still find it useful to distinguish between LTM and STM, so long as it is possible to avoid the implication that these necessarily involve successive and physically separable stages. The contents of STM roughly correspond to "what is being remembered" by a person at a given time, and form a kind of "working memory" that temporarily retains both newly-perceived environmental information and information retrieved from LTM, while the information from both these sources is being used by the individual to cope with the demands of a task. A computing system such as the human brain needs to possess stores or "registers" where information is temporarily retained whilst mental operations are being performed on it.

Short-term memory provides a holding mechanism that stores data at the interface or working area where items that the individual has just perceived and information that he already possesses are brought together in order to deal with cognitive tasks. Differences between people in the functioning of STM, which may reflect either individual variability or developmental changes, influence the likelihood that events to which a person is exposed will contribute to the body of relatively permanent knowledge and skills that determine his intellectual competence. In addition, individual differences in the contents of LTM and in the retrieval of materials that are stored there affect the way in which new information will be experienced in the future.

Implicit in the concept of a working memory is the view that the processing capacity that is used to meet demands for retaining material in STM is shared by the demands for other concurrent intellectual functions. Baddeley and Hitch (1974) found that having to retain information in STM imposes a load that can restrict performance at other tasks that are being attempted at the same time, since the total shared information processing capacity is restricted. In one experiment Baddeley and Hitch compared the effect of varying the levels of concurrent memory load on the ability to comprehend prose passages being presented at the same time. The memory task consisted of lists of three or six digits, presented visually. The subjects, who were undergraduate students, had to retain the digit lists for two or four seconds, and then attempt written recall. A control condition incorporated presentation of the identical materials, which subjects had to write down, but without needing to retain the items in memory. The comprehension tasks were based upon 120-word prose passages which were read aloud to the subjects, who subsequently attempted to answer questions concerning the meaningful contents. The authors found that comprehension scores were not affected by a three-item memory load, but having to store six digits in memory did reduce scores on the comprehension test to a level significantly lower than scores in the control condition.

In a further experiment Baddeley and Hitch investigated the effects on a STM load of performance at a concurrent task of verbal reasoning. Each reasoning task involved a letter pair, A B, for example, which was preceded by a sentence, such as "A is not preceded by B". Subjects had to judge whether the sentence was a *true* or *false* description of the pair of letters. The forms of sentences were varied in a number of ways by alternatively using positive or negative statements, active or passive verbs, and the alternative terms "precedes" and "follows". In the condition that included a memory load, subjects listened to a list of six letters and had to retain them whilst they were given the reasoning task. Subjects in the control condition received similar memory tasks, but did not have to keep items in memory at the same time as they were trying to solve the reasoning test. The authors found that those subjects who were informed that it was important to ensure that recall was accurate took significantly longer to perform the reasoning task than subjects who were not burdened with STM load. The reasoning test speeds of subjects who were told to ensure that the problems were completed as accurately as possible were not affected by memory load, but those individuals recalled the items very inaccurately.

These experimental findings indicate that it is valid to speak of a working memory which makes use of a limited processing capacity that is shared by the task requirement of operations such as reasoning and comprehending, as well as straightforward memory demands. It might be argued that comprehension and reasoning processes compete with memory for the use of such shared capacity only in so far as each competing task necessitates information being retained. However, this simply serves to emphasize that the temporary retention of items in a form in which they are immediately available for various kinds of mental processing is essential for a variety of mental tasks.

III. Fitting the Task to the Learner by Reducing the Demands upon Memory

Methods for improving remembering provide the major means of surmounting those limitations on learning and other educational processes that are due to memory limitations. An alternative means of making use of what is known about the psychology of human memory in order to produce educational improvements is to adapt educational tasks to conform to the memory limitations of learners. An illustration by Miller (1956a) gives an indication of the possible value of this kind of approach. Miller poses the problem of discovering the area of a right-angled triangle, given only the length of the baseline (b) and that of the hypotenuse (h). He shows one solution, as follows:

(1) $h + b = v$
(2) $h - b = w$
(3) $v \times w = x$
(4) $\sqrt{x} = \pm y$
(5) $+y \times b = z$
(6) $z/2 = $ area.

The problem can be solved quite satisfactorily by the above method. However, it is an inconvenient method for learners to use, not because of any intrinsic difficulty in the equations, but because it is necessary to remember all the six steps. Retaining the steps imposes a burdensome load on memory. The only alternative is to consult a printed copy of the six steps each time the method is to be used, and this may not be at all convenient. Owing to these difficulties, Miller describes the above task solution as an "ugly" one, and he compares it unfavourably with a second solution, which involves memorizing fewer steps, as follows:

(1) Find the altitude by theory of Pythagoras.
(2) Find the area of the triangle from multiplying base times altitude and dividing by two.

This alternative method puts a smaller load upon the user's memory.

Miller describes it as an "efficient" solution, and it is certainly a more practical one for everyday use.

Other things being equal, if the teacher presents materials that are to be learned in a manner that makes light demands upon students' STM capacities, learning will be easier than if STM demands are heavy. This principle should be considered whenever instructional materials are being designed. Case (1975) emphasizes the importance of ensuring that demands in learning tasks are within young learners' capacities. He reports that learning problems are frequently caused by a mismatch between the capacities of the learner and the demands of instruction. Such problems can be eliminated by redesigning the instructional sequence to reduce the amount of information that has to be processed within a fixed time.

IV. Factors Underlying Individual Differences in Remembering

Having established the widespread necessity for remembering in tasks that are encountered in the process of education, we shall introduce evidence concerning the detailed characteristics of effective memory. What kinds of attributes or strategies are associated with high levels of success at tasks that demand human remembering? Data that are obtained from our attempts to answer this question can be used to help people to remember materials more effectively, and hence to perform better at many if not most of the tasks that are encountered in the process of becoming educated.

Most of the available information concerning individual differences in the detailed characteristics of human memory comes from developmental research comparing performance by children at different ages. Investigations into cultural differences, research into mental retardation, and studies of individuals with exceptional abilities to remember has yielded further evidence concerning the factors underlying successful remembering. We shall concentrate on the findings of developmental research, since they provide the most detailed and systematically organized body of knowledge about the detailed forms of differences in memory. First, however, we shall consider a few pertinent findings from other kinds of research.

Exceptional Memory

Analysis of the abilities of really exceptional memorizers has produced many interesting findings, although it does not always yield insights that can be applied to helping normal people to remember more. The well-known mnemonist S, who Luria (1968) describes in his book "The Mind of a Mnemonist", appeared to have a memory system that made great use of visual imagery and worked on principles that were different from the mechanisms of memory in ordinary people. Although S's ability to memorize was undoubtedly phenomenal, it is worth noting that the operation of his memory appears to have been counter-productive for him in certain important respects, as is evident from his frustration at the omnipresent concrete images that made abstract thought virtually impossible for him. On the whole, Luria's account of memory in S offers little that can contribute to useful improvements in ordinary people's remembering. Similarly, other descriptions of remarkable memorizers, such as a girl described by Coltheart and Glick (1974) who possesses the unusual ability to speak words backwards immediately upon hearing them, suggest that their rare feats of memory depend upon mechanisms that operate in ways that are very different from the workings of normal memory. Knowing about the methods followed by such individuals has had limited value for attempts to improve remembering in normal individuals.

Of greater relevance to our wish to improve remembering is Hunter's (1962; 1977, see also Chapter 1) description of Professor A. Aitken, a mathematician who had an outstanding ability to remember numerical symbols. He used this ability to perform a variety of feats of mental calculation; for instance, he could recall the value of π to 1000 decimal places. A key to Aitken's mnemonic abilities lay in his extensive knowledge about the items he was remembering. This enabled him to perceive lists of numbers as being far more meaningful than they are for most people. As Hunter notes in Chapter 1, Aitken's considerable resources of LTM were brought into operation to reduce the effort necessary for calculation. Thus, on hearing the sequence 1961, Aitken immediately recognized it as being the product of 37×53, and the sum of either $44^2 + 5^5$ or $40^2 + 19^2$.

The importance of a person knowing about the items he is trying to retain becomes increasingly clear as one makes further comparisons between the circumstances of more and less successful attempts to remember. Brown (1975) draws attention to the finding that excellent chess players can remember the positions of around 24 chess pieces without great difficulty, so long as the positions are legitimate ones in the game of chess. Unskilled amateur players can only remember around ten positions. Reitman (1976) observed similar differences between beginners and master players in memory for the positions of pieces in the game "Go". Chi (1978) found that children aged ten who were keen chess players recalled the positions of chess pieces more accurately than adults who could play chess but had limited knowledge of the game. It is clear that sheer degree of knowledge about chess makes an enormous difference in situations of this kind. When the chess pieces are randomly placed on the squares of a chessboard, an unskilled amateur player can remember just as many of the positions as an advanced chess master. The superior performance of the latter at remembering legitimate chess positions is partly due to the ability to make correct inferences, based on existing knowledge about the game. Brown also mentions Bartlett's account of a cowherd who could recall the identifying marks and the prices of hundreds of animals long after they had been sold. Again, the degree of knowledge about the particular items being remembered appears to have been a crucial consideration. However, other studies of individual differences in memory suggest that knowledge about the items being retained is by no means the only source of variability in memory performance. In the following section, which describes developmental research into the components of human memory, we shall encounter a number of important other factors.

Since about 1965 a substantial amount of research into the development of human memory has been undertaken, and as a result it is now possible to give a reasonably complete answer to the question, "Why do adults and older children remember more than young children?". As it happens, many of the researchers who have investigated the factors underlying developmental changes in memory have also been interested in the trainability of memory functions. Studies have been undertaken to discover if teaching young children to use strategies that are associated with the higher levels of memory task performance obtained by older children can produce improvements in remembering by the young children. For reasons of convenience we shall defer consideration of training studies until later.

Causes of Developmental Improvements in Remembering

Broadly speaking, we can distinguish four categories of possible causes of age-related improvements in memory. First, it is conceivable that there are *capacity* changes in the basic physiological hardware of memory systems. Thus the number of "slots" (Chi, 1976) for storing information in STM might increase with age, or the speed at which memory traces fade might decrease. As it happens, the available evidence suggests that changes in basic memory capacities after early childhood are small or non-existent. However, it appears that each of the three other factors does make a contribution to age-related improvements in remembering.

The second category refers to the strategies individuals use when attempting to remember. It is contended that there are important age-related differences in strategies of labelling, mediation, organization and rehearsal for example, and that older individuals profit from adopting more effective strategies. The third kind of change underlying developmental memory improvements is in the knowledge individuals possess concerning the materials being remembered. The examples of chess players and numerical calculators we have already mentioned demonstrate that the degree of knowledge a person possesses about particular items may considerably affect the probability of remembering them. It appears that the increases in knowledge that occur as children get older make a contribution to their increasing ability to remember. Increases in knowledge may raise the possibility of a person being able to relate newly-perceived items to existing knowledge. It can also raise the effectiveness of retrieval plans and improve the accuracy of the inferences that people make when trying to reproduce information on the basis of partial retention.

Fourthly, there appear to be considerable age-related changes in the extent to which children can deliberately adopt plans to help them remember things. As they get older, children become increasingly aware that it may be necessary to make an effort to remember things. They begin to understand that the use of appropriate plans or strategies can lead to increased remembering. To refer to this kind of knowledge about how to remember, Flavell (1971) introduced the term "Metamemory Processes". The young child is at first barely able to make a distinction between perceiving something and trying to remember it. Age-related increases in the ability to make deliberate efforts to remember and to select and pursue memory strategies have marked effects on performance. The growing child acquires increasingly effective "executive control" over the activities and processes that facilitate remembering. Although the basic hardware of memory does not change, the ability to make effective use of it increases very considerably.

It is important to realize that this convenient and useful categorization of the factors underlying memory changes is not entirely satisfactory in every respect. One problem is that the categories of change are not completely independent. For instance, the operation of a *strategy*, such as one involving rehearsal, may depend to a marked extent upon the *knowledge* an individual possesses. Another difficulty is that it is not always easy to decide into which category a particular process best fits.

For example, some of the plans that individuals adopt clearly fit into the strategies category but in other cases it is hard to decide if the strategies or metamemory category is most appropriate. Similarly, it is not always possible to distinguish with certainty between what appear to be basic memory capacities and certain acquired processes. The latter may initially have taken the form of deliberate strategies, but with experience, have become completely automatic and entirely outside the conscious control of the individual. It is important to realize that the fact that a process may take place completely automatically, and without the individual being aware of it, provides no reliable evidence for it being unlearned or controlled by basic hardware of the memory system. In fact, the majority of processes which form individuals' strategies in memory tasks are performed automatically and without awareness. It is well known that the products of conscious experience provide few reliable guidelines and many false clues about the operation of human cognition (Pylyshyn, 1973).

The possibility of changes in basic capacity

Recent empirical research has offered no firm support for the view that increases in basic capacities for retaining or processing information form a major cause of developmental memory changes after early childhood. The finding that older children and adults can remember more items than young children does not appear to be due to structural changes in the capacity available for retaining information or in the rate of decay of information from memory. It would be very difficult to provide conclusive proof that no structural alterations in capacity occur at all, but two kinds of evidence indicate that even if such changes do take place, they do not make a marked contribution to memory development after the earliest years. First, it is found that when children of different ages are compared at tasks in which the influence of factors other than basic capacity are minimized, young children tend to perform as well as adults. Secondly, the evidence appears to suggest that developmental changes in memory can be adequately accounted for by age-related improvements in the use of strategies and metamemory processes, and by differences in knowledge about items to be remembered (see Harris, 1978). In the following paragraphs we shall discuss evidence concerning the influence of these factors.

Strategies

A considerable body of research findings indicates that the control processes which students undertake when confronted by a task that necessitates information being retained have marked effects upon performance (see Chapter 2). We shall refer to such activities as strategies, bearing in mind that the use of a strategy does not necessarily imply any conscious intention to do so. The strategies that a person acquires can take many forms, for instance labelling, elaborating, various kinds of coding processes, using mediators, organizing items, rehearsal and various other planned activities. A number of illustrations will serve to demonstrate the fact that the more successful memory performance of older children than younger children reflects greater use of effective strategies.

The strategy of rehearsing items is a control process that has been investigated by a number of researchers. The fact that rehearsal can be consciously controlled makes it relatively amenable to investigation. One effect of rehearsal is to maintain items in STM. As a result, information remains available and may be incorporated into the individuals body of permanently stored knowledge. Other things being equal, the individual who rehearses will recall more information than a person who does not rehearse, and items that a person rehearses are more likely to be recalled by him than items which he does not rehearse.

Young children under about five years of age do not rehearse spontaneously. As a result, their performance at memory tasks suffers. To gain a rough indication of the amount of rehearsal that children undertake, Flavell et al. (1966) observed the lip movements of children who were trying to remember the names of some common objects. Lip movements were observed in 17 out of the 20 ten-year-old subjects, but in only two out of 20 five-year-olds. Within each age there was a positive relationship between the presence of lip movements and the number of items recalled. A further experiment was undertaken by Keeney et al. (1967) to discover it the above relationship involved a causal link between rehearsal and recall. Children aged six and seven years were observed as they attempted to recall item lists. As in the previous study those children who made mouth movements, indicating rehearsal, recalled more items than the other children. Next, these children who did not spontaneously rehearse were given careful instructions to do so, by whispering the names of the pictures during the interval between presentation and recall. The children were able to follow this instruction without difficulty. When they did so, their level on recall improved to that of the children who did rehearse spontaneously. This finding clearly supports the assertion that rehearsal causes improved performance. It appears that young children who do not rehearse are not necessarily unable to do so. There may be what Flavell and his co-researchers term a "production deficiency", whereby some children have not yet acquired the habit of making use of a skill that already lies within their competence.

A source of difficulty in interpreting the above findings is that it is not absolutely clear whether the beneficial effects related to the children's lip movements were due to rehearsal as such or were effects of naming or labelling the objects (which must precede verbal rehearsal) or of both naming and rehearsal in combination. Subdivision of children's memory strategies into different types is at best a somewhat crude process, and the actual control processes that people use tend to involve a number of components. However, the evidence does indicate that naming or labelling activities can influence recall even when they are not followed by rehearsal. Hagen and Kingsley (1968) specifically instructed some of their child subjects to speak aloud the names of objects represented by pictures. In children aged six, seven and eight years instructions to say the words did lead to increased recall, but recall in older children, aged ten, and in very young children, aged four, was not influenced by this instruction. A possible explanation of the absence of an effect in the oldest and youngest subjects is that ten-year-olds name items spontaneously (presumably silently) and four-year-olds are too young to benefit from a naming strategy.

The findings of a number of experiments indicate that the effectiveness of rehearsing depends on the particular kind of rehearsal strategy that is followed. For example, Kingsley and Hagen (1969) found that children who rehearsed the names of picture objects in a cumulative manner, repeatedly rehearsing the complete list up to the item most recently presented, recalled more items than children who simply rehearsed each single item as it was presented, one at a time. In general, children do not gain the habit of naming and rehearsing items spontaneously until some time after they have reached an age when they could profit from doing so. They have to learn how to time their rehearsals appropriately to take advantage of the intervals between presentation of the separate items (Hagen et al., 1973) and to rehearse cumulatively, rather than one item at a time (Ornstein et al., 1975). Activities such as rehearsing are by no means all-or-none strategies. Experience contributes to a developing ability to select and follow forms of rehearsal that are well suited to each particular task.

The other kinds of strategies that enable the older child and adult to remember larger quantities of information than younger children include various organizing, grouping and categorizing activities, linking processes for forming connections between separate items, techniques that involve forming visual images of materials to be remembered, and plans for allocating time efficiently between different items. The strategy that is followed in a particular task may involve a combination of some of the above activities, and in the course of a task an individual may alter the strategies he employs. Research into developmental changes in the kinds of strategies that are used is reviewed by Chi (1976), Huttenlocher and Burke (1976) and Hagen and Stanovich (1977).

The fact that simply telling children to undertake simple strategies such as naming and rehearsing items can produce marked increases in remembering, encourages us to expect that instruction and training in strategic activities may lead to considerable improvements at a variety of other tasks in which the memory requirement is important. As we shall see later, this does seem to be the case.

Knowledge

Developmental increases in children's knowledge provide a further age-related factor that contributes to remembering. Improvements in ability to remember verbal materials are due in part to increases in the capacity to identify and encode the items that are to be remembered. In turn, this capacity is related to the extent of the individual's knowledge about the items. Huttenlocher and Burke (1976) press this view more strongly, arguing that there is no firm support for the view that strategies as such lead to increases in memory. They claim that improved memory strategies are simply a byproduct of increased knowledge about the items being retained in memory. Chi (1978) advances a similar view. She considers that most of the age improvements observed in memory-related tasks may be traced to differences between children and adults in the amounts of information stored in memory.

It is undoubtedly true that some strategies can only be undertaken if the individual possesses appropriate knowledge. For example, in order to pursue an organizational strategy in which words are grouped into semantic categories, it is essential for the person to know about those attributes of the items that serve as a basis for semantic grouping. Similarly, a strategy of rehearsing items in meaningful groups can only be followed if the individual has the knowledge on which item grouping is based. Our view is that both the use of appropriate strategies and possession of appropriate knowledge contribute to age-related increases in memory. In some circumstances, however, a child who acquires the knowledge about items that is necessary in order to make use of a certain strategy may adopt the strategy in the absence of any deliberate training in the strategic activity as such. In one experiment by Stephen Ceci (Howe, 1976) children aged three and four years were shown pictures of animals, and it was explained to the children that the birth of each animal occurred in one of three different ways. After learning about the methods of birth, the children were shown pictures of some of the animals again, and they were later asked to recall these items. On examining the order in which the animals were recalled, it was found that the children to whom the methods of birth had been explained spontaneously clustered the animals on this basis. Moreover, these children recalled more items than children who had not been so instructed.

The more a person knows about meanings of an item stored in his memory the more easily the item can be retrieved. This is partly because a larger number of related items can serve as possible retrieval cues. Thus, when we have to retrieve from memory the retained word *cow*, various kinds of knowledge about cows can serve to provide retrieval cues. Knowing that a cow is a mammal, an animal, a quadruped, a provider of milk, is large, is similar to a bull, is found on farms, and so on, can serve as cues or "tags" via which access to the word may be facilitated. A young child who knows only a few of these semantic attributes has a smaller quantity of potential tags available to him than an older person. That is, the number of potential items which can provide access routes to retrieve the word is smaller than the number available to an adult. Hence, the probability that a related item will function as an effective recall cue is lower in the case of a young child than an adult. With increasing age, a child's knowledge enlarges, and the number of routes via which a particular item may be located increases. When items simply have to be recognized, and not recalled, however, the number of meanings or tags possessed by the individual is less important as a determinant of success at retrieving items.

Another reason for the finding that increases in knowledge are accompanied by more accurate remembering lies in the fact that when people try to remember things, they often make use of inferences. Estimates or guesses about what is to be remembered are made on the basis of what is known to be true. The greater the degree of knowledge an individual possesses in relation to what he is trying to recall, the greater the probability that such inferences will be correct.

There is considerable evidence that children and adults do make use of inferences based on existing knowledge when they are trying to remember information. Following Bartlett, recall can be regarded as a partly reconstructive process. In the circumstances of everyday life, exact reproduction is rare; the individual unconsciously incorporates existing knowledge. Piaget and Inhelder (1973) place a similar emphasis on the function of inference-making in memorization, and they refer to memory as being essentially constructive. Thus when

Paris and Carter (1973) presented sentences to children aged seven and ten years, and subsequently presented novel sentences that were semantically consistent with the premises of the original sentences, the children incorrectly reported that the new sentences were the ones that had been presented originally. There was a similar finding when pictures were shown. Paris and Mahoney (1974) presented children with sets of thematically related sentences and pictures. In a subsequent recognition test children reported having previously perceived sentences and pictures that were in fact new to them, providing that the meanings of the contents of the new items were consistent with those of the original items. The kinds of inferences that led to "errors" in the above experiments have a very positive role in real-life remembering.

When we have to remember things in everyday life it is often necessary to make inferences, elaborations and organizations that incorporate both the information that has just been made available to a person and the stored information that forms his personal body of knowledge. In a typical brief conversation between friends, for instance, each participant will extract meaning from what is said by making a variety of inferences and assumptions that are based upon his existing knowledge (Hagan *et al.*, 1975; see also Bernstein, 1962). Even in those circumstances in which it is commonly supposed that narrative accounts are repeated word-for-word, within an oral tradition of story-telling, close analysis reveals that exact reproduction is generally absent, and that inferences are plentiful. Brown (1975) discusses an investigation of the oral recitation of South Slavonic songs. The singers deliver songs throughout the forty nights of Ramadan, and the basic themes and the structures of the songs, which are very significant to the listeners, are traditional. Considerable feats of memory are involved, and the singers report that they sing each song precisely as they received it from other singers. However, this is not actually the case; close analysis reveals that each individual singer considerably modifies the details of the songs. Every performance of the song is essentially the singer's own construction, based on a constant structure of central themes and ideas to which the singer contributes details in an individual manner (see also Chapter 1).

Methodological difficulties make it hard to establish precisely how the contribution of inferential factors to memory is affected by child development, but it is clear the marked developmental changes take place in the inferential operations that influence remembering (Paris and Lindauer, 1976). Paris and Upton (1976) found that when children listened to stories and were then questioned about the contents, older children not only remembered more accurately than younger subjects, but they also obtained the highest scores on questions that involved inferred presuppositions and consequences of the stories. In another experiment it was observed that children who made consistent inferences tended to perform most accurately on a test of free recall for stories. Ability to make correct inferences was a good predictor of accuracy of remembering, and increasingly so among the older children, suggesting that the functional value of making such inferences may increase with age.

Metamemory

The final category of factors contributing to memory that shows systematic differences between children and adults form what Flavell calls "Metamemorial Processes". He uses this term to refer to awareness of the need to remember and knowledge about importance of selecting effective methods for remembering something.

As children grow older, they become increasingly more adept in knowing how to remember what they need to retain. The things that a person does in order to remember information and events can be regarded the "tools for the job" of remembering, and metamemory processes control decisions concerning the tool to use for a particular memory task.

Metamemorial processes vary considerably in complexity and sophistication. A very young child may be hardly aware of the distinction between simply seeing something and attending to it closely, and making him aware of this may appreciably improve remembering. A slightly older child may be helped by being made aware of the value of making some kind of deliberate attempt to remember. In older children and adults a degree of knowledge of these distinctions can be taken for granted. Individual differences related to metamemorial processes may reside in the suitability of the methods and the strategies that a person adopts in order to deal with a particular task. The sophisticated adult learner possesses a repertoire of effective strategies and can choose a strategy that will be maximally effective for a task at hand, altering the strategy he is using when ever it is useful to do so. High levels of success reflect the ability to select a particular strategy that provides "the right tool for the job" in a variety of situations, rather than in the possession of any one particular strategy that is not available to the less successful. As Campione and Brown (1977, p. 374) note, "different strategies are effective in different situations, and the mature memorizer is able to evaluate the task demands accurately enough to come up with an appropriate choice".

The magnitude of developmental performance differences in a memory task will depend upon the degree to which a deliberate strategy is necessary (Brown, 1975). In recognition tasks, strategic intervention is not required to any great extent and it is generally found that developmental differences are small or non-existent, as are differences between normal and retarded subjects (Campione and Brown, 1977). Training or instruction does not produce large improvements.

Flavell's use of the term "metamemory" is very broad. It can refer to a person being aware of memory and knowing anything that is pertinent to information storage and retrieval (Flavell and Wellman, 1977). Amongst the manifestations of possessing metamemory are knowing that some things are easier to remember than others and being aware that one item is on the verge of recall while another is quite irretrievable. Rudimentary metamemory capabilities are present at as young as three years of age. In one experiment by Wellman *et al.* (1975), three-year-olds watched a toy being placed under one of a number of identical cups. After a 45 second delay, the children were told to find the toy. The experimenter had left the room during the delay period, having previously instructed the child either to *wait* with the toy or to *remember* where the toy was located. During the delay period, the children who were specifically told to remember where the toys were situated showed more behaviour that suggested they were attempting to retain the items or preparing to retrieve them than the children who were simply told to wait. Furthermore, under some conditions the children who were told to remember recalled the items more accurately than the other children. There was a positive correlation between accuracy of recall and the numbers of behaviours during the delay period that appeared to be directed towards remembering the items.

Knowing about how to remember increases with age, and performance at tasks that involve memory is thereby improved. Kreutzer *et al.* (1975) found that some of the six-year-olds and most of the seven-year-olds they tested realized that increases in the amount of time available to study pictures would result in higher levels of recall. Similarly, eight-year-olds in an investigation by Rogoff *et al.* (1974) studied picture items for longer if they were first told that they would be expected to remember them over a period of at least one day, than if they had to remember them for only a few minutes. However, six- and four-year-olds did not study the items carefully when they were told that lengthy retention was required.

Most of the ten-and eleven-year-olds observed by Kreutzer *et al.* (1975), but very few of the six- and seven-year-olds, realized that word pairs made of opposites (for example: *hard, easy*) would be easier to learn than pairs of random words. Older children were also more likely to perceive that presentation of items in narrative form would lead to increased remembering. Flavell *et al.* (1970) found that children aged seven to ten years were much better at estimating when they were ready to recall items accurately than four to six-year-olds. Age-related differences were found in the accuracy of "feeling of knowing" judgements (in which people who cannot recall the answer to a question predict whether or not they will be able to recognize it when it is displayed within a list of other items) and in the related "tip of the tongue" experience (Flavell and Wellman, 1977). Children aged nine were better than five-year-olds at predicting whether they would recognize items. Even in five-year-olds, however, a child's answers to questions about whether an item that the child was unable to name had been seen before proved to be quite accurate predictors. This finding is consistent with the view that the younger child's inability to assess whether they would recognize things was not due to a lack of appropriate cues. Rather it is a failure to appreciate that awareness of having previously seen an item increases the likelihood of subsequent recognition.

A number of metamemorial capacities that increase with age are related to children's knowledge about the effectiveness of retrieval strategies. In the study by Kreutzer *et al.* (1975) children were asked to try to think of all the things they could do in order to try to find a jacket they had lost while at school. Most children could think of at least one sensible search strategy, but the older children were able to imagine a larger number of possible retrieval strategies than the younger ones, and the older children were more likely to produce relatively sophisticated strategies, such as retracing the day's activities from the place where the child last remembered being aware of the jacket. Older children were also more successful at thinking of strategies to retrieve information about when a particular event had taken place.

V. Increasing the Ability to Remember

We have established that memory requirements provide a major source of the difficulty of many, if not most, of the circumstances that contribute to a person's education. We have also shown that individual and developmental differences in remembering are largely determined by the strategies that are followed, by the learner's state of knowledge about the materials to be remembered, and by awareness of the processes and activities that lead to effective remembering. Since improvements in the accuracy of remembering can bring about numerous educational gains, it will be clear that any success that is obtained at improving memory performance has considerable practical value in education. In some of the studies we have discussed, simple instructions to perform a memory task in one way rather than another produced marked improvements in remembering. This finding encourages us to expect that in a variety of circumstances training procedures that have been specifically designed to yield such improvements will be successful.

To demonstrate that age-related improvements in memory are largely due to increasingly effective strategies, knowledge and metamemorial processes, we have considered the effects of the three kinds of phenomena separately, but in the practical circumstances of everyday life they typically combine together to influence memory. Two of the three categories, strategies and metamemorial processes, refer to activities that are rapidly acquired, through learning, and which once acquired can be applied in a variety of situations. Nevertheless, it is necessary to distinguish between acquiring the *ability* to use an effective strategy and gaining the *habit* of regularly doing so.

In a number of investigations it has been found that even when children have been taught an effective strategy that clearly raises performance levels, the children do not continue to use the strategy when specific instructions to do so are no longer provided. Furthermore, young children tend not to apply a newly-learned strategy to situations different from that in which it was acquired, even though, from an adult viewpoint, the value of doing so might appear to be obvious. It is important to realize that the habit of following a new procedure, however valuable it may be, may take time and practice to acquire.

There is little doubt that most of the activities that go under the general headings "strategies" and "metamemorial processes" can be acquired through learning. It follows that the memory improvements that are due to improved strategies and metamemory processes can be induced by appropriate training. Concerning the contribution of increased knowledge to remembering, however, the situation is somewhat different. The problem is that the effects on memory of acquiring a particular item of knowledge tend to be specific to the remembering of particular kinds of information. Thus, if a child's lack of knowledge about a word prevents him utilizing a potentially useful organizational strategy, acquiring further knowledge about that word might enable him to adopt the strategy, and help him to learn the items. However, the newly-acquired knowledge would be little or no help for learning an entirely different set of materials.

Studies of Memory Training

We shall next describe some studies that have been undertaken to discover whether various memory skills can be improved by appropriate training. The findings support the view that training can produce improvements in important aspects of human memory. Since memory is a limiting factor in numerous educationally significant task situations, successful techniques for improving memory skills have considerable practical value.

Rehearsal training

Rehearsal is one activity that has been examined in experimental research investigating the effects of instructing children to engage in memory strategies. Following the observation of Flavell *et al.* (1966) that developmental and individual differences in children's recall are related to differences in the amount of spontaneous rehearsal (assessed by measuring lip movements), Keeney *et al.* (1967) established that when five- and six-year-old children who did not spontaneously rehearse were encouraged to do so, their recall of the names of pictures they were shown rose to the higher levels obtained by children who did spontaneously rehearse. However, these investigators remarked that after a child had profited from following rehearsal instructions, he did not necessarily continue to rehearse. A child may need prompting to rehearse at the appropriate moment (Hagen *et al.*, 1973), and when young children do rehearse they do not always do so in an effective manner (Ornstein *et al.*, 1975). In other words, effective rehearsal depends not only on a person being able to rehearse, but also upon his knowing when and how to rehearse most advantageously and gaining the habit of rehearsing.

Mentally retarded individuals often benefit from rehearsal instructions similar to those that are effective with normal children. Brown *et al* (1973) found that after retarded adolescents had been trained to rehearse they remembered more items, and their general pattern of performance after training became more similar than previously to those of normal subjects who rehearsed spontaneously. Butterfield *et al.* (1973) trained subjects to rehearse in a particular manner the six items that were presented to them in a self-paced task. Subjects were taught to pause after the third item, then rehearse the first three items, and then briefly expose the final three before the recall test. Adopting this strategy produced large improvements in recall. We shall return later to this interesting study.

Training in Organization

Various kinds of organizing and grouping activities have been shown to lead to improvements in remembering. When lists of unrelated items have to be remembered, simple temporal grouping into twos and threes can lead to marked improvements. Many kinds of organizational activities involve detecting relationships between the items, or coding the materials in a manner that effectively reduces the number of separate items to be retained and subsequently retrieved. The advantages of coding information was demonstrated in a well-known experiment by S. Smith, reported by Miller (1956b). Pairs and triplets of the items that formed lists of binary digits were recoded into shorter sequences of decimal digits. (For example, 00 might be recoded as 0, 01 as 1, 10 as 2, 11 as 3.) The outcome of requiring subjects to recode the binary items in this manner was to increase the length of list that each person could remember correctly. Slak (1970) showed that recoding digits phonemically can also lead to increases in the number of items retained in memory. However, learning the code used in Slak's study was an arduous task.

Considerable evidence exists that young children's memory performance improves when they are taught or encouraged to use organizational strategies involving grouping or categorizing activities which they do not adopt spontaneously. Liberty and Ornstein (1973) required nine-year-old children to sort items into an organized pattern used by adults. These authors found that retention levels increased, and items were retained with a higher degree of organization. Lange and Hultsch (1970) and S. K. Northrop (Moely, 1977) observed that children aged from five to 11 years who were told to sort picture items into groups recalled them more accurately than children who were simply told to examine the pictures. In Northrop's study the improvement was maintained over a period of one week. Moely et al. (1969) found that children as young as five years old were able to arrange items into categories, but they did not spontaneously do so when they were trying to learn the items. However, when appropriate instructions were provided these children could use their categorizing skills to improve recall. Training in the use of category organization also led to improved remembering in six- and seven-year -old children observed by Moely and Jeffrey (1974). In training sessions, the experimenter suggested to the children that items could be divided into groups of things that went together or were alike in some way, and she provided necessary practice and assistance. Following training the children's recall performance improved: they remembered a larger number of categories and more items in each category.

As in the case of rehearsal strategies, it appears that children sometimes exhibit a "production deficiency" in categorizing. Although they have the ability to organize verbal materials into categories, an activity that would lead to improvements in remembering, they by no means always do so. Just as we found to be true for rehearsal strategies, it appears that simply possessing an organization skill is not sufficient to guarantee that a person gains the habit of actually applying organizational strategies that are appropriate to the requirements of a particular task. In fact, young children may be quite unaware of the fact that organizing items into semantic categories can lead to improved recall. Moynahan (1973) found that children aged nine years and over were considerably more likely than seven-year-olds to predict that a list of items organized into categories would be easier to remember than a similar quantity of unrelated items.

A number of factors may influence the likelihood of a person adopting the kinds of organizational strategies that improve retention, in the absence of explicit instructions to form groups or categories. One is the presence of a deliberate intention to learn, and this will be discussed later, as an instance of metamemory. Another is the form of the activities required when the material is presented. When children participating in an experiment by Jenkins (1974) had to engage in activities such as providing modifiers for words or rating their pleasantness, which necessitate the meanings of the items being comprehended, they subsequently recalled more words than children who were given tasks at the time of presentation that involved attending only to formal attributes of the words, such as their sounds. A similar finding was obtained in an investigation by Turnure *et al.* (1976), to be described later. Murphy and Brown (1975) observed that four-year-olds who had previously had to identify the appropriate semantic group of each item recalled more items than children who simply noted their colour or sound.

Training verbal mediation

Situations in which the use of organizational strategies results in improved remembering typically involve the learner detecting relationships or similarities between list items. Doing so involves extensive cognitive functioning by mental processes that "mediate" between the input and output of information. The term "mediation" refers to any of a wide range of cognitive events underlying human information-processing. In memory research the word may refer to activities that function to form links between materials that need to be remembered. In "elaborative mediation" the individual inserts information (in the form of a sentence or a visual image, for example) that adds to what is to be retained. This results in what may appear to be a paradoxical situation, in which it is apparently easier for the individual to retain a body of information that is longer and more complex than the array that was originally presented. The basic reason why such strategies are successful is that the task ceases to be one of retaining a number of entirely separate items, since they become connected within an already structured body of meaningful knowledge.

An early demonstration of the effectiveness of a strategy involving elaborative mediation was provided by Jensen and Rohwer (1963). They found that mentally retarded adults performed considerably better at a paired-associate word learning task if they were given sentences that had the function of joining the words that formed each pair. Training in the use of sentence mediators also leads to improvements in normal children up to about seven years old, but not in older children and adults (Jensen, 1971), because older individuals spontaneously introduce similar strategies or other activities that are equally successful. It was noted by Peterson (1973) that seven-year-old children were less likely to produce elaborative mediation in a word learning task when a time restriction was placed upon them.

In general, until cognitive strategies become well established the individual has to invest a considerable amount of time and conscious effort in them. The ability to follow strategies in a manner that appears to be effortless and automatic is acquired only as a result of considerable practice. It might be desirable for classroom teachers to give priority to helping children's newly acquired strategies to become firmly established.

Rohwer and Dempster (1977) point out that there are marked individual differences in elaborative activities at all ages. Elaboration, in common with other strategies, is by no means always undertaken in those circumstances in which it would be advantageous. Rohwer and Dempster note that people may adopt the practice of constructing stories that have the mediating function of helping to join initially separate and unconnected items. The effects of specifically instructing young adults to follow such a strategy can be dramatic, as is shown in the findings of an experiment by Bower and Clark (1969). They presented 12 successive lists of ten nouns and instructed subjects to form narratives that effectively connected the items. The following is a typical narrative. The ten nouns forming the original list appear in capitals.

A VEGETABLE can be a useful INSTRUMENT for a COLLEGE student. A carrot can be a NAIL for your FENCE or BASIN. But a MERCHANT of the QUEEN would SCALE that fence and feed the carrot to a GOAT.

When recall of each list was requested immediately following presentation, there were no substantial differences between subjects who had been instructed to make narrative sentences and other subjects (forming a control group) who received no such directions. Both groups achieved near perfect recall. However, after all the lists had been presented the participants were required to recall as many items as they could from all lists. At this stage there was a large difference between the groups. Those individuals who had been told to form narrative recalled 93% of the words, on average, whereas subjects in the control condition recalled only 13% of the words. This pattern of findings should serve to remind us that the effect (or lack thereof) of a strategy on performance at a test of immediate recall may not always serve as a reliable indicator of its long term influence.

Visual imagery

Remembering can also be increased by following instructions to use elaborative mediation that is based upon visual imagery. Verbal mediators and visual images function in combination in some circumstances, and it is not invariably easy to separate their effects. Nor is it always clear whether the improved recall that may follow the construction of a sentence which joins items to be remembered is due to the actual semantic qualities of the sentences or to concrete images they evoke. Reese (1965) examined the separate and combined influences on word retention of instructions to form visual images and the provision of sentence contexts. He showed children aged from two to six years some pictures that illustrated pairs of objects interacting together, for example a chicken waving a flag. Other children listened to sentences that described the same interaction but they did not see pictures. A third group of children heard the sentences and saw the equivalent pictures as well. Children in a fourth control condition simply saw the word pairs, without any materials or instructions designed to encourage the formation of mediating links.

The children in the control condition required more trials to learn the words than did the subjects in any of the three experimental groups. The youngest children, averaging three-and-a-half years, learned most rapidly in the sentence condition, and the older children were aided equally by the picture mediators and the sentences. A possible reason for the relative ineffectiveness of pictures for the younger children was that since verbal recall was required, the need to transform picture images into words may have proved a source of difficulty.

Older children's recall may also benefit from instructions to form visual images (Levin *et al.*, 1973), but such instruction appears to be relatively ineffective with young children. Wolff and Levin (1972) found that eight-year-olds who were carefully instructed to form mental images of pairs of toys "playing together" retained items more accurately than children in a control condition who were simply told to remember which toys were paired together. The children in the imagery condition performed just as well as subjects in conditions that involved actual manipulations of the toys. However, the performance of younger children aged five in the imagery condition was on a par with that of subjects of the same age in the control condition, and appreciably below that of five-year-olds who either watched the experimenter make each pair of toys interact or actually manipulated toys themselves.

Improving Memory: General considerations

The findings that we have been discussing demonstrate that appropriate instructions or training can produce marked improvements in remembering in a variety of circumstances. Indeed, relatively short and simple instructions were found to be sufficient in most of the investigations that we have described. Lengthy training procedures have rarely been necessary. It is heartening to observe that many improvements can be rapidly achieved.

Why do instructions work? Belmont and Butterfield (1977, p. 462) consider that an approach will succeed if it "leads children to use particular cognitive programs" that are suited to the task and are based on an understanding of the child. This can only be achieved if the researcher understands the requirements of the task in some detail and knows a fair amount about the processing limitations of the learner. It is then possible to develop plans that are within the individual's capacity.

Such an approach was followed in the successful attempt by Butterfield *et al.* (1973) to improve STM performance in mentally retarded adolescents. The subjects were trained to follow a sequence of steps, starting with input and ending with a correct response. The task involved six-item lists which were followed by a probe item, and subjects had to indicate the position of the probe item in the list. In training the adolescents were taught to form a group or "chunk" from the early items in each list, and then to rehearse these as a single group. The purpose of these activities was to ensure that the early items would be retained in memory in a relatively consolidated form. Next, the adolescents were instructed to attend to the later items in each list, so that these could subsequently be held, albeit briefly, in STM. When the probe item was presented the subjects were to immediately check whether that item matched any of the later items. If it did, the subject responded by stating the correct position. If the probe item was not among the final items temporarily stored in STM, the subject was to search the early items. Since these had been rehearsed as a group they had been retained in memory in a relatively consolidated form, and were not greatly affected by the delay and interference caused by presenting the final items and having to search through them when the probe was presented.

This procedure was successful because it made use of memory processes that the adolescent retarded subjects already possessed, for instance, STM capacity and the ability to rehearse. It had been established in advance that neither of these was impaired. The procedure contributed an important element that the mentally retarded subjects lacked, namely coordination between the memory processes. Essentially, each subject learned a plan for making use of his existing capabilities in a coordinated and organized fashion that was more effective than any plan he could have produced spontaneously when confronted by the task. In this respect, most memory training procedures are similar to the one above. That is, the aim is not to alter basic memory processes, but to introduce plans for deploying the capacities which a person already possesses in an organized and coordinated manner that is maximally effective for meeting the demands of a particular task.

The outcome of such plans does not depend upon the individual deliberately following any programme or strategy. He need not be aware of following any plan, and he does not even have to make a deliberate effort to remember something. In a study by Turnure et al. (1976) instructions to generate sentence to join pictures of common objects were found to be relatively ineffective for aiding five-year-old normal and retarded children to remember the items. However, when the children were told to answer "What?" questions about the items, for example, "What is the soap doing under the jacket?" (soap and jacket being the two objects), or "Why?" questions, such as "Why is the soap hiding in the jacket?" both the normal and the retarded children recalled around four times as many of the items as were recalled in either a conventional sentence generation condition or in a condition in which the children used sentences that were supplied for them by the experimenter, and about ten times as many items as children who simply provided work labels for the items as they inspected them. The questioning procedure was also found to be equally effective in a study conducted on children in Israel. None of the children knew at the time of the training phase (in which some children produced mediating sentences, some copied sentences, some labelled the items and others answered questions) that they would subsequently be asked to recall the items. In fact, none of the children were given any indication that they were participating in an experiment that tested memory. This knowledge is not always essential; what seems to be more important is the requirement to engage in some activity that involves processing the items in a meaningful way. In the present study the children were induced to do so by the instruction to answer questions about the relationship between the two items in each pair. A similar finding was obtained in some research conducted in the USSR by Istomina (1975). She found that children were much better at recalling items that they encountered in the context of meaningful play activities that involved objects in a toy shop than at recalling the same items in a laboratory task. The plans for remembering were understandable to the children since they were communicated within the context of practical activities and play situations that had goals which were meaningful to the children.

VI. Memory Research and Classroom Realities

At this point we shall pause to ask if we have achieved the aim of exploiting knowledge about human memory in order to achieve educationally valuable goals and purposes. The answer must be yes and no. On the positive side, we have amply demonstrated that it is possible to produce marked improvements in remembering. Since, as we have shown, memory limitations are crucial in numerous tasks that contribute to a child becoming educated, including comprehension, numeracy and other important skills, and since individual differences in memory are important determinants of individual variability in achievements, we might well be tempted to conclude that our main aims are achieved. We have demonstrated, after all, that memory abilities which are crucial in education can indeed be improved. It appears to follow that we can make use of what is known about memory in order to produce marked increases in educational achievements.

Further reflection suggests that this is too optimistic a view of the present situation. One indication that our aims are not so completely achieved lies in the observation that very few of the tasks in which memory improvements have been observed are ones that can be regarded as "educational" in the practical sense of being the kinds of task that are frequently encountered in a school classroom. There are a number of difficulties. First, most of the experiments that we have described involve materials which are somewhat different from those which are usually taught at school. Secondly, most (but not all) of the experiments reported in the memory research literature involve deliberate intention to remember on the part of the participants. Many of the school situations in which materials are learned and retained do not necessitate the students making deliberate efforts to remember. Thus, although comprehension and reasoning do necessitate information being retained, when such tasks are encountered in school contexts, they are not usually accompanied by the "Try to remember . . ." instructions commonly used in psychological experiments. Thirdly, as we have just noted, most of the school tasks that require children to remember things do not only involve remembering. Other capacities are also required and remembering is achieved in the context of additional activities. In many memory experiments this added context is lacking. It is possible that contextual considerations influence retention in ways that cannot be predicted from a knowledge of experimental research into human memory.

Clearly, it would be premature for us to conclude that memory research has arrived at a stage at which we can make detailed pronouncements about all the educational circumstances in which people have to retain information. Further investigation would be necessary before we can establish whether all of the factors that have been found to improve remembering in experimental research are as effective in the broader contexts of everyday education in real life as they are in the more circumscribed, restricted and controllable circumstances in which most of the research has been conducted.

There is now considerable awareness of the importance of contextual factors among investigators studying child memory. Some of the reported research has taken full account of the complexities of classroom learning. The techniques developed by R. C. Atkinson and others (Atkinson, 1975; Raugh and Atkinson, 1975; Pressley, 1977a; Raugh *et al.*, 1977) to facilitate vocabulary acquisition in second-language learning provide a good illustration of the kind of applied study that is required. (A fuller description is provided in Chapter 2.) Briefly, these authors devised an ingenious procedure in which, as a first step, spoken English words are linked to English "keywords", each of which is chosen on the basis of being similar in sound to part of the foreign word that is to be learned. To learn the Spanish word for *duck*, for example, which is *pato*, pronounced roughly *pot-o*, the English word *pot* was chosen as the keyword. The second step involves forming a visual image that links the keyword to the English word. For instance, to join *pot* and *duck*, the learner might have a vivid visual image of a large duck trying to hide behind a flower-pot. Thus the English word becomes linked to the English keyword via the image, and indirectly to the similar-sounding Spanish equivalent.

Cumbersome though this method may appear to be, it has been shown to be highly effective in practice. A series of experiments has demonstrated that American students following the method have been considerably more successful at learning Russian and Spanish words than students who followed a conventional rote-learning technique. The arduous and time-consuming vocabulary learning that is necessary for acquiring new languages is made easier by following the method. Its value lies in its applicability to learning in everyday circumstances. The fact that using imagery can facilitate learning has been amply demonstrated in research by Alan Paivio (1971) and numerous other investigators. Imagery makes important contributions to a number of learned abilities, including reading (Pressley, 1976, 1977b; Jorm, 1977) sentence retention (Andre and Sola, 1976) and remembering objects in real scenes (Dirks and Neisser, 1977). The method devised by Atkinson and Raugh has shown that it is possible to make use of knowledge about the effects of forming visual images in order to produce a technique that has a practical value in everyday education.

VII. General Conclusion

We have progressed a considerable way, but not all the way, towards establishing that the findings of scientific investigations of human memory can have widespread practical applications for school learning. We have demonstrated that retention is essential in a variety of the skills and achievements that contribute to the process of education. We have shown that the degree of difficulty of many educational tasks (other than ones that are ostensibly "memory" tasks) is closely related to the burdens of remembering they impose. We have also found that individual differences between people's achievements at a variety of skills are closely related to differences in the ability to remember.

Furthermore, research has made it possible to describe in some detail the factors that underlie differences in achievements on memory tasks, both by different adults and by children varying in age. Using this knowledge, it has proved possible to describe a number of procedures that enable individuals, usually after relatively short periods of instruction, to improve their performance at memory tasks quite considerably.

What remains to be established on a widespread basis is the possibility of applying our ability to improve remembering to those educational circumstances in which retention of information is essential, but in which (a) deliberate remembering is not attempted, (b) the materials to be acquired are more characteristic of those encountered in daily classroom circumstances than are the somewhat artificial verbal materials that tend to be found in the psychological laboratory of the memory researcher and (c) the educational tasks are broader, less circumscribed and are less narrowly "memory tests" than the ones encountered in much research into memory. In other words, we need to establish how far what we know about improving remembering can be applied to the varied and numerous educational circumstances in which memory is a crucial requirement. Investigations such as the studies of imagery techniques in foreign language acquisition have provided a useful and encouraging indication of the type of practical development that needs to be undertaken. As usual, the conclusion that further research is necessary is inescapable. There is a need for more demonstrations of the practical applicability to education of the real gains that have recently been established.

References

Andre, T. and Sola, J. (1976). Imagery, verbatim and paraphrased sentences, and retention of meaningful sentences. *J. educ. Psychol.* **68**, 661–669.

Atkinson, R. C. (1975). Mnemotechnics in second-language learning. *Am. Psychol.* **30**, 821–828.

Atwood, M. E. and Polson, P. G. (1976). A process model for water jar problems. *Cognitive Psychol.* **8**, 191–216.

Baddeley, A. D. and Hitch, G. (1974). Working memory. *In* "The Psychology of Learning and Motivation" (G. H. Bower, Ed.). Vol. 8, Academic Press, New York and London.

Belmont, J. M. and Butterfield, E. C. (1977). The instructional approach to developmental cognitive research. *In* "Perspectives on the Development of Memory and Cognition" (R. V. Kail and J. W. Hagan, Eds). Erlbaum Associates, Hillsdale, New Jersey.

Bernstein, B. (1962). Social class, linguistic codes and grammatical elements. *Language and Speech* **5**, 221–240.

Bower, G. H. and Clark, M. C. (1969). Narrative stories and mediators for serial learning. *Psychonomic Sci.* **14**, 181–182.

Brown, A. L. (1975). The development of memory: Knowing, knowing about knowing, and knowing how to know. *In* "Advances in Child Development and Behavior" (H. W. Reese, Ed.). Vol. 10. Academic Press, New York and London.

Brown, A. L., Campione, J. C., Bray, N. W. and Wilcox, B. L. (1973). Keeping track of changing variables: Effects of rehearsal training and rehearsal prevention in normal and retarded adolescents. *J. exp. Psychol.* **101**, 123–131.

Butterfield, E. C., Wambold, C. and Belmont, J. M. (1973). On the theory and practice of improving short-term memory. *Am. J. Mental Deficiency* **77**, 654–660.

Campione, J. C. and Brown, A. L. (1977). Memory and metamemory development in educable retarded children. *In* "Perspectives on the Development of Memory and Cognition" (R. V. Kail and J. W. Hagen, Eds). Erlbaum Associates, Hillsdale, New Jersey.

Case, R. (1975). Gearing the demands of instruction to the developmental capacities of the learner. *Rev. educ. Res.* **45**, 59–87.

Chi, M. T. H. (1976). Short-term limitations in children: Capacity or processing deficits? *Memory and Cognition* **4**, 559–572.

Chi, M. T. H. (1978). Knowledge structures and memory development. *In* "Children's Thinking: What Develops?" (R. Siegler, Ed.). Erlbaum Associates, Hillsdale, New Jersey.

Coltheart, M. and Glick, M. J. (1974). Visual imagery: a case study. *Q. J. exp. Psychol.* **26**, 438–453.

Dirks, J. and Neisser, U. (1977). Memory for objects in real scenes: the development of recognition and recall. *J. exp. Child Psychol.* **23**, 315–328.

Flavell, J. H. (1971). First discussant's comments: What is memory development the development of? *Hum. Develop.* **14**, 272–278.

Flavell, J. H., Beach, D. R. and Chinsky, J. M. (1966). Spontaneous verbal rehearsal in a memory task as a function of age. *Child Develop.* **37**, 283–299.

Flavell, J. H., Friedrichs, A. G. and Hoyt, J. D. (1970). Developmental changes in memorization processes. *Cognitive Psychol.* **1**, 324–340.

Flavell, J. H. and Wellman, H. M. (1977). Metamemory. *In* "Perspective on the Development of Memory and Cognition" (J. W. Hagen, Eds). Erlbaum Associates, Hillsdale, New Jersey.

Hagen, J. W., Hargrave, S. and Ross, W. (1973). Prompting and rehearsal in short-term memory. *Child Develop.* **44**, 201–204.

Hagen, J. W., Jongeward, R. H. and Kail, R. V. (1975). Cognitive perspectives on the development of memory. *In* "Advances in Child Development and Behaviour" (H. W. Reese, Ed.). Vol. 10. Academic Press, New York and London.

Hagen, J. W. and Kingsley, P. R. (1968). Labelling effects in short-term memory. *Child Develop.* **39**, 113–121.

Hagen, J. W. and Stanovich, K. G. (1977). Memory: Strategies of acquisition. *In* "Perspectives on the Development of Memory and Cognition" R. V. Kail and J. W. Hagen, Eds). Erlbaum Associates, Hillsdale, New Jersey.

Harris, P. (1978). Developmental Aspects of Children's Memory. *In* "Aspects of Memory". (M. M. Gruneberg and P. E. Morris, Eds). Methuen, London.

Howe, M. J. A. (1976). Good learners and poor learners. *Bull. Br. Psychol. Soc.* **29**, 16–19.

Hunter, I. M. L. (1962). An exceptional talent for calculative thinking. *Br. J. Psychol.* **53**, 243–258.

Hunter, I. M. L. (1977). An exceptional memory. *Br. J. Psychol.* **68**, 155–164.

Huttenlocher, J. and Burke, D. (1976). Why does memory span increase with age? *Cognitive Psychol.* **8**, 1–31.

Istomina, Z. M. (1975). The development of voluntary memory in preschool-age children. *Soviet Psychol.* **13** (4), 5–64.

Jenkins, J. J. (1974). Remember that old theory of memory? Well, forget it! *Am. Psychol.* **28**, 947–961.

Jensen, A. R. (1971). The role of verbal mediation in mental development. *J. Genet. Psychol.* **18**, 39–70.

Jensen, A. R. and Rohwer, W. D. (1963). Verbal mediation in paried-associate and serial learning. *J. Verb. Learn. Verb. Behav.* **1**, 346–352.

Jorm, A. F. (1977). Effect of word imagery on reading performance as a function of reader ability. *J. educ. Psychol.* **69**, 46–54.

Keeney, T. J., Cannizzo, S. R. and Flavell, J. H. (1967). Spontaneous and induced verbal rehearsal in a recall task. *Child Develop.* **38**, 953–966.

Kingsley, P. R. and Hagen, J. W. (1969). Induced versus spontaneous rehearsal in short-term memory in nursery school children. *Develop. Psychol.* **1**, 40–46.

Labouvie, G. V., Frohring, W. R., Baltes, P. B. and Goulet, L. R. (1973). Changing relationship between recall performance and abilities as a function of stage of learning and timing of recall. *J. educ. Psychol.* **64**, 191–198.

Kreutzer, M. A., Leonard, C. and Flavell, J. H. (1975). An interview study of children's knowledge about memory. *Monogr. Soc. Res. Child Develop.* **40**, (1, Serial no. 159).

Lange, G. W. and Hultsch, D. F. (1970). The development of free classification and free recall in children. *Develop. Psychol.* **3**, 408.

Levin, J. R., Davidson, R. E., Wolff, P. and Citron, M. A. (1973). A comparison of induced imagery and sentence strategies in children's paired-associate learning. *J. educ. Psychol.* **64**, 306–309.

Liberty, C. and Ornstein, P. A. (1973). Age differences in organization and recall: The effects of training and categorization. *J. exp. Child Psychol.* **15**, 169–186.

Luchins, A. S. (1942). Mechanization in problem solving. *Psychol. Monogr.* **54**, (Whole no. 248).

Luria, A. R. (1968). "The Mind of a Mnemonist". Basic Books, New York.

Miller, G. A. (1956a). Information and memory. *Scient. Am.* August.

Moely, B. E. (1977). Organizational factors in the development of memory. *In* "Perspectives on the Development of Memory and Cognition" (R. V. Kail and J. W. Hagen, Eds). Erlbaum Associates, Hillsdale, New Jersey.

Moely, B. E. and Jeffrey, W. (1974). The effect of organization training on children's free recall of category items. *Child Develop.* **45**, 135–143.

Moely, B. E., Olson, F. A., Halwes, T. G. and Flavell, J. H. (1969). Production deficiency in young children's clustered recall. *Develop. Psychol.* **1**, 26–34.

Moynahan, E. D. (1973). The development of knowledge concerning the effect of categorization upon free recall. *Child Develop.* **44**, 238–246.

Murphy, M. D. and Brown, A. L. (1975). Incidental learning in preschool children as a function of level of cognitive analysis. *J. exp. Child Psychol.* **19**, 509–523.

Ornstein, P. A., Naus, M. J. and Liberty, C. (1975). Rehearsal and organizational processes in children's memory. *Child Develop.* **46**, 818–830.

Paivio, A. (1971). "Imagery and Verbal Processes." Holt, Rinehart and Winston, New York.

Paris, S. G. and Carter, A. Y. (1973). Semantic and constructive aspects of sentence memory in children. *Develop. Psychol.* **9**, 109–113.

Paris, S. G. and Lindauer, B. K. (1976). The role of inference in children's comprehension and memory for sentences and pictures. *Cognitive Psychol.* **8**, 217–227.

Paris, S. G. and Mahoney, G. J. (1974). Cognitive integration in children's memory for sentences and pictures. *Child Develop.* **45**, 633–642.

Paris, S. G. and Upton, L. R. (1976). Children's memory for inferential relationships in prose. *Child Develop.* **47**, 660–668.

Peterson, C. C. (1973). The effect of time on mediation deficiency in children and adults. *J. exp. Child Psychol.* **3**, 279–288.

Piaget, J. and Inhelder, B. (1973). "Memory and Intelligence." Basic Books, New York.

Pressley, G. M. (1976). Mental imagery helps eight-year-olds to remember what they read. *J. educ. Psychol.* **68**, 355–359.

Pressley, G. M. (1977a) Children's use of the keyword method to learn simple Spanish vocabulary words. *J. educ. Psychol.* **69**, 465–472.

Pressley, G. M. (1977b). Imagery and children's learning: putting the picture in developmental perspective. *Rev. educ. Res.* **47**, 585–622.

Pylyshyn, Z. W. (1973). What the mind's eye tells the mind's brain: a critique of mental imagery. *Psychol. Bull.* **80**, 1–24.

Raugh, M. R. and Atkinson, R. C. (1975). A mnemonic method for learning a second language vocabulary. *J. educ. Psychol.* **67**, 1–16.

Raugh, M. R., Schupbach, R. D. and Atkinson, R. C. (1977). Teaching a large Russian language vocabulary by the mnemonic keyword method. *Instructional Sci.* **6**, 199–221.

Reed, S. K. and Johnson, J. A. (1977). Memory for problem solutions. *In* The Psychology of Learning and Motivation." (G. H. Bower, Ed). Vol. 11. Academic Press, New York and London.

Reese, H. W. (1965). Imagery in paired-associate learning in children. *J. exp. Child Psychol.* **2**, 290–296.

Reitman, J. S. (1976). Skilled perception in GO: Deducing memory structures from inter-response time. *Cogn. Psychol.* **8**, 336–356.

Rogoff, B., Newcombe, N. and Hagan, J. (1974). Planfulness and recognition memory. *Child Develop.* **45**, 972–977.

Rohwer, W. D. and Dempster, F. N. (1977). Memory developmental and educational processes. *In* "Perspectives on the Development of Memory and Cognition." (R. V. Kail and J. W. Hagan, Eds) Erlbaum Associates, Hillsdale, New Jersey.

Slak, S. (1970). Phonemic recoding of digital information. *J. exp. Psychol.* **86**, 398–406.

Trabasso, T. (1977). The role of memory as a system in making transitive inferences. *In* "Perspectives on the Development of Memory and Cognition." (R. V. Kail and J. W. Hagan, Eds) Erlbaum Associates, Hillsdale, New Jersey.

Turnure, J., Buium, N. and Thurlow, M. (1976). The effectiveness of interrogatives for promoting verbal elaboration productivity in young children. *Child Develop.* **47**, 851–855.

Wellman, H. M., Ritter, K. and Flavell, J. H. (1975). Deliberate memory behaviour in the delayed reactions of very young children. *Develop. Psychol.* **11**, 780–787.

Whimbey, S. E., Fischhof, V. and Silikowitz, R. (1969). Memory span: a forgotten capacity. *J. educ. Psychol.* **60**, 56–58.

Wolff, P. and Levin, J. R. (1972). The role of overt activity in children's imagery production. *Child Development* **43**, 537–547.

4. Memory Systems and the Reading Processes

G. UNDERWOOD

Department of Psychology,
University of Nottingham, UK

I. Cognitive Skills in the Reading Process: An introduction

The purpose of this chapter is to describe some of the uses of our memory system and processes during the reading of text, and the purpose of this section is to outline the argument which will be presented. A major problem centres around the issue of whether phonological encoding is necessary during reading, and looks at the relationship between this transformation of print, the processes of word recognition and the derivation of text meaning. The particular route which is used when the skilled reader inspects a sentence for a few seconds, and comes to understand the meaning intended by its writer, is of interest not only to the cognitive psychologist, but also to the educational psychologist whose concern lies with the design and evaluation of schemes for the teaching of reading. The discussion of the uses of phonological encoding will therefore make reference to the more popular methods of teaching reading, and will come to some tentative conclusions about the application of our knowledge of the reading process.

Some reading schemes implicitly hold the view that meaning is accessed through the sounds of words, and indeed, some cognitive psychologists explicitly hold this same view. The access route to the semantic lexicon, or "word memory", may involve the production of the sound of the word which is being read, and if so, then phonologically mediated reading schemes are well grounded theoretically. If we can establish that meaning can be available without phonological mediation, then it would appear that such schemes are introducing extra difficulty for the beginning reader, by asking him to perform an unnecessary and distracting task. The early part of the present discussion of "The Access Route to the Lexicon" is an analysis of the possible ways in which the meaning of words might be made available by first converting the print into a corresponding sound. This is achieved through a description of how the reader might be able to transform each and every word he sees into a unique phonological form. This unique form would then be used to access the meaning of the word. The model immediately fails, of course, by the very existence of heterographic homophones—words with more than one meaning but which sound the same (e.g. SEAS and SEES; FEET and FEAT; SIGHT, CITE and SITE). By the time a phonological form of these homophones has been generated then the visual features which distinguish them are lost and cannot be used to aid in the derivation of meaning (see e.g. Sperling, 1960). Homographic homophones are words with more than one meaning and where the visual *and* phonological forms are identical, such as MINT, LIGHT, BALL and PORT. These words pose a problem for any theory of lexical access, but once we have conceded that the meanings of other words allows us to distinguish between the meanings of homophones, then the problem of homophones is solved. The question of whether lexical access is achieved through the use of phonological encoding must look further than the case of homophones for its evidence, and the stumbling block is provided by the exception words. No system of rules has been described which can lead to the correct pronunciation of all words in the English language, without recourse to the meanings of those words. The homographic heterophones are a case in point here: LEAD, INVALID, TEAR and ROW have two pronunciations, one regular and one irregular or exceptional. Words with only one pronunciation are a problem enough however, for the rules which govern how the letter combination PH should be pronounced cannot be specified without using the meanings of the components of the word. To distinguish between the PH sound in PHYSICS and PHRASE and that in SHEPHERD and UPHILL we need to know that the P and the H in the last two words belong to different units of meaning, or morphemes. Pronunciation depends upon meaning.

The failure of the hypothesis of phonological encoding route for lexical access leads us to investigate the alternative hypothesis of direct visual access. By this route meaning is accessed directly, and attention to the auditory characteristics of the word is unnecessary for this process. In such cases we may be affected by the meanings of words even when we are unaware of the words themselves. This is one way in which we are able to show that lexical access does not require phonological encoding, for if the reader is unaware of a word he is clearly not attending to how it might be pronounced. A number of phenomena are reported which show just this effect, and the implications for theories of lexical access and for theories of selection attention are outlined. An alternative method of demonstrating that phonological encoding is unnecessary has been to have readers use the meanings of words in experimental tasks where they are unable to generate the phonological form of a word because they are engaged with a vocalization suppression technique. Word meanings can still be appreciated when the articulatory apparatus is occupied, although sentences are best understood when a phonological form is available.

Evidence suggesting that phonological encoding is used, even though this strategy is not essential for lexical access, causes us to consider the possible benefits for the reader who chooses to transform print into speech. Good readers show distinct signs of a preference for this strategy, and even employ it in artificial laboratory tasks quite unrelated to normal reading practice. Three advantages of this strategy are discussed here. In the first case, the comprehension of long or complicated sentences requires a storage device, and such a device is provided by the relatively long lasting traces of auditory memory. By transforming print into speech we make available a memory of the print which will last for a few seconds—until we have read the rest of the sentence. The integration of words' meanings from sentences is a task requiring the storage of early presented words until later words are available, and phonological encoding facilitates this process. The second advantage of this strategy is that when print is converted into a speech-like form a structure of intonation and stress can be impressed upon the otherwise uniform message, and this may aid the disambiguation of the sentence and its encoding in memory. Thirdly, the problem of organizing the spatial display into a temporal sequence is solved by transforming the print. We cannot hope to process all the information on a page at the same time. (Whether we are limited capacity processors or whether we act as if we are, the fact remains that there is a limit to the amount of information which we can understand at a given instant.) Accordingly, we need to take the information off the page in a sequence, and this process is controlled and regular and in the same order in which it was written if the reader phonologically encodes the print word by word and sentence by sentence.

Phonological encoding is therefore useful during reading. It provides a memory, a prosodic structure and a sequential ordering of the text, but it does not provide access to meaning so much as provide an opportunity for us to gain access.

II. The Recognition of Words

Before engaging in the discussion of how words are recognized it is worth pausing to mention one of the more popular notions in cognitive psychology—the internal lexicon. The lexicon is the total store of all of our word memories. An account of the process of word recognition involves the description of how lexical access is achieved or how the printed (or spoken) word can gain access to the memory of what it means. This store of words and their meanings—the lexicon—is a notional concept and does not necessarily correspond to any structure in the brain. The use of the term lexicon is simply a convenient way of talking about the composite memory of word meanings.

When a word is presented to the eyes or to the ears then it may contact its representation in the lexicon, it may be recognized by the lexicon. This section is concerned with the conditions which are necessary for this process of recognition by the lexicon, and a part of the discussion will touch upon the question of the conditions necessary for the individual perceiver to be aware of the recognition (see p. 112). There appear to be two recognition stages—one in which the word contacts the lexicon and is recognized, and a consequent process whereby the word appears to awareness. The first of these stages can be demonstrated without the second.

The lexicon, then, is a word-store, but according to Murrell and Morton (1974) it does not contain the words themselves so much as the morphemes upon which the spoken and written words are based. The units which are stored in the lexicon, and which are often called *logogens*, after Morton (1969), are said to be the stems of meanings which are central to a word (SUIT, SUITING, SUITED and SUIT-CASE and all have a morpheme in common, as do SICK, SICKLY, SICKNESS and SEASICK). Murrell and Morton (1974) concluded that the lexicon stores morphemic units of meaning rather than words, on the basis of an experiment in which recent experience of one word (e.g. BORED) facilitated the recognition of words with the same morphemic stem (e.g. BORING). Words similar in sound and shape (e.g. BORN) but different in morphemic origin did not facilitate recognition. This experiment does not compel us to accept the conclusion that the lexicon is a collection of morphemes, however, and an equally likely explanation of the result might be that associates facilitate each other. BORED might facilitate BORING, but does it also facilitate TEDIOUS or DULL, or for that matter LECTURE? We have available a large number of demonstrations of the associate-priming phenomenon from a wide variety of experimental situations (e.g. Bradshaw, 1974; Dallas and Merickle, 1976; Jacobson, 1973; Meyer and Schvaneveldt, 1971; Underwood, 1976a; Underwood et al., 1978), and the Murrell and Morton result may be another example of short term activation of a logogen facilitating the processing of the associates of that logogen.

Recognition of a word entails the activation of the logogen, or lexical representation, by sufficient information to exceed a certain threshold level. Logogens may differ in the amount of information needed for their activation as a result of their long term probability of presentation (the word CAT may have a lower threshold than the word CAM, for instance) or as a result of short term changes in the context information preceding presentation. For example, in the context WHEEL, FLANGE, PISTON, MOTION, COG, the word CAM may be more easily recognized than the word CAT. Information is accumulated in the lexicon until sufficient activation has been produced, and when the threshold has been exceeded the word is said to be recognized. (Note that this does not necessarily mean that the perceiver will be aware of the word, for a number of effects of the perceptual defence phenomenon may be a result of the uncorrelated operation of the recognition and awareness thresholds. Emotional or unpleasant words may have average (or even lower-than-average) *lexical recognition* thresholds but higher-than-average *awareness* thresholds. See for instance, Dixon, 1971 and Underwood, 1976b.)

The Access Route to the Lexicon

Two general groups of theories of lexical access have been proposed, and these might be called *the direct visual access route* and *the phonological encoding route*. The possibility of either route being used is reflected by the controversy in the classroom regarding the use of phonics in the teaching of reading. A large number of schemes exist which attempt to teach reading skills through the use of phonological encoding (e.g. "Fun with Phonics", "Functional Phonetics", "Reading with Phonics", "The Royal Road Readers" and "Speech-to-Print Phonics"). These and many similar schemes emphasize the sound of words, and discrimination between the visual patterns of print is made with the aid of differences in pronunciation. These schemes use words and letters as the adult reader would recognize them, but a sub-group of these reading schemes rely upon the transcription of English into an ortho-graphically regular script (e.g. "i/t/a", "UNIFON" and "Fōnetic English"). These schemes are used in part recognition of a difficulty with other phonological methods in that English orthography, being irregular, tends to confuse the novice. Compare, for instance, the sounds produced by the italicized letters in the following groups of words: *F*USE, *PH*ASE and SHE*PH*ERD; or BR*EA*D, M*EA*L, CR*EA*TE, R*EA*L and R*EE*L; or even more simply, GIN*G*ER, SIN*G*ER and LIN*G*ER; and C*A*KE, C*A*LM and C*A*T. For any letter or group of letters in English there exists the possibility of more than one pronunciation, and furthermore, for any sound in English there exists the possibility of more than one orthographically legal spelling. This latter problem is the case of the heterographic homophones such as FEET/FEAT, SIGHT/SITE/CITE and ROAD/RODE which have one sound for a number of different words, each with their own spelling and meaning. To get around the problem of the irregularity of the English orthography, reading schemes such as i/t/a first introduce the child to an artificial but regular orthography based upon a phonetic script. Each letter in the i/t/a orthography has one and only one pronunciation, and so the child does not miscue his pronunciation as he does regularly when learning to use standard English or t.o. (tradi-tional orthography).

Rather than introducing the child to the sound equivalents of a phonetic or traditional orthography to emphasize differences between words on the basis of their pronunciations and the decoding of the word into its constituent sounds, a second group of reading schemes prefers to have the child learn the meanings of whole words in the context of their use. These linguistic schemes accustom the child to the use of printed words in relation to the meanings of other words (e.g. "Break-through to Literacy", "Chandler Reading Program" and "Language Experiences in Reading").

The phonological and linguistic reading schemes represent the two extremes in the population of reading methods, with many schemes lying between these extremes in their emphases. Whereas they differ in the extent to which words are placed in their general linguistic context, and in the extent to which they require the reader to break up each word into its constituent graphemes and phonemes, they all depend to some extent upon the child reading out aloud the words which he sees. Learning to read is heavily dependent upon phonological decoding, whether it is the phonemes of the word which are pronounced or the whole word itself. However, methods such as "Fun with Phonics" and the "Royal Road Readers" scheme of Daniels and Diack (1956) are most compatible with the theory of lexical access which considers that the readers must phonologically encode the printed word in order to gain access to its meaning. Methods such as "Breakthrough to Literacy" do not consider that an appreciation of the phonemic structure of a word is necessary for its discrimination and semantic analysis, and so might be seen to be more in sympathy with the notion of direct lexical access without phonological mediation.

The phonological encoding hypothesis

Evidence in favour of the phonological encoding hypothesis, other than the (unreliable) subjective evidence of our sometimes hearing ourselves subvocalizing whilst reading, came first from a study of immediate remembering by Conrad (1964). When subjects were presented with lists of letters to remember over short intervals the pattern of errors was specific, and implicated phonological encoding. The letters were presented visually for the viewers to read to themselves, and report was by writing the letters so at no time was it necessary for the subjects to vocalize. The result which suggests that they were nevertheless using some form of phonological mediation was that similar sounding letters were confusable in recall (e.g. B,C,D,G) but that letters which did not sound similar were less often recalled in error for one another (e.g. A,F,N,Y). In an experiment tracing the developmental course of this strategy of phonologically encoding words which need to be remembered, Conrad (1972) found that words which sound the same have no recall disadvantage for young children but at age five and six a slight advantage was apparent for the dissimilar sounding words. After this age the advantage of dissimilarity became quite noticeable. Interestingly enough, Conrad did not present his subjects with words as such, but with pictures of objects whose *names* either sounded similar or dissimilar. This developmental trend, therefore, is one of the strategies by which pictures are best remembered if they are given names, and the names remembered phonologically.

A piece of evidence more clearly related to a reading task is provided by an experiment reported by Corcoran (1966) who simply had subjects read through a passage silently while crossing out instances of the letter "*e*". The implication of phonological encoding in this case comes again from the pattern of errors—readers tended to miss more "*e*'s" which are not pronounced in speech, even though they read silently. So, the second "*e*" in BREATHE would have been more likely to be missed than the first "*e*".

It is arguable that the experiments of Conrad and of Corcoran both involve more than lexical access—Conrad's experiments require storage in memory, and Corcoran's experiment requires the detection of a feature of some words—and that the phonological encoding which was uncovered was necessary for processes other than lexical access. One way around this problem is to rely upon a task which involves only lexical access, the lexical decision task. In an experiment reported by Rubenstein *et al.* (1971) subjects were shown strings of letters and asked to decide whether or not they formed words. Thus the letter-string HOUSE gains a "yes" response and the letter-string HOVSE gains a "no". The interesting result of the Rubenstein *et al.* experiment was that the response times to non-words differed according to whether they were pronounceable. Letter-strings which could not be pronounced were easiest to reject as being non-words (e.g. RKME), those which were pronounceable were slower (e.g. RAME), but those which were pronounceable and homophomic with actual words were slowest of all (e.g. RANE). Their conclusion was that the subjects were generating a phonological code of each letter-string, and comparing this code with the entries in the lexicon. If a code could not be constructed, through orthographic illegality, then the letter-string was not a word, and a decision could be taken earlier than when a code was generated. For the case of non-words which sounded as if they could be words, a match in the lexicon would be found, and only by the additional process of checking the spelling could a correct, but slower, response be executed.

It is clear that adult readers can use a phonological encoding strategy when processing verbal material. In a wide range of experimental situations this strategy can be seen to be influencing performance, and it would be reasonable to assume that it is a preferred strategy (it is used even when it leads to errors). It is debatable whether we can go further than this, to argue that is it essential for performance whenever reading is required, for a model which depends entirely upon a phonological code must explain how we can pronounce English words which are orthographically illegal, how we can pronounce new words and non-words, and how we can pronounce and understand the different meanings of homographs. The models of lexical access through phonological encoding are mentioned in the following section, but a complete exposition of the possible models and their problems will be found in a discussion by Coltheart (1978).

Models of phonological mediation

A large number of models have been proposed which depend upon the generation of a phonological code of the word prior to lexical access (e.g. Gough, 1972; Hansen and Rodgers, 1968; Liberman *et al.*, 1972; Mark *et al.*, 1977; Rubenstein *et al.*, 1971; Spoehr and Smith, 1973). The common feature of these models is that they all propose that when a word is read it is translated into a phonological code, and it is the phonological representation which gains access to the lexicon and enables the reader to extract the meaning of the word. The principal evidence in favour of these models is cited in the previous section, together with evidence of muscle recordings such as that provided by Hardyck and Petrinovich (1970) using electromyographic recordings from the larynx. The suppression of vocalization made comprehension more difficult when speech recoding was too slight to be observable by the electromyographic measure. Comprehension was not affected by vocalization suppression when readers were given easy material.

Lexical access through phonological mediation could be achieved theoretically through one of two routes, the production of grapheme–phoneme correspondences, or through the production of grapheme–syllabic correspondences. These two routes will be discussed briefly here, although Coltheart (1978) has described their operation in considerable detail elsewhere (Coltheart also discusses a third route of access, using a second, phonological lexicon. The phonological lexicon would contain a list of rules of pronunciation, but the model contains the faults of the other two routes).

If the reader is capable of applying a list of grapheme–phoneme correspondence (GPC) rules to words then he will be able to translate the written word into a spoken word without knowing what it means. In this way the phonological form of a written word can be generated before meaning is given to the word, and this phonological code then be used to access the lexicon. The GPC rules dictate how a word should be pronounced by assigning a particular phoneme to each grapheme. However, decoding of a word into its graphemes requires that a regular relationship should exist between the letters in a word and its phonemes. This is not the case, as we have already seen. The letter combination PH is sometimes one grapheme and one phoneme (e.g. in PHASE), and is sometimes part of two graphemes and two phonemes (e.g. in UPHILL). It is the morphemic base which dictates which in each case, and the morphemic base is not accessed by this model until *after* generation of the phonological code. English orthography is in the main regular, but the existence of exception words, which are in frequent usage and which are clearly recognizable, pose a serious problem for the GPC model. The differences between regular and exception words were investigated by Baron and Strawson (1976). Subjects were required to read out aloud a list of regular or exception words. If the list was composed of regular words the subjects read them faster than if the words all had irregular spelling. This result led Baron and Strawson to suggest that whereas regular words may be processed with a GPC procedure, the exception words had to be accessed first through the semantic lexicon. After gaining lexical access the phonological code could be generated, but not by the application of the GPC rules alone. Similarly, it might be argued that the different phonological forms of homographs such as LEAD, TEAR, INVALID, READ and ROW can only be discovered after the meaning is apparent.

An alternative model of phonological encoding has proposed that printed words are translated not into sequences of phonemes but into syllables (Hansen and Rodgers, 1968; Spoehr and Smith, 1973). The advantage of the syllable production model over a GPC model is that the latter assumes that consonants are phonemes unaccompanied by vowels. As unaccompanied consonants cannot be pronounced they must be abstract, and without a phonological correspondence. Syllables, on the other hand, can be pronounced and this problem is avoided by considering the basic unit of analysis to be the syllable. After analysis of the word into its constituent syllables, the pronunciation of the syllables is derived and the syllables blended. Only then is the complete phonological representation used to gain lexical access. Hansen and Rodgers propose a series of rules which dictate how the pronunciation of the syllables should be completed, and if lexical access with one pronunciation fails then the next combination of syllables is tried as a match for a word in the lexicon. For example, the rules governing a word with a CVCCVCC combination of consonants and vowels dictate that it should be first parsed as CVC + CVCC, and so FASTING becomes FAS + TING, which is correct. However, by the same rule PASTING becomes PAS + TING, for which there is no match in the lexicon. The next rule to be tried is CV + CCVCC, which produces PA + STING, and a successful match is made. Coltheart's (1978) excellent treatment of Hansen and Rodger's model points out several flaws with the parsing rules, and one of his examples is the word COVER. A CVCVC combination of consonants and vowels should be first parsed as CV + CVC, according to the model, but this produces CO + VER, and the attempt at lexical access fails. The next attempt is with a CVC + VC combination (i.e. COV + ER) but this also fails. No correct pronunciation is available by this model which produces a new organization of syllables each time one organization fails, even when a new *pronunciation* would be more appropriate.

Another serious problem with the Hansen and Rodgers model occurs at the final stage of lexical access, after a pronunciation has been derived. For example, as mentioned above, a CVCCVCC combination is parsed as CVC + CVCC. Therefore the word WORKING comes out as WOR + KING and pronounced as WARKING. Lexical access is therefore achieved, but for the wrong word. Similarly, homophones produce a problem, for the model cannot distinguish between the meanings of words with the same pronunciation. Neither does the model distinguish between regular and exception words, but Baron and Strawson (1976) have demonstrated that regular words can be read and pronounced more easily than exception words.

Given that phonological encoding prior to lexical access cannot account for the variety of behaviour which can be exhibited with exception words, with homophones, and with homographs, then we must conclude that access is not preceded or mediated by recoding the script into its phonological form. Our problem then becomes one of accounting for the variety of evidence which has led us to consider the phonological encoding hypothesis of mediated reading. It is necessary for a non-mediation model to account for Conrad's acoustic confusion effect, Corcoran's acoustic letter cancellation effect, and Rubenstein's pseudohomophone effect. The alternative model, and some suggested explanations of these phonological effects, will be discussed in the following section.

Direct visual access in reading

An experiment reported by Bradshaw (1974) may be instructive here as a demonstration that the meanings of words can be accessed when no phonological representation is available. Subjects were asked to read a briefly presented word, and to assign a meaning to it. The word was a homograph such as PALM which could be interpreted as being associated with anatomy or botany, and was accompanied by two other letter strings, one to either side. One letter string was a collection of consonants, and the other was a disambiguating word—in the case of PALM the word might have been HAND or TREE. The presence of a disambiguating word, which was not read and for which there was insufficient opportunity for phonological encoding, did nevertheless affect reading performances. Subjects preferred the meaning of the homograph which was indicated by the disambiguating word, *even when they were unable to report the disambiguating word*. The meanings of words can be effective when they are not available to awareness, and when a phonological representation has not been generated. (The discussion of experiments similar to Bradshaw's will be continued on p. 111 in the context of the relationship between attention and word recognition.)

Evidence of direct access to the lexicon comes from a different source in the experiments reported by Kolers (1970). When reading text which is inverted, adult, skilled readers made a large number of errors which maintained the meaning of the sentence. Instead of reading "Emerson once said that . . ." one subject said "Emerson has said that . . .", and another, "Emerson once suggested that . . .". Children can be observed to make similar semantic substitution errors when learning to read. These errors which maintain the semantic form of the text are another indication that the meanings of words can be available before the graphemes have been transformed into phonemes or syllables.

If we can gain access to the lexicon without using a phonological transformation of the print, and indeed without necessarily being aware of the words which we are reading, then presumably the graphemic features of the word are sufficient to define its address in the lexicon. Not all of the features of the word are necessary for recognition of the whole: Pillsbury's (1897) subjects reported words which they had not seen, in that FOYEVER was read as FOREVER, and FASHXON as FASHION. The beginnings and ends of words seem particularly useful for recognition (Bruner and O'Dowd, 1958; Rayner, 1975), but these findings may be a reflection of nothing more than the influence of lateral masking: letters in the centre of a word have more letters to the side of them, than do letters at either end. Whatever information is used to identify a word and distinguish it from all others, it appears to be the case that it is *visual* information which is used to access the meaning stored in the lexicon.

If this is so, and a phonological representation is unnecessary for lexical access, then it remains to account for the appearance of effects of phonological encoding in reading tasks. One clue to the use of phonological encoding is provided by Kleiman (1975) using an experiment in which subjects were unable to articulate the words they were to read. While making a variety of decisions about printed words they shadowed (repeated back) lists of digits and so were unable to phonologically encode the print. Whenever a decision was to be made whilst shadowing, the decision time was slower than when not shadowing, but "phonemic" decisions about pairs of words (i.e. "do these two words sound the same?") were affected more by simultaneous shadowing than were "graphemic" decisions (i.e. "do these two words look the same?") or "semantic" decisions (i.e. "do these two words mean the same?"). Graphemic and semantic decisions could be performed without phonological recoding. In a further experiment Kleiman asked his subjects to make decisions about the words in sentences, whilst shadowing. For a "graphemic" decision, they were asked whether one word (e.g. BURY) looked similar to any words in the sentence (e.g. YESTERDAY THE GRAND JURY ADJOURNED). For a "phonemic" decision they were asked whether the word (e.g. SOUL) sounded like any word in the sentence (e.g. THE REFEREE CALLED A FOUL). In addition Kleiman introduced "category" and "acceptability" decisions. Subjects were asked if any word in the sentence (e.g. EVERYONE AT HOME PLAYED MONOPOLY) was a member of the category indicated by the word (e.g. GAMES) or were asked if the sentence was semantically acceptable (e.g. WORRIED FENCES PROTECT LITTLE CHILDREN). The first three of these types of decisions produced evidence similar to Kleiman's first experiment: graphemic and category decisions were considerably less affected by shadowing than were phonemic decisions. Interestingly, the acceptability decision was more affected than any other by the requirement to shadow, and Kleiman concluded that the processing of *sentences* requires them to be recoded phonologically.

From Kleiman's experiment there is an indication of the role of phonological encoding in reading. Skilled readers can extract the meanings of words by a visual route to the lexicon, but if they need to integrate the meanings of these words to derive an understanding of the sentence as a whole, then they need to employ some storage device. Such a storage device, or what Baddeley and Hitch (1974) call "working memory" may use the relatively long decay function of the articulatory loop.* By translating print into a phonological code, then, we give ourselves more time to work upon the meanings of the words in the sentence. Kleiman's acceptability decision, and sentence comprehension in general, requires that the first word he retained until all words have been presented before the schematic meaning can become apparent. Differences between sentence constructions can create differences in the required memory load. Self-embedded sentences such as:

(1) THE RABBIT THE HAWK THE HUNTER SHOT SWOOPED UPON DISAPPEARED and left-branching sentences such as

(2) ALMOST BUT NOT ALL OF THE CURRENT TOP-CLASS TRACK AND FIELD ATHLETES AVAILABLE LAST MONTH WENT ON TOUR are both more difficult to understand and to remember than right-branching sentences such as

---

* I have argued elsewhere that the use of the term "memory store" to refer to a long decay function is at the least misleading (Underwood, 1976b). Memory by this view is a process of retention, and no structure exists in which items may be "placed" as if in some cognitive receptacle. Accordingly the present discussion will continue to refer to a storage "device" rather that a storage "system", to draw the distinction between a structural view which is unnecessary, and a processing view which is sufficient.

(3) THE HUNTER SHOT THE HAWK WHICH SWOOPED
UPON THE RABBIT WHICH DISAPPEARED.

Whenever a word and its qualifiers are separated, or a word and its referents are separated, then we need to hold that word in a temporary storage device until the phrase is completed. The phonological code provides just such a device, and an adaptive strategy when reading sentences is to convert the print into this code to gain thinking time (Underwood, 1976b). A further advantage of returning the print to speech is that the addition of prosodics can then be used to imprint the syntactic structure upon the sentence (Liberman *et al.*, 1977), and so gain a further source of access to the schematic meaning.

If there exists an advantage for the strategy of generating a phonological code then we may find it difficult to avoid using it for laboratory tasks in which we are penalized for using anything but a visual access and storage strategy. The acoustic confusion effect and the acoustic letter cancellation task may both be products of the use of a phonological encoding *strategy* which is not essential for task performance, but which is habitual when presented with verbal materials. It may even be necessary for the efficient performance of these memory tasks, but it is clearly not necessary for the lexical access of words. The pseudohomophone effect has no memory load inherent in the task, however, and is a little more difficult to explain without recourse to the suggestion that a phonological encoding process is necessary for the lexical decision task. Coltheart *et al.* (1977) have suggested an explanation which assumes that both routes of access are used simultaneously. If visual access is attempted at the same time as the reader attempts to apply GPC rules, and if visual access is faster than phonological encoding, then the lexical access of words will always be completed via the visual route. In the case of non-words, however, when the attempted visual access fails, then the phonological code will sometimes be generated before the "no" response is made.

The repeated appearance of effects of acoustic similarity in a number of different experimental situations—the pseudohomophone effect is dependent upon acoustic similarity between a non-word and a word which is known to the reader—demands that we take account of the phonological encoding strategy in a complete model of the reading process. Although we can demonstrate that phonological encoding is unnecessary for the meaning of the word to be gained from its printed form it does appear to be a necessary part of skilled reading. By recording print into its phonological form a memory trace of longer duration is made available, and an advantage of extra thinking time is gained over a reader who depends upon his relatively short duration visual memory. To relate the meanings of words in sentences with difficult or ambiguous surface structure the reader must be able to recall the first words of the sentence after the whole sentence has been presented. For this purpose alone it would seem useful to have available a longer lasting phonological representation. An additional advantage of phonological recoding of the print is that the prosodic structure can be returned to the message. Intonation is of clear advantage in the interpretation of meaning (see Taylor, 1976) and the differences between "did *YOU* get the book?", "did you *GET* the book?" and "did you get *THE BOOK*?" can be appreciated best in their spoken form.

A third and final advantage is that by recoding the print we are imposing our own attention control, and we are compelled to process each word on the page. It is all too easy when reading to realize the meanings of individual words while attending, not to the schematic meaning of the text, but to something more interesting. On arriving at the bottom of the page we then have no idea of what the passage was about, although upon re-reading the passage will seem very familiar. We can read for word meanings, or we can read for text meanings. The relationships between word recognition, reading and attention are the subject of the next section.

Attentional Strategies and Word Recognition

Although the historically early theories of attention appeared on the surface to be concerned with perception as a whole, they have only ever been sub-theories of word recognition. The only materials used regularly in experimental studies of attention have been verbal materials—words and letter-names—for the very simple reason that these are the easiest materials to manipulate. (Although experiments concerned with "subliminal perception", are clearly related to theories of attention, they have rarely been seen as concerning these theories—but see Dixon (1971) for an exception. These experiments have regularly used non-verbal stimuli in their demonstrations of perception prior to awareness. The subliminal perception effect demonstrates that neither of the two main theories of attention are complete.)

The "perceptual-selection" theories of attention proposed by Broadbent (1958) and Treisman (1960) suggest that words may be processed to an appreciation of their gross physical characteristics without the need to attend to them (pitch of the speaker's voice, colour of the lettering, size of the print, direction of the sound, etc.). Words can only be understood for their meanings, however, by attending to them. Attention is then defined as a process of selecting words for access to a recognition system which has limited capacity—only one word can be recognized at a time.

As a result of a number of demonstrations of the occasional processing of the meanings of unattended words (Moray, 1959; Treisman, 1960), the "strong" form of this theory (Broadbent, 1958) gave way to the "weak" form suggested by Treisman (1960). Rather than postulating that unattended messages receive *no processing* for meaning, the weaker theory maintains that they receive *attenuated processing*. Whereas attended messages are fully available for comprehension and for volitional determination of the response, unattended messages are said to be attenuated, or analysed incompletely for meaning. Treisman has never been able to specify the characteristics of this "attenuation", but appears to be suggesting that the "important" aspects of the meaning are analysed and the "unimportant" aspects ignored. Importance may vary temporarily (as the context of a sentence changes), or may be more permanent (certain words or events may always be perceived, for instance). The important feature of both of these theories is that attention is held to be essential for perception—when events are unattended they cannot be perceived, or understood, or integrated with conscious life, or used to organize volitional responses.

An alternate group of theories claims to explain the occurrence of the semantic processing of unattended words not by recourse to the notion of attentuation, but by first arguing that attention is not required for perception so much as response organization (Deutsch and Deutsch, 1963; Norman, 1968).

These are the "response-selection" theories of attention, and they maintain that whereas we can perceive without the need to attend, we do need to attend to the organization and execution of volitional responses.

The two things which can be said of these two classes of theories of attention are that they are confusable, and that they are both wrong.

They are confusable in the sense that they are both defined so incompletely that the process of comprehension may be viewed as perception by one theory and as preparation for response by the other theory. Accordingly, predictions from the two theories are identical regarding the level of semantic processing of an unattended word. Both theories predict reduced processing in comparison with attended words, but for different reasons. These reasons have been impossible to verify empirically, and as yet we have no evidence to distinguish between the two theories. A discussion of the statement that they are both wrong is the subject of the next section.

Is attention necessary for the recognition of words?

It is a matter of historical record that whereas the 1960s were plagued by a series of attempts to distinguish between the two principal classes of theories of attention, the 1970s have seen a return to the original question: can we recognize words without attending to them? The revised theory of attention which is presented here is an account of the data collected in an attempt to answer the question. The implications of this theory for a general model of the reading process are outlined in the next section, but for the present we shall restrict the discussion to the analysis of single words.

As a part of the debate between perceptual-selection and response-selection theories of attention, Joe Lewis (1970) at Oregon published a report using what has proved to be a very productive method. Rather than attempting to determine the use of attention directly, Lewis observed the effects of unattended messages upon the processing of attended messages: he only ever looked at the success of the listener's performance with the attended message. The attended message was always a list of words, and the subjects were asked to shadow them quickly and accurately. The shadowing latencies were recorded as a function of the semantic association between a shadowed word and an unattended word presented at the same time. When a relationship existed between the shadowed word and the simultaneous unattended word, then the speed of shadowing was affected. The particular pattern of results from Lewis's experiment is confusing, but the basic effect has been found now a number of times. These experiments have been discussed in some detail elsewhere (Underwood, 1978), and we can conclude that unattended spoken words are analysed for their semantic content to a sufficient extent that the shadowing latencies to attended words may be influenced.

Two similar results will be mentioned before moving away from spoken words to the effects of printed words and to the synthesis of these effects into a model of attention and word recognition. Although using dissimilar techniques, Corteen and Wood (1972) and Mackay (1973) both offer support for Lewis's basic finding that unattended words gain lexical access. Words which have been associated previously with electric shocks tended to continue to elicit a galvanic skin response (GSR) when they appeared in an unattended message (Corteen and Wood, 1972), and furthermore, associates of these words also tended to elicit GSR responses. In an interesting sequel to this experiment, Corteen and Dunn (1974) asked their subjects to indicate by pressing a key whenever they heard a shock-associated word. In the course of the experiment a GSR response was observed on 42 occasions, but on only one of these occasions was the key pressed to indicate awareness of the critical word. We shall return to this result later. The reliability of the effect has received some criticism (Wardlow and Kroll, 1976; Neisser, 1976), but it has been replicated often enough to be regarded as a real effect (e.g. von Wright *et al.*, 1975; Forster and Govier, 1978).

The third experiment to demonstrate that unattended words gain access to the lexicon of word meanings, was reported in 1973 by MacKay. Subjects heard ambiguous sentences together with an unattended message which offered a resolution of the ambiguity of the attended message. The variable of interest here was the source of the ambiguity, and the dependent measure was the extent to which the unattended message influenced the interpretation of the ambiguous sentence. MacKay found that lexical ambiguity was resolved by unattended words (as did Bradshaw with printed ambiguous words), but that deep structural ambiguity was unaffected. The sentence THEY THREW STONES TOWARD THE BANK YESTERDAY was affected by the presentation of the word MONEY or the word RIVER, as only one word is ambiguous, and the deep structure is consistent whichever interpretation we choose. Sentences such as THEY THOUGHT THE SHOOTING OF THE HUNTERS WAS DREADFUL, which have an ambiguity of deep structure, were not so easily disambiguated. Unattended messages such as SPORTSMEN SLAIN did not influence the interpretation away from a comment upon the hunter's aiming at *their* targets. This again is a fascinating result with implications for the reading process and for the attention process, and will be discussed later in this chapter.

Printed words can also be demonstrated to gain access to the lexicon when they are not being attended. Underwood (1976a, 1977) reported that the time taken by an observer to name a simple line drawing is increased if a related word is printed to one side (e.g. the word CREAM printed next to a picture of a cat), in comparison with those occasions when the word is unrelated to the picture. Philpott and Wilding (1979) have recently reported similar results for the case of drawings accompanied by subliminally presented words. Awareness of the word was suppressed by presenting it with dim illumination at the same time as the shape was presented under bright illumination. Underwood *et al.* (1978) have extended the finding to the influence of words upon other words. The facilitating effect of context prior to the exposure of a word which is to be recognized can be increased if a related word accompanies the target word. From these results, and that of Bradshaw

(1974) it appears that printed as well as spoken words can be recognized at the level of lexical activation, and without the reader being aware of them. Bradshaw found that his subjects were liable to the effect of disambiguating words whether or not they could report them afterwards, and Underwood (1977) found that whereas an effect was still apparent when the viewers could not report the "unattended" word the pattern of influence upon picture-naming between related and unrelated words was reversed when they were aware of the word and could report it. The subjects tested by Philpott and Wilding were clearly unaware of the interfering words.

The model of attention has become well-defined as a result of these experiments which investigated the effects of unattended words upon on-going activity, and we can summarize its necessary features as follows:

(1) single words gain lexical access without the need to attend to them (viz. Bradshaw, 1974; Lewis, 1970; Underwood, 1976a).

(2) single words create a different pattern of influence when the subject becomes aware of them, and so we can distinguish between lexical access and awareness of lexical access (viz. Corteen and Dunn, 1974; Philpott and Wilding, 1979; Underwood, 1977).

(3) schematic meaning or deep structural meaning cannot be appreciated without attention (viz. MacKay, 1973).

Attention, then, is not necessary for the recognition of words in isolation, and at the level of lexical activation words may be recognized without our being aware of them. If we need to use those words, then we also need to attend to them. When we do attend, or when we become aware of them for some other reason, the words interact differently with the material of which we are already aware.

In some respects this model resembles the perceptual-selective theories of attention, and in others it resembles the response-selection theories. This model considers that words are recognized *prior* to a level of processing which is synonymous with the subjective state of awareness. In this sense it is a response-selection model, because the state of awareness might be argued to be necessary for the organization and choice between available responses (Underwood, 1978). We do, however, need to attend to words in order to integrate them with other stimuli, as MacKay's (1973) demonstrations with deep structural ambiguity indicate. Accordingly the model might be called a perceptual-selection theory, because the understanding of words in their general contexts can only follow their selection by the attention process. The problem can be summarized as follows: what constitutes *perception* and what is the function of our becoming *aware* of stimuli? Neither the perceptual-selection nor response-selection theories can offer help here, and are incomplete theories as a result. Both of these classes of theories can therefore be rejected by the same set of data: the demonstrations that words can be recognized prior to selection, but need to be selected to be integrated with other words. In the following discussion this set of data is related to the reading process.

The influence of unattended print during reading

We can demonstrate that unattended words gain lexical access without being selected and without the reader being aware of them, but is this of any use when reading prose or is it (another) result which is restricted to laboratory conditions? The straightforward answer is that we are still in the process of finding out, but there do exist a few pointers to indicate that the effect does have some "ecological validity".

Willows and MacKinnon (1973) and Willows (1974) have developed the "reading-between-the-lines" paradigm to investigate the attentional strategies used by good and poor readers. In this paradigm readers are told to attend to, and read, alternate lines of prose. Between the lines are printed distracting words which the readers are told to ignore. In one such passage used by Willows (1974) the material to be read started: "ALL OF US ADMIRE THE GREAT SKILL OF A GOOD TRUCK DRIVER. HE HAULS MANY TONS OF THINGS ALMOST DAILY, INCLUDING DANGER-OUS EXPLOSIVES". Printed in red between the lines in Willows's "selective reading" condition, were the words: "TRANSPORT DRIVERS", "STRANDED MOTORISTS", "SLIPPERY ROADS", "DYNAMITE", etc. and each of these words and phrases appeared during a subsequent comprehension test. The words between the lines (which were presumably unattended) were all plausible ans-wers to the multi-choice comprehension questions, and indeed appeared as alternatives. For the question "About whom is this para-graph?" the alternatives were "transport drivers, van drivers, truck drivers, semi-trailer drivers, pickup truck drivers, bus drivers". For the question "What does he haul that makes his trip dangerous?" the alternatives were "gun powder, dynamite, bombs, combustibles, explosives, gasoline". The dependent measure in this experiment was the number of comprehension errors, as a function of whether or not any words were printed between the lines, and as a function of the skill of the reader as assessed by the Gates-MacGinitie Reading Test. The subjects were around 11 years old, and were divided into two groups: those who were reading to a level predicted by their non-verbal I.Q.

("good" readers), and those who were reading below that level ("poor" readers). The result was quite startling. As expected in the "control reading" condition, in which no words appeared between the lines, there was little difference between the two groups of readers for the number of intrusion errors produced. (As intrusion error counted as erroneously responding to a comprehension question with a word that would have appeared between the lines.) In the "selective reading" condition however the good readers actually produced more intrusion errors than the poor readers. It appears that a characteristic of good reading habits is to focus one's attention widely. We can explain the result if the poor readers were attending very closely to each word which they were to read out, and if the good readers were accepting more information from the page then they needed to read out. Unattended words influenced the good readers but not the poor readers, but this is the limit to our conclusion. It is unclear, for instance, whether the good readers are good because they accept information from the parafovea (that part of the retina within a few degrees of the fovea) or even the periphery of vision, or whether accepting parafoveal information is a product of a general strategy and is quite incidental to the skill of reading. This argument resembles the issue of whether good readers have a particular pattern of eye movements as a result of a general strategy, or whether that pattern of eye movements necessarily produces a good reader. Whether the conclusion, that the general strategy produces useful eye movement habits, will also be applicable to the issue of the use of parafoveal information still remains to be seen.

As well as this inherent difficulty in the explanation of the effect of parafoveal information upon good readers, there exist a number of methodological problems with the free-reading situation used by Willows. The principal problem is that it is impossible to say whether or not the good readers were more affected by the words between the lines simply because they looked directly at them (Underwood et al., 1978). They would have had more time to investigate the words printed in red than would the poor readers, and the pattern of eye movements was not recorded. Even if a direct fixation was not made upon these words, a suitably long fixation within a few degrees of visual angle would enable the words to be recognized well.

A second experiment using a free-reading task did record the pattern of eye movements (Kennedy, 1978a), and indeed the durations of fixations, location of fixations, and time to fixate upon critical words were the dependent measures taken. Kennedy had his adult skilled readers look at short passages while recording their eye movements, before they indicated comprehension. Three sentences comprised each paragraph, and two types of paragraphs were used. In one type two highly associated words appeared (e.g. HILL and MOUNTAIN), one word in the first sentence and one in the third sentence, and in the other type of paragraph the associate in the first sentence was replaced with a word which was contextually appropriate but which was not a high associate (e.g. TRACK and MOUNTAIN). Kennedy observed the pattern of eye movements up to the critical word in the third sentence for these two types of paragraphs. Three measures indicated the influence of this relationship between the critical word and its associate: (1) if an associate was present in the first sentence, then readers arrived at the critical word faster than if no associate had been present; (2) readers fixated more upon the critical word if an associate had been present earlier; (3) readers fixated less on function words (prepositions, articles, pronouns etc.) when the two associates were present.

Curiously, when the associates were both present the readers took longer to indicate that they have understood the passage than when only one of them was included. This is a result which makes the pattern more difficult to understand, for by providing a high associate the passage becomes more homogenous, more uniform and more redundant, and yet comprehension took longer to achieve. Kennedy did not report any measures of a comprehension test, but if the effects of parafoveal words are adaptive then we would predict that the presence of an associate in the parafovea or periphery would be to ease the general comprehension of the paragraph. Comprehension was slower in this condition, but it may have been richer.

Unattended or parafoveal words can be shown to affect performance in tachistoscopic single-fixation tasks and in free-reading tasks. The question to be asked now concerns the relationship between these parafoveal influences and the strategies used by skilled readers. Both the pattern of eye movements and the pattern of influence from parafoveal words change as the reader develops his skill. Whether these are *intentional* and *volitional* changes, or a *consequence* of other changes in the reading strategy is a complicated question. Eye movements appear to change as a consequence of other changes, but we have no answers to the problem of whether the skilled reader intentionally accepts parafoveal information. The question of what such information might be used for is the subject of the following discussion.

The use of unattended print during reading

A popular notion in the study of visual perception is that we achieve an understanding of our visual world through a series of approximations.

These are hypotheses about what the object or event under scrutiny really is. We can never know what is really there, of course, because the perceiver like the scientist can only disconfirm his hypothesis and it is not possible to confirm that what we perceive coincides with what is really out there. Richard Gregory's (1970, 1973) views apart, the reader does have a problem of attempting to discover the meaningful content of the text before him. The text might be described as an approximation of what the writer intended to convey, and the method of conveyance is a code. The task for the reader is to decode the written symbols and then put together the individual word meanings in an attempt to reconstruct the general meaning once held by the writer. In this sense reading is a task of hypothesis formation: the reader may hold a series of approximate meanings of the text before he comes to understand the meaning as intended by the writer. As he sets off down the page he encounters information ("evidence") which can be used initially to set up an hypothesis of what the passage concerns, and later to confirm or disconfirm the hypothesis.

If this view of reading as a process of hypothesis formation and testing is appropriate, then we may ask from where does the reader gain the evidence used to evaluate his hypothesis? He certainly can look at specific words and phrases to judge the acceptability of these specific meanings to the general meaning-hypothesis. In view of the evidence presented in the preceding sections we may suppose that it is also possible for him to use information ahead of fixation. Parafoveal meanings, if not the specific parafoveal words themselves, may be used to bias the interpretations of words being attended to, to aid the formulation or evaluation of the hypothesis of the text meaning, or, more simply, to guide the future pattern of eye-movements in the search for useful information in the text. This theory of the use of parafoveal or unattended print during reading is a theory of strong control—unattended meanings are said to control the understanding of the text directly and indirectly. Direct control is possible by the disambiguation of alternative meanings and by the integration of unattended meanings with the hypotheses under scrutiny, whereas indirect control is possible by the attraction of future fixations to page locations which contain hypothesis-related information. Evidence in support of this theory has been presented in earlier discussions here, but may be summarized as follows:

    (1) the meanings of parafoveal words can influence the processing of words being read intentionally (Underwood *et al.*, 1978), and can disambiguate the meanings of those words (Bradshaw, 1974).

(2) the meanings of parafoveal words can affect the time taken to comprehend short lists of sentences (Kennedy, 1978a,b) and affect the nature of comprehension errors (Willows, 1974).

(3) the meanings of parafoveal words can affect the pattern of eye-movements prior to fixation upon those words (Kennedy, 1978a).

Whether we can find evidence to support or reject the principal statement of this theory, that it is a meaning-hypothesis which is affected by unattended words, remains to be seen.

The theory is closely bound up with theories of the control of eye-movements. The difference is a change of emphasis from our looking at the uses to which non-fixated information might be put. The view here, closely related to the "cognitive control" theories of eye-movements described by Hochberg (1970) and Kennedy (1978a), is that word-meanings ahead of fixation influence the comprehension of what is being fixated upon and influence the future pattern of fixations. This is a very sophisticated form of control, and clearly would be apparent only in the behaviour of the skilled reader. Again, it remains to be seen whether we can demonstrate a relationship between the extent of a reader's skill and the extent to which parafoveal meanings are effective, are appreciated, and are used during reading to guide the search for further information.

III. The Application of Reading Strategies: Some conclusions

Although word recognition may proceed passively it is clear that the integrated task of reading is an active process which requires a great deal of attention. The scrutiny afforded by attending to a complex visual display such as a page of text can lead to a variety of strategies of inspection and understanding. We can be aware subjectively of our selection of different strategies, and of their outcomes. When distracted by some sequence of events unrelated to the page of text, for instance, we may be unable to give any attention to the task of forming hypotheses about the text-meaning. In such a case word may be read passively, and in one sense the text may be said to have been read. A consequence of this strategy is that the reader fails to grasp the underlying meaning of the passage. Upon re-reading the page he may have a strong feeling of familiarity with the words attended to now for the first time.

The use of different strategies of reading has been investigated in a number of experimental situations, and one of the clearest demonstrations is provided by Levin and Cohn (1968) using the eye–voice span method. When reading aloud the eyes are visually a few words ahead of the voice: if sight of the text is removed by turning off the lights for instance, then the reader can still produce a few words from the text. This lag between looking at the printed words and saying them is called the eye–voice span (EVS). Levin and Cohn looked at the development of the EVS in children between the ages of six and 15 years, as a function of different reading instructions. The instructions might be considered to lead to different reading strategies, and varied from "read normally as though you are reading out loud to a friend", to "read carefully in preparation for questioning" and "read right through for the general idea". These instructions produced changes in the EVS even for the youngest readers. When they were reading carefully the smallest EVSs were apparent, and instructions to read for the general idea produced the largest EVSs. Beginning readers, then, are aware of different styles of reading, and can manipulate their own styles to match the requirements of the specific task.

Oddly enough, adult skilled readers do not show such dramatic differences in performance as a consequence of using different reading strategies. McConkie *et al.* (1973) had groups of undergraduates read passages from the *Scientific American* in preparation for a few questions. The questions themselves were designed to produce differences in the strategies used, and varied from subject group to subject group. Some subjects received factual, numerical questions about their passages each time and others received "higher order questions" requiring the reader to draw inferences about the passage, and to think up a suitable title. Whereas these manipulations produced differences in the speed of reading, similar questions after the final passage failed to show any differences in the comprehension achieved by the various groups of readers. By the time the final passage was presented the reading strategies would have become well established by repeated questioning of the same style. After the final passage had been read the same test questions were presented to all groups, but each group appeared to have understood the passage as well as any other group. It is arguable of course that gross strategy differences would not have been encouraged by an experiment in which all readers know that they were to be questioned on the passages. Comparisons with groups who had been instructed to "read quickly to obtain an idea of the general meaning" or to "read carefully to check for any inconsistencies in the argument" might well have produced differences on the final comprehension test of the kind administered by McConkie *et al.*

A variety of reading strategies can be demonstrated in children beginning to read (Levin and Cohn, 1968; Schwartz, 1977), and in the child's methods of learning to read (Francis, 1977), even though the manifestation of these strategies in the behaviour of the adult skilled reader has been more difficult to demonstrate. The question asked here is, why do readers cling to the phonological encoding strategy? (which has been discussed on pp. 101–105), when it is clear that words may be recognized without this form of mediation.

Kleiman's (1975) experiment indicated that adult skilled readers do not need to subvocalize when reading single pairs of words for meaning, but that if they need to make judgments about the meanings of sentences then interference with their ability to subvocalize interferes with the judgment. Barron and Baron (1977) have a similar result for beginning readers. Children aged between six and 14 years made "same-different" judgments about picture-word pairs on the basis of whether the picture and word rhymed (e.g. picture: HORN, word: CORN) or whether they had related meanings (e.g. picture: PENCIL, word: PAPER). Asking the subjects to perform a simultaneous vocalization suppression task (they had to say "double, double, double . . ." at the same time as making the judgment) *did* interfere with "rhyming" judgments, but *did not* interfere with "meaning" judgments. Even the youngest children were able to derive the meanings of the word and the picture and compare them, without use of a phonological encoding strategy. Why then do they insist upon using it when reading normally?

A further experiment recently reported by Barron (1978) makes the task of explanation possibly worse. In a study of young readers he found that the better readers were those who used phonological encoding on a task as unrelated to normal reading as the lexical decision task. The pseudohomophone effect ("is PHACE a word?") is an indicator of phonological encoding, and was more apparent in 11- and 12-year-old readers who are classified as "good" than in those classified as "poor". Furthermore, the size of the pseudohomophone effect was positively correlated with the reading speed of this same group of children. The reluctance of some cognitive psychologists to accept the argument that phonological encoding is unnecessary on the grounds that they "can hear themselves whilst they are reading", appears to be well grounded, and supported by these experiments of Barron (1978), Barron and Baron (1977) and Kleiman (1975). Phonological encoding is clearly of *some* use, even though it is unnecessary for the task of word recognition and analysis of single word meanings.

In putting together Barron's result (1978) and the finding reported by Lunzer (1978), that the best predictor of reading achievement was the ability to recall sequences of objects, Underwood and Holt (1978) suggested that phonological encoding is used because it enforces a temporal sequence upon the spatial display of a page of text. The reader must attend to the relationships between *sequences* of words, and their order is of vital importance. Before we can understand the meaning of a paragraph or even a sentence we must become aware of the sequential relationships between the events coded in the words. It makes a great deal of difference whether "THE BUSY POLICEMAN IGNORED AN APPROACHING CHILD" or "THE BUSY CHILD IGNORED AN APPROACHING POLICEMAN", and having a reader count quietly from one to ten while reading (vocalization suppression condition) affects the difficulty of distinguishing (Levy, 1977). In Levy's experiment a lexical change (from POLICEMAN to OFFICER) was also disturbed by vocalization suppression, although this result is in conflict with results by Kleiman (1975) and Barron and Baron (1977).

Phonological encoding may be helpful in asserting a temporal order on the events being described in a sentence—the relationships between words may be best appreciated when they are considered as a sequence. This is certainly not always the case, and in many abstract sentences a single temporal order of description may actually hinder comprehension. In simple reading tasks comprehension may be improved by subvocalization however, but this is not the full extent of the benefit gained by phonologically encoding the written text. A second use is suggested by Kleiman who found that when a full sentence was to be understood then subvocalization helped performance. He concluded that when reading sentences we need the use of Baddeley and Hitch's (1974) "working memory". This is basically a phonologically based short term storage device for remembering about three words for a few seconds. Disruption of this "articulatory loop" is said to interfere with some reading tasks because short term storage is necessary when relating the beginning of sentence, for instance, to the end of a sentence. (This device is discussed on pp. 107–109.) In addition, Liberman *et al.* (1977) have suggested that subvocalization aids comprehension in a third use by affording the opportunity to return a prosodic structure to the otherwise uniform print. Sub-groups of the population with specific reading problems (e.g. "dyslexics", the deaf, adult illiterates) may be found to have a deficiency with the use of the phonological encoding strategy for any or for all three of its uses during reading. Demonstrations that these groups can nevertheless perceive word meanings are awaited eagerly, but so far we have only studies of "phonemic dyslexic" patients who appear to know the meanings of words without being able to *say* what those words are (Marshall and Newcombe, 1973; Shallice and Warrington, 1975).

If phonological encoding is of some use during reading, and three uses are suggested here, but of no use in the recognition of individual word meanings, then cognitive psychology is in a position to comment upon the attempts made by educational psychologists to introduce the "ideal" scheme for teaching reading. Clearly, those schemes which require the child to break down each word into its component sounds are to be criticized by the evidence presented here, unless they can demonstrate that the Phonic method aids word recognition in some indirect way. Phonic methods do at least make the task of producing a phonological code easier when only 40 sounds (for letters) are to be chosen initially rather than the tens of thousands of sounds (for complete words) used by the more direct methods described as "Look-Say" schemes. Choosing between 40 sounds may be easier, but it gives the child an extra process before he gets to the sound of the complete word. This extra task is, arguably, a distraction from the main purpose of reading: to derive inferences about the meaning of the print. The sound of the complete word will not aid lexical access, and is quite unnecessary for the derivation of word meanings. In this sense the emphasis placed upon the sounds of words by the "Look-Say" methods is inappropriate. Sounds do not produce meanings, but they do form a short-lived memory trace which will retain a version of the word while its precise meaning is being found and being qualified by its accompanying words. This retention function, a sequencing function, and a prosodic return function, give a distinct advantage to those readers who can easily generate a phonological version of the whole words and strings of words. Whilst the sounds are available to allow the opportunity for lingustic processing, they do not perform the processing itself, and only by emphasizing to the beginning reader the *functions* of words in a broad linguistic context can any linguistic skill develop. The phonological encoding strategy can be seen best as a tool which may mediate an appreciation of written language. It does not provide the appreciation, but allows other processes to occur which are involved more directly in the derivation of meaning.

References

Baddeley, A. D. and Hitch, G. (1974). Working memory. *In* "The Psychology of Learning and Motivation" (G. A. Bower, Ed.). Vol. 8. Academic Press, New York and London.

Baron, J. and Strawson, C. (1976). Use of orthographic and word-specific knowledge in reading words aloud. *J. exp. Psychol: Human Perception and Performance* **2**, 386–393.

Barron, R. W. (1978). Reading skill and phonological coding in lexical access. *In* "Practical Aspects of Memory" (M. M. Gruneberg, P. E. Morris, and R. N. Sykes, Eds). Academic Press, London and New York.

Barron, R. W. and Baron, J. (1977). How children get meaning from printed words. *Child Develop.* **48**, 587–594.

Bradshaw, J. L. (1974). Peripherally presented and unreported words may bias the perceived meaning of a centrally fixated homograph. *J. exp. Psychol.* **103**, 1200–1202.

Broadbent, D. E. (1958). "Perception and Communication". Pergamon Press, Oxford.

Bruner, J. S. and O'Dowd, D. (1958). A note on the informativeness of parts of words. *Language and Speech* **1**, 98–101.

Coltheart, M. (1978). Lexical access in simple reading tasks. *In* "Strategies of Information Processing" (G. Underwood, Ed.). Academic Press, London and New York.

Coltheart, M., Davelaar, E., Jonasson, J. T. and Besner, D. (1977). Acess to the internal lexicon. *In* "Attention and Performance" (S. Dornic, Ed.). Vol. VI. Erlbaum Associates, Hillsdale, New Jersey.

Conrad, R. (1964). Acoustic confusion in immediate memory. *Br. J. Psychol.* **55**, 75–84.

Conrad, R. (1972). The developmental role of vocalizing in short-term memory. *J. Verb. Learn. Verb. Behav.* **11**, 521–533.

Corcoran, D. W. J. (1966). An acoustic factor in letter cancellation. *Nature* **210**, 658.

Corteen, R. S. and Dunn, D. (1974). Shock-associated words in a non-attended message: A test for momentary awareness. *J. exp. Psychol.* **102**, 1134–1144.

Corteen, R. S. and Wood, B. (1972). Automatic responses to shock-associated words in an unattended channel. *J. exp. Psychol.* **94**, 308–313.

Dallas, M. and Merikle, P. M. (1976). Semantic processing of non-attended visual information. *Can. J. Psychol.* **30**, 15–21.

Daniels, J. C. and Diack, H. (1956). "Progress in Reading". Institute of Education, University of Nottingham, Nottingham.

Deutsch, J. A. and Deutsch, D. (1963). Attention: Some theoretical considerations. *Psychol. Rev.* **70**, 80–90.

Dixon, N. F. (1971). "Subliminal Perception: The Nature of a Controversy". McGraw-Hill, London.

Forster, P. M. and Govier, E. (1978). Discrimination without awareness? *Q. J. exp. Psychol.* **30**, 289–295.

Francis, H. (1977). Children's strategies in learning to read. *Br. J. educ. Psychol.* **47**, 117–125.

Gough, P. (1972). One second of reading. *In* "Language by Eye and by Ear" (J. P. Kavanagh and I. G. Mattingley, Eds). M.I.T. Press, Cambridge, Massachusetts.

Gregory, R. L. (1970). "The Intelligent Eye." Weidenfeld and Nicolson, London.

Gregory, R. L. (1973). The confounded eye. *In* "Illusion in Nature and Art" (R. L. Gregory and E. H. Gombrich, Eds). Duckworth, London.

Hansen, D. and Rodgers, T. S. (1968). An exploration of psycholinguistic units in initial reading. *In* "The Psycholinguistic Nature of the Reading Process" (K. S. Goodman, Ed.). Wayne State University Press, Detroit, Michigan.

Hardyck, C. D. and Petrinovich, L. F. (1970). Subvocal speech and comprehension as a function of the difficulty level of the reading material. *J. Verb. Learn. Verb. Behav.* **9**, 647–652.

Hochberg, J. (1970). Components of literacy: Speculations and exploratory research. *In* "Basic Studies on Reading" (H. Levin and J. P. Williams, Eds). Basic Books, New York.

Jacobson, J. Z. (1973). Effects of association upon masking and reading latency. *Can. J. Psychol.* **27**, 58–69.

Kennedy, A. (1978a). Reading sentences: Some observations on the control of eye-movements. *In* "Strategies of Information Processing" (G. Underwood, Ed.). Academic Press, London and New York.

Kennedy, A. (1978b). Eye-movements and the integration of semantic information during reading. *In* "Practical Aspects of Memory" (M. M. Gruneberg, P. E. Morris and R. N. Sykes, Eds). Academic Press, London and New York.

Kleiman, G. M. (1975). Speech recoding in reading. *J. Verb. Learn. Verb. Behav.* **24**, 323–339.

Kolers, P. A. (1970). Three stages of reading. *In* "Basic Studies on Reading" (H. Levin and J. P. Williams, Eds). Basic Books, New York.

Levin. H. and Cohn, J. A. (1968). Studies of oral reading: XII. Effects of instructions on the eye-voice span. *In* "The Analysis of Reading Skill (H. Levin, E. J. Gibson and J. J. Gibson, Eds). Cornell University, Ithaca, New York.

Levy, B. A. (1977). Reading: Speech and meaning processes. *J. Verb. Learn. Verb. Behav.* **16**, 623–638.

Lewis, J. L. (1970). Semantic processing of unattended messages using dichotic listening. *J. exp. Psychol.* **85**, 225–228.

Liberman, A. M., Mattingly, I. G. and Turvey, M. T. (1972). Language codes and memory codes. *In* "Coding Processes in Human Memory" (A. W. Melton and E. Martin, Eds). Winston, Washington D.C.

Liberman, I. Y., Shankweiler, D., Liberman, A. M., Fowler, C. and Fischer, F. W. (1977). Phonetic segmentation and recoding in the beginning reader. *In* "Toward a Psychology of Reading" (A. S. Reber and D. Scarborough, Eds). Erlbaum Associates, Hillsdale, New Jersey.

Lunzer, E. A. (1978). Short term memory and reading, Stage 1. *In* "Practical Aspects of Memory" (M. M. Gruneberg, P. E. Morris and R. N. Sykes, Eds). Academic Press, London and New York.

MacKay, D. M. (1973). Aspects of the theory of comprehension, memory and attention. *Q. J. exp. Psychol.* **25**, 22–40.

Mark, L. S., Shankweiler, D., Liberman, I. Y. and Fowler, C. A. (1977).

Phonetic recoding and reading difficulty in beginning readers. *Memory and Cognition* **5**, 623–629.

Marshall, J. C. and Newcombe, F. (1973). Patterns of paralexia: A psycholinguistic approach. *J. Psycholing. Res.* **2**, 175–199.

McConkie, G. W., Rayner, K. and Wilson, S. J. (1973). Experimental manipulation of reading strategies. *J. educ. Psychol.* **65**, 1–8.

Meyer, D. E. and Schvaneveldt, R. W. (1971). Facilitation in recognizing pairs of words: Evidence of a dependence between retrieval operations. *J. exp. Psychol.* **90**, 227–234.

Moray, N. (1959). Attention in dichotic listening: Affective cues and the influence of instructions. *Q. J. exp. Psychol.* **11**, 56–60.

Morton, J. (1969). Interaction of information in word recognition. *Psychol. Rev.* **76**, 165–178.

Murrell, G. A. and Morton, J. (1974). Word recognition and morphemic structure. *J. exp. Psychol.* **102**, 963–968.

Neisser, U. (1976). "Cognition and Reality". Freeman, San Francisco.

Norman, D. A. (1968). Toward a theory of memory and attention. *Psychol. Rev.* **75**, 522–536.

Philpott, A. and Wilding, J. (1979). Semantic interference from subliminal stimuli in a dichoptic viewing situation. *Br. J. Psychol.* (in press).

Pillsbury, W. B. (1897). A study in apperception. *Am. J. Psychol.* **8**, 315–393.

Rayner, K. (1975). The perceptual span and peripheral cues in reading. *Cognitive Psychol.* **7**, 65–81.

Rubenstein, H. R., Lewis, S. S. and Rubenstein, M. A. (1971). Evidence for phonemic recoding in visual word recognition. *J. Verb. Learn. Verb. Behav.* **10**, 645–657.

Schwartz, R. M. (1977). Strategic processes in beginning reading. *J. Read. Behav.* **9**, 17–26.

Shallice, T. and Warrington, E. K. (1975). Word recognition in a phonemic dyslexic patient. *Q. J. exp. Psychol.* **27**, 187–199.

Sperling, G. (1960). The information available in brief visual presentations. *Psychol. Monogr.* **74**, (whole no. 498).

Spoehr, K. T. and Smith, E. E. (1973). The role of syllables in perceptual processing. *Cognitive Psychol.* **5**, 71–89.

Taylor, J. (1976). "Introduction to Psycholinguistics". Holt, Rinehart and Winston, New York.

Treisman, A. M. (1960). Contextual cues in selective listening. *Q. J. exp. Psychol.* **12**, 242–248.

Underwood, G. (1976a). Semantic interference from unattended printed words. *Br. J. Psychol.* **67**, 327–338.

Underwood, G. (1976b). "Attention and Memory". Pergamon Press, Oxford.

Underwood, G. (1977). Attention, awareness and hemispheric differences in word recognition, *Neuropsychologia* **15**, 61–67.

Underwood, G. (1978). Attentional strategies and behavioural control. *In* "Strategies of Information Processing" (G. Underwood, Ed.). Academic Press, London and New York.

Underwood, G. and Holt, P. O'B. (1978). Analyzing the reading process. *In* "Practical Aspects of Memory" (M. M. Gruneberg, P. E. Morris, and R. N. Sykes, Eds). Academic Press, London and New York.

Underwood, G., Parry, R. S. and Bull, L. A. (1978). Simple reading tasks are affected by unattended context. *In* "Practical Aspects of Memory" (M. M. Gruneberg, R. N. Sykes and P. E. Morris, Eds). Academic Press, London and New York.

Wardlow, K. A. and Kroll, N. E. A. (1976). Autonomic responses to shock-associated words in a non-attended message: A failure to replicate. *J. exp. Psychol: Human Perception and Performance* **2**, 357–360.

Willows, D. M. (1974). Reading between the lines: Selective attention in good and poor readers. *Child Develop.* **45**, 408–415.

Willows, D. M. and MacKinnon, G. E. (1973). Selective reading: Attention to the "unattended" lines. *Can. J. Psychol.* **37**, 292–304.

von Wright, J. M., Anderson, K. and Stenman, U. (1975). Generalization of conditioned GSRs in dichotic listening. *In* "Attention and Performance" (P. M. A. Rabbitt and J. Dornic, Eds). Vol. V. Academic Press, London and New York.

5. Memory and Ageing

E. MILLER

Department of Clinical Psychology,
Addenbrooke's Hospital,
Cambridge, UK

It is commonly accepted that memory fades with age and that this is an inevitable part of the ageing process. In addition some older people suffer degenerative changes in the central nervous system and develop dementia. Dementia produces changes in many aspects of cognitive functioning. Prominent amongst these are memory impairments which commonly become bad enough to represent a serious handicap by themselves. Even in the case of older people who are not dementing, that common saying that "You cannot teach an old dog new tricks" conveys the almost universal prejudice that old people are almost incapable of learning and remembering new skills and ideas.

The relevant literature on memory and ageing is extremely large and an exhaustive coverage would be beyond the scope of this chapter. The discussion will therefore concentrate on a number of key issues. In particular this chapter will attempt to answer four questions:

(1) Does memory really decline as a function of age and, if so, by how much?
(2) If normal people do show changes in memory as they get older what are these changes?
(3) What changes in memory occur in older people who develop dementia?
(4) What can be done to ameliorate the effects of memory impairments in the elderly?

Before proceeding with these questions it is useful to clarify the terminology. In this chapter "old" and synonymous terms like "elderly" will be used to refer to people of above retirement age (i.e. 60 to 65 and older). The term "young" will always be used in connection with young adults.

I. Does Memory Decline with Age?

To the reader not familiar with research on ageing this question must seem rather provocative. This chapter would not appear in a book like this unless it is believed that something happened to memory as people get older. The question does memory decline with age, is posed in this form because it illustrates some important methodological considerations which arise in all psychological research into ageing. The only illustrations of some of these methodological issues come from the study of psychological functions other than memory. For this reason this section, unlike the rest, will refer to some work which does not bear directly upon memory.

In general terms it is true to say that almost every investigator who has given the same memory task to both older subjects and younger adults has found that the older sample perform less well. It is tempting to use such findings, and they exist in great profusion, as incontrovertible proof of a decline in memory with age. There are a number of objections that could be entered against such a conclusion. Basically these centre around the point that groups of older and younger subjects may well differ on other variables in addition to that of age.

A common argument is that the older subject is likely to be less well motivated to do as well on the experimental tasks and the poorer performance may be at least partially a reflection of this. It is impossible to rule out poor motivation as a partial explanation of some findings but the balance of evidence is very much against attributing all differences in performance to motivation. One way of investigating this proposition has relied on the argument that introducing special manipulations in the experiment which are designed to enhance motivation should have a greater effect on older subjects. The prediction is that the older subject, being naturally poorly motivated, has more room to improve when motivation is increased. The younger subject, with better motivation, will be nearer his peak performance and has less scope for improvement. I know of no such experiment using a memory task as the main dependent variable but the strategy has been applied to other functions alleged to decline with age (e.g. reaction time and performance on cognitive tests). Such experiments have consistently failed to support the notion of age-related decline being an artifact of lowered motivation (Botwinick *et. al.*, 1957; Ganzler, 1964). Inglis *et al.* (1968) have also argued that if motivation is the main variable affecting performance on memory tasks then it would be expected to have a similar effect on all measures of memory performance. This was not the case in the Inglis *et al.* investigations where one dependent variable turned out to be very sensitive to age changes whilst the other was relatively insensitive. It must be concluded that poor motivation is inadequate as the sole, or even the most important, cause of the observed differences in memory performance between old and young subjects.

Probably the most convincing argument for not taking differences between old and young groups entirely at face value comes from the possible parallel with studies of age changes in intelligence test scores (see: Miller, 1977a; Savage, 1973). In the standardization of the major intelligence tests, such as the Wechsler Adult Intelligence Scale (WAIS), the test is administered to a cross-section of the population including sub-groups at different age levels. Comparison of the raw scores obtained by groups at different ages, typically gives the impression that intellectual ability increases through childhood but levels off by about the age of 20 years. It then remains static for only a decade or so before it starts to decline. This decline is slow at first but starts to accelerate as the individual reaches the end of middle age.

An alternative to the cross-sectional approach is to study age changes longitudinally, ideally by repeatedly assessing a group of subjects throughout their adult life. The difficulties inherent in such longitudinal studies do not need to be laboured here and it is hardly surprising that data from longitudinal investigations covering the whole of adult life from maturity to old age are conspicuous by their absence. However some relevant information can be obtained. For example, Owens (1966) reported on a sample of males first tested on the Army Alpha test at around the age of 50 years. The sample was retested 11 years later. Using subjects of that age there should be a very definite deterioration in test performance between the two testings if the results from cross-sectional studies give us a true picture of intellectual decline. In fact Owens's subjects showed only the slightest trend towards lower scores on retesting and this was nowhere near statistical significance.

Of even greater interest is the much more sophisticated investigation reported by Schaie and Strother (1968a; 1968b). They used a mixed cross-sectional and longitudinal design. Samples of subjects at each 5-year age interval between 20 and 70 were tested on the Primary

Mental Abilities Test and all were retested seven years later. Examining the data from the initial testings alone, revealed the conventional view of intellectual decline as derived from cross-sectional studies. When account was taken of each group's change (or lack of it) over the 7-year retest interval the picture confirmed that cross-sectional data do exaggerate the amount of intellectual decline except where speed plays a very important part in performance.

In retrospect it is easy to see why cross-sectional studies might overestimate the decline with age. Consider a cross-sectional study carried out in 1970. The 70-year-olds in the sample would have been born in 1900. This was at a time when diseases related to nutritional deficiencies, such as rickets which were not uncommon, and educational opportunities were much less favourable than they would have been for 20-year-old subjects born in 1950. It is known that both nutritional deficiencies and educational opportunities can affect scores on intelligence tests (e.g. Husen, 1951). In fact Schaie and Gribbin (1975) have argued that the point at which decline in intellectual functioning starts to become manifest is moving up the age scale with each successive generation.

It is obviously dangerous to generalize too much from one psychological function to another. I know of no data obtained from the use of memory tasks which would allow any assessment of what the decline in memory with age would look like if it were to be studied longtitudinally. Nevertheless the experience with intelligence tests cautions that purely cross-sectional data obtained from separate samples of old and young subjects should be treated with some suspicion. In support of this there are a few indications in the literature that the ability to learn new skills in people of advancing years may not be as poor as common prejudice would have it. Investigations of the ability of middle aged workers to learn new skills have generally shown that the apparent impairments are small. These are sometimes at least partially the consequence of other factors than poor learning *per se* and can be compensated for by the use of appropriate training strategies (Belbin, 1958; Belbin and Downs, 1964; Birren, 1964). In addition an Australian report has claimed good levels of learning among retired people attending classes in German (Naylor and Harwood, 1975).

It can be seen that trying to decide whether memory declines with age is rather more complicated than it seems at first sight. Since the available data on memory is solely derived from cross-sectional studies it is probably fair to conclude that we have no adequate scientific demonstration that memory does decline with age! However, this is not the important issue because we can be reasonably certain that an individual's memory at, say, 80 years is not what it was as a young adult. These methodological difficulties and inadequacies also mean that it is impossible at present to draw any conclusion as to when memory starts to decline and by how much. It is this sort of information that it would be useful to have. Yet another complication of the methodological problems will be taken up at the start of the next section on the nature of the memory change.

Before leaving this section with its methodological concerns it is worthwhile drawing attention to the nature of age as a variable. Age is not a causal variable. Changes do not occur because of the passage of time but because time allows other variables the opportunity to act. Although this point is fairly obvious it is all too easy to lapse into the assumption that the passage of time can be used to explain any demonstrated changes with age. It is necessary to remember that age-related changes must be related to other variables if causes for the change are being sought.

II. The Nature of the Memory Change with Age

Whatever view of memory is taken most theorists would agree that memory is a complex process. Inevitably any discussion of the nature of the memory change associated with ageing is going to make comments about how any one aspect of the total memory process is alleged to have changed with respect to another. This will be the case whether it takes the form of suggesting that, say, primary memory is more affected than secondary memory, or that the older subject has a greater difficulty in achieving the deeper, semantic forms of coding. If the argument in the previous section is accepted to the effect that the straight comparison of old and young subjects can lead to a distortion in the amount of decline, then it is far from unreasonable to take it a step further. It could be that the distortion due to cross-sectional data may be more marked on some measures of memory than others (just as cross-sectional studies of intelligence exaggerate the decline in unspeeded but not heavily speeded tests). In order to look at the available evidence at all it is necessary to assume that this latter possibility is not the case, at least to any appreciable degree.

It is difficult to find a satisfactory way of subdividing and classifying the very large quantity of evidence relevant to the topic of normal memory change with age. The most obvious way is to follow the theoretical bent of most of the work published in this field. This involves a multi-stage model of memory. Incoming information is alleged to pass through a very brief sensory store and into a short-term (or primary) memory (STM). The usual assumption is that STM is of limited capacity and that most information arriving at this stage will be lost irretrievably fairly quickly. Some information will be passed on from the (STM) into long-term (or secondary) memory (LTM) for more permanent storage (see Murdock, 1967). Initially it will be convenient to start by following the outline of this model. In recent years this type of model of memory has started to attract increasing criticism (e.g. Craik and Lockhart, 1972) and theoretical ideas have tended to focus upon a more continuous model of memory and the levels of processing alleged to be carried out upon the to-be-remembered material. (The small amount of work relevant to this latter type of approach will also be discussed.)

There is very little evidence relating to sensory (iconic or echoic) memory in older people. With regard to the visual modality Schonfield and Wenger (1975) studied the exposure time required for subjects to identify a string of letters presented tachistoscopically. There was a considerable increase in the time required to identify the letters when the number of letters was raised from four to five in older subjects. With younger subjects the jump from six to seven letters had to be reached before there was any comparable increase in the time required for identification. Kline and Szafran (1975) found that older subjects were much more susceptible to backward masking from a "visual noise" field when trying to identify tachistoscopically presented digits.

Walsh and Thompson (1978) used a rather different technique to look at sensory memory. Subjects saw the letter "O" presented in two brief flashes. The inter-stimulus interval was then adjusted to find the longest interval for which the subject would report seeing a continuous stimulus. This interval was found to be reliably longer in younger subjects thus suggesting a more rapid decay of information in sensory memory in the older group. Thus all three experiments point to the possibility that older people may have a less efficient iconic memory.

There is no direct evidence with regard to auditory sensory memory (echoic memory). A complex experiment by Clark and Knowles (1973) used the dichotic listening technique (involving the simultaneous presentation of messages to each ear) varying method and order of report in order to tease out whether previously established age changes were the result of registration, retention or retrieval deficits. Clark and Knowles concluded that the older subject was especially impaired in the initial perception or registration of information. Taken at face value this study suggests that echoic memory might be worth exploring.

Undoubtedly one of the most popular hypotheses has been that older subjects are impaired in the acquisition of new information especially at the level of STM. Inglis *et al.* (1968) have described a series of experiments using the dichotic listening technique. It was consistently found that older subjects were impaired in the recall of digits to the ear that was reported second. No differences between old and young occurred for the first ear that was reported. The argument was that reporting from the second ear was affected because the set of digits produced second had to be held in some form of short-term store whilst those reported first were being read out.

Later experiments (e.g. Clark and Knowles, 1973; Schonfield *et al.*, 1972) have differed in that losses have also appeared in digits from the ear reported first. Craik (1977) discusses the possibility that the difference between earlier and later results may lie in a procedural difference. In general the later investigations specified the ear to be reported first, whereas the earlier ones left it to the subject to decide which to report first. Thus when the order of report is unspecified older subjects may concentrate unduly on their favoured (usually right) ear and neglect the other thus producing the results described by Inglis *et al.* (1968). Regardless of the details, a major problem with these experiments on dichotic listening is that the output from one ear can no longer be safely equated with output from a short-term store (Broadbent, 1971; Craik, 1977).

More recent approaches to the study of STM or primary memory have not provided convincing evidence of a deficit at this level in the elderly. It has been held that the recency effect in free recall (i.e. the last items presented tend to be better recalled) can be used to give a relatively pure measure of primary memory (Watkins, 1974). Neither Craik (1968) nor Raymond (1971) were able to get evidence of decreased primary memory in older subjects as based on recency in free recall. In any case there are again theoretical difficulties with this technique (e.g. Baddeley and Hitch, 1974).

A variation on the STM deficit hypothesis is that older subjects may be more prone to decay of material or interference in STM. One way to examine these factors is to use the Peterson and Peterson (1959) experimental paradigm whereby the subject is given stimuli to remember (e.g. three letters or words) immediately followed by a counting task in which the subject has to participate quite actively. After a given interval of counting, the subject is required to recall the "to-be-remembered" stimuli. In this situation efficiency of recall declines as a function of the time interval before recall is requested. The typical finding with older subjects is that they show no increase in the rate of forgetting in this type of experiment (e.g. Kriauciunas, 1968).

A final point in relation to STM is that it has been claimed (e.g.

McGhie *et al.*, 1965) that STM for visually presented material is more vulnerable to disturbance with age than is the case for material presented in the auditory modality. Others, like Marcer (1974), have built this apparent finding into a key position in their overall theoretical analysis of memory change with age. Taub (1975) has indicated a major methodological inadequacy in the crucial experiments in that no proper attempt was made to equate the material presented through the two modalities. In Taub's own experiment it was found that all subjects found it easier to recall material presented through the auditory modality as compared with visual presentation. However this modality effect seemed to have nothing to do with age in that it was equally apparent in young and old subjects.

The evidence considered so far gives little encouragement to the idea that older people have a particular impairment in STM. Following the "modal model" it is now appropriate to examine LTM or secondary memory. In experiments utilizing free recall there is a very definite diminution in the ability of elderly subjects to recall items from the earlier part of the lists (e.g. Raymond, 1971). It is the recall of items from this part of the list that has often been held to reflect output from secondary memory.

It has been suggested that the elderly are particularly impaired on recall tasks as opposed to those based on recognition. Schonfield and Robertson (1966) required subjects at several different age levels to learn a list of 24 words, with retention being examined by both recall and recognition tests. In this experiment recognition showed no decline with age but recall declined almost linearly with age. One minor criticism of this experiment is that the oldest subjects were only in their sixties and the finding of no decline in recognition might not hold in extreme old age. Usually experiments designed to examine this further do agree in showing recall to be more affected by age but, despite Schonfield and Robertson, there is good evidence that deficits do occur in recognition as well as recall (e.g. Erber, 1974).

It may be that this recall-recognition difference is merely due to recognition tests being less sensitive than recall tests but there are other possible implications. It can be argued that recall requires a much more active retrieval process than recognition. If the retrieval process is prone to become less efficient with ageing then Schonfield and Robertson's (1966) finding of greater decline on tests of recall might be expected. There is also other evidence that has been held to be consistent with the view that ageing might affect the ability to retrieve information from secondary memory.

Laurence (1967) presented a list of 36 words to her subjects. The

words fell into six categories (names of flowers, birds, etc.) Giving
subjects the names of these categories at the time of recall helped
the older subjects but not the younger. In fact it enhanced the recall of
the older group to such an extent that it equalled that of the younger.
The argument then runs that if this kind of cue produces normal levels
of recall then the material to be learned must have reached secondary
memory with normal facility otherwise giving the cue at the time of
recall could not have had the observed effect. The other possible
hypothesis is that the category cue may assist at the time of recall
because the material to be learned was coded in an inappropriate way.
This is a little less plausible in this context because giving the category
cues at the time of learning had no benefit.

On the other hand there is evidence that is difficult to fit into any
hypothesis postulating retrieval difficulties as being an explanation of
memory loss with age. For example, Drachman and Leavitt (1972)
compared young and old subjects on a number of different memory
tasks. They found no deficit on their particular test of retrieval of old
memories (supplying members of different categories such as flowers).
Cueing at the time of recall, by giving the initial letters of the words to
be recalled, did assist older subjects but to no greater degree than it did
for the younger. There is no evidence of retrieval problems here but
Drachman and Leavitt did find the older group to be impaired in the
learning of supra-span lists of digits. They conclude that older people
suffer from problems of storage rather than retrieval.

It can be seen that work on secondary memory, like that on primary
memory, has not led to very satisfactory conclusions about the nature of
the change in memory that occurs with age. There is a difficulty in
getting pure measures of the various aspects of the multi-stage model of
memory. Different experiments also seem to highlight different aspects
of the overall system. It could be simply that this is because most
aspects of the system do deteriorate with age and just which is shown up
at any one time is determined by the characteristics of the particular
experiment. An alternative is to argue that if the overall model does not
lead to clear conclusions, as the multi-stage model certainly has not,
then it might be better to explore the value of other approaches to
memory.

In recent years interest has started to switch to "level of processing"
as the main explanatory construct in verbal memory (e.g. Craik and
Lockhart, 1972). Memory is assumed to be a continuum rather than a
set of discrete stores and the durability of memory is assumed to depend
upon the "depth" or level of encoding that has been carried out. It is
also usually considered that the extraction and storage of the semantic

features of the to-be-remembered material involves a deeper level of processing than the elaboration of its more physical attributes (e.g. the acoustic characteristics of a word).

On the basis of this approach an attractive theory of memory change with age revolves around the idea that older people are less able to process information at the deeper, more semantic, levels. As yet there is little evidence relating directly to this hypothesis. Eysenck (1974) presented words to his subjects and asked them to carry out various processes with the words. Some involved shallower levels of processing (counting the number of letters in the word). Others allegedly involved deeper processing by generating appropriate adjectives or images for each word. Subjects were led to believe that this was all that the experiment involved although a later instruction to recall the words was given. All subjects recalled the words alleged to have been subjected to the deeper levels of processing better than the rest. When compared with younger controls older subjects were especially impaired in recalling words subjected to deeper processing. Eysenck considered that his results demonstrated a deficit in semantic processing in the older group.

Unfortunately other work has not given such unequivocal support for the hypothesis. White (cited by Craik, 1977) carried out an experiment rather similar to that of Eysenck (1974). The differences that White demonstrated between older and younger subjects were consistent with Eysenck's data when the test for later memory was based on recall. When this later test involved recognition of the words that had been used in the earlier part of the experiment the differences between old and young in the critical conditions tended to disappear. Again this may be because recognition gives a less sensitive measure than recall. Otherwise it might point to a problem in retrieval as well as in encoding.

Mistler-Lachman (1977) attempted to look at encoding in the memories of older subjects using the "release from proactive inhibition" technique as developed by Wickens (1970). In essence this involves studying a situation (the STM task first used by Peterson and Peterson, 1959) which is known to be heavily prone to proactive interference. After several trials using "to-be-remembered" stimuli of a similar nature in order to build up proactive interference, a further trial is given in which the stimuli differ in some way from those used previously. Recall of this latter stimulus is much better than if no such shifts in the type of stimulus had been made. It is this effect that is known as "release from proactive inhibition". The interference between items that builds up to produce the proactive inhibition must occur along some dimension of encoding. To the extent that the elderly lose the ability to classify and process information so they should show a lower build of proactive inhibition and much less of a release effect. In Mistler-Lachman's (1977) experiment a sample of elderly subjects drawn from the community showed no less release from proactive inhibition than the normal controls. The release effect did not occur in a group of elderly living in rest homes but the obvious question can be raised as to whether these were really a sample of normal elderly people.

The notion that the older person's memory may suffer because of an impaired ability to utilize the deeper levels of processing is initially appealing but the findings obtained so far are not wholly encouraging apart from Eysenck (1974). Memory encoding in the elderly has not yet been explored in sufficient detail to justify any final conclusion on this hypothesis. It could be argued that that the few experiments carried out so far have not covered all the possible dimensions along which processing and encoding might occur. When this is done the levels of processing hypothesis might appear in a much more convincing light.

All in all this selective review has not led to any firm conclusions about the nature of the memory change with age. Even when pains are taken to take into account a much larger proportion of the extensive literature than space has permitted here (e.g. Craik, 1977) this does not lead to any clearer decisions. This unsatisfactory position is not likely to be resolved until two major underlying problems have been resolved. The first is methodological. As has already been indicated it is unsatisfactory that data on memory changes with age should come solely from cross-sectional studies with their known ability to bias the picture. This problem could be overcome in time especially by the use of the mixed longtitudinal and cross-sectional design as developed by Schiae and Strother (1968a,b). The other problem is more difficult. It is simply that it is impossible to give an account of the memory changes with age until we have a satisfactory model upon which to base that account.

From the point of view of trying to deal with the practical problems posed by memory impairments in the aged it can be argued that the kind of research discussed in this section is not of the most immediate use. Almost without exception research has been directed to examining the nature of the *change* that has occurred in memory as a result of ageing. To help ameliorate any memory problems that the aged may have it might not be of any value to know what changes have occurred over the individual's adult life. It is more apposite to know under what conditions the elderly person's memory will perform at its best and at its worst. In other words research that compares the performance of different groups of elderly subjects under different conditions is likely to have greater practical value than that which compares the old with the young under the same conditions.

III. What Changes Occur in Dementia?

Dementia is a common disorder in old age and is found in about 10% of those over the age of 65 years (Pearce and Miller, 1973). In most cases (so-called "senile dementia") this appears to be produced by an abnormally rapid atrophy of the brain with the brain also showing an exaggeration of the pathological changes that are found in extreme old age (e.g. senile plaques). Senile dementia also seems to be more or less identical with the rarer form of pre-senile dementia known as Alzheimer's disease which has a very similar pathology. Patients with dementia of this type are liable to a large range of psychological dysfunctions (Miller, 1977a). General intellectual deterioration occurs as do changes in mood and personality. Memory impairments are particularly prominent and are commonly the thing that first alerts others to the fact that the slow, insidious dementing process has started. This section will outline what is known about memory in dementia. A more comprehensive, overall discussion of psychological changes in dementia is available in Miller (1977a).

Again it is easiest to approach the nature of memory deficits in dementia with the multi-stage model in mind. Miller (1977b) required demented subjects and normal controls to report the letters contained in an array of six when these were viewed tachistoscopically. The exposure time was varied but each exposure was followed by a "visual noise" field to give a backward masking effect. For any given length of exposure of the letters (the experiment used a range of values between 50 and 250 ms) the dements were able to report fewer letters than the controls. This result is consistent with the idea that the earliest levels of registration and processing might be impaired in dementia but the finding needs to be confirmed and explored further.

As was the case with normal memory changes with age it has been hypothesized that the source of the memory problem in dementia lies in STM. Inglis and his associates (see Inglis, 1970) have applied the dichotic listening technique to elderly demented patients. The results formed a parallel with those described in the previous section on normal ageing in that the elderly dements when compared with age matched normal controls were impaired in recalling digits from the ear reported second. The same problems as previously discussed, also arise in trying to equate the findings with a deficit in STM.

Miller (1971) reported two experiments based on the free recall of lists of words. Recall of words from the end of the list was less efficient in the demented group and this was held to be consistent with a deficit in STM or primary memory. Recall of items from the beginning of the list was also affected. A possible explanation for this is that the impaired STM of the dement is unable to process words at the beginning of the list rapidly enough and so they do not get through STM and into LTM. To check on this Miller compared the effects of two rates of presentation of items in the list. If impaired STM was the sole cause of the reduced primacy effect a slower rate of presentation would give the dement a better chance to process the first words in the list, through into long-term storage and recall from this part of the list and ought to be enhanced. In fact, this did not occur to any discernable degree in the demented group, although the controls did show better recall of the early words in the list with slower rates of presentation. On the basis of these results Miller (1971) suggested that both STM and LTM must be affected in dementia.

This interpretation depends upon the plausibility of the short-term versus long-term store interpretation of free recall which has recently been challenged (Baddeley and Hitch, 1974). In fact a further experiment based on a very different technique has also led to a similar conclusion. Miller (1973) had subjects learn lists of words that were just above the length that could be correctly repeated after a single presentation. Demented subjects were found to be clearly impaired in supra-span learning and this is again consistent with the idea that LTM is implicated. The actual "word spans" were also reduced in dementia which could be considered to reflect a poor STM.

In attempting to look at LTM or secondary memory in dementia, Miller (1975) required subjects to learn lists of words over a number of presentations. After a delay, retention was tested for by means of the conventional types of recall and recognition tests and by a partial information procedure. This latter involved presenting the subjects with the initial letters of the words that had to be recalled. The dements showed appreciable impairments on the conventional recall and recognition tests but, unlike the controls, recall was enhanced by the partial information condition.

In fact there was no significant difference between the dements and controls with partial information. Since partial information assisted dements and not controls and is provided at the time of recall the results suggest the possibility of a retrieval deficit in dementia. A major puzzle in these results is, why providing the subject with the initial letter should be so helpful, whilst giving the entire word in the context of a conventional recognition test still leaves the dements apparently impaired.

Two possible explanations can be advanced for the beneficial effect of partial information. One is that the demented patient codes new information in a bizarre form. In order for this to be subsequently retrieved it is necessary that an appropriate cue be given. A second explanation, advanced by Warrington and Weiskrantz (1970) to explain similar findings in patients with the amnesic syndrome, appeals to the concept of disinhibition. It can be argued that successful recall, especially of something like a list of common words, depends to some extent on the ability to inhibit the retrieval of potential responses that are incorrect (i.e. other common words in the subject's vocabulary). If this ability to inhibit the recall of incorrect responses is lost then the recall of correct responses may be impeded and the subject may match incorrectly retrieved words with the filler items provided in the recognition test. Hence the poor recognition performance. Providing the initial letter of the word assists the dement by severely restricting the number of responses which might be considered adequate without actually providing an incorrect response which might correspond to an inappropriately retrieved item.

Preliminary investigations have not really supported either of these explanations. An experiment designed to examine the types of error that dements make in recognition testing yielded no evidence of any peculiarities in encoding (Miller, 1974). A prediction derived from the disinhibition hypothesis relating to the differential effect that altering the number of alternatives would have on the recognition of demented subjects was upheld. On the other hand, in the same paper Miller (1978) examined the occurrence of intrusions in recall. The disinhibition hypothesis would predict that demented subjects would produce many more intrusions but this does not seem to occur. The finding by Woods and Piercy (1974) that partial information can be similarly effective in normal subjects when the trace is weak raises the possibility that the partial information effect in dementia may simply be the consequence of poor acquisition leading to a weak trace.

The effect of dementia on memory has not been a popular area of study and there have been few attempts to examine the problem systematically. As was the case with normal memory changes with age the data do not fit any straightforward explanation based upon the multi-stage model of memory. As yet no work has been published which is based on the level of processing approach to memory. Again it can be argued that, from a practical point of view, trying to describe how memory in dementia differs from that in normal healthy subjects may not lead to the most useful research. What would be much more relevant are studies comparing groups of demented subjects under different conditions to determine under what conditions memory and learning are relatively enhanced or impaired. As yet this approach has been totally neglected but the finding that partial information can differentially assist recall in dementia might prove an interesting starting point.

IV. What Can Be Done About Memory Impairment in the Aged?

Memory impairments, especially when they get more marked as in dementia, can be extremely handicapping. The crucial practical problem is what can be done to alleviate them. This section concentrates on psychological approaches but physical methods ought to be briefly mentioned. Drugs such as the alleged cerebral vasodilators, hyperbaric oxygen and other techniques have been tried (see Miller, 1977a). These show very little in the way of convincing evidence of efficacy. Even preparations like cyclandelate which have shown promising results in the early clinical trials subsequently seem to succumb to negative results (e.g. Davies *et al.*, 1977). As things are at present the beneficial effects of physical methods of treatment must be regarded as minimal at best, and probably even non-existent.

In turning to possible psychological methods of reducing memory impairments the picture seems to be equally gloomy at first. If the aim is to improve memory performance in elderly persons in a way that might be considered as moving towards a "cure" of memory disorder then this is certainly not possible. In the present state of knowledge about memory and its impairments there seems to be no hope of any technique that will produce a general improvement in memory, at least within the foreseeable future. This does not mean that there is nothing that can be done to help but it does suggest that it is necessary to set rather different and more limited objectives. Instead of trying to improve memory as such, the aim has to be the amelioration of the effects of memory disorder. Given that the individual may have a memory impairment it is necessary to seek out ways of ensuring that it has a minimal impact on the person's everyday living and quality of life.

The first approach to ameliorating the effects of memory disorder is apparently obvious, although it often tends to be overlooked by those who work with the elderly. Memory disorders typically have a much more profound effect upon the acquisition of new information and skills than they do on the ability to retain and utilize old skills and ideas, especially if the latter have been heavily overlearned. The place with which the old person is most familiar and where most overlearned skills will be in evidence (especially in the case of women) is in the home. This has a number of implications for work with the mildly demented elderly. Occupational therapists, who are usually the group who deal with and assess "activities of daily living", may be concerned to decide whether an old lady is capable of looking after herself if she returns home on leaving hospital. Assessing the patient's ability to prepare meals in the Occupational Therapy Department kitchen could give an estimate of performance that is misleadingly low. The same lady in her own kitchen, where she is familiar with the location of everything, may reveal an adequate ability to prepare food. Similarly the same lady may shop reasonably well in the local supermarket where a perambulation round the familiar shelves may provide the necessary cues as to the sort of things that need to be bought. Another supermarket may be a bustling and incomprehensible confusion.

Maintaining the familiar environment may help to minimize the impact of a memory disorder. This can be supplemented by the use of special props for memory such as lists of things to do prominently displayed in the kitchen or having a helpful neighbour remind the patient when certain things need to be done. However it is not possible to entirely avoid the need to register new information even if this is just a modification of old skills. It sometimes happens in clinical practice that an old person could achieve a more satisfactory and rewarding way of life if only they could learn, or relearn a particular skill. For example an old person admitted to hospital may have partly lost the ability to dress him/herself and this could well be for reasons that have nothing to do with the basic skills and abilities required in dressing. If this important self-help skill could be reinstated then the individual might be able to leave hospital and live in, say, a local authority residential home for the aged. Under such circumstances it may be possible to mobilize the person's remaining capacity to learn so that the goal can be achieved.

It is in just this context that research which compares learning and retention in demented groups under different learning conditions would come into its own. Unfortunately there is very little sound information to fall back upon although there are a few leads that are worth following up. Early studies of operant learning have shown that demented subjects, unlike the normal aged, give low, erratic response rates and are insensitive to changes in reinforcement contingencies (Mackay, 1965). Further investigations using a human analogue of the Skinner box situation have been reported by Ankus and Quarrington (1972). In the latter investigation the authors were particularly careful to establish the appropriateness of the reinforcer for each subject. When this was done even the demented subjects showed good learning and they were also very sensitive to changes in the schedules of re-inforcement in exactly the same way as the normal controls.

Ankus and Quarrington's work suggests that, given the use of appropriate reinforcers which need to be established separately for each subject, operant techniques (behaviour modification) might have potential for use with the memory disturbed elderly. Preliminary appli-cations in the clinical setting give rise to cautious optimism. Mueller and Atlas (1972) set up small discussion groups of demented old people. After establishing baseline response levels, group members were reinforced (initially by means of primary reinforcers such as sweets but later tokens) for speaking. Group verbal interaction increased appreci-ably and ward staff claimed that this carried over into the general ward setting. Other accounts of the application of behaviour modification techniques with the elderly can be found in Hoyer (1973) and Hoyer et al. (1974).

Another finding with possible practical significance comes from more conventional studies of memory. The experiment of Miller (1975) has already been described. Briefly it was shown that after the learning of a list of words, conventional tests of recall and recognition showed very poor retention in a demented group. When partial information was provided (the initial letters of the words that were to be recalled) recall was not significantly less than normal in the demented group. In fact this finding parallels a similar result obtained previously by War-rington and Weiskrantz (1970) using patients with the amnesic syn-drome and including cases with Korsakoff's syndrome.

In studying a single case with Korsakoff's syndrome (a condition most frequently encountered in alcoholics and whose most prominent feature is a severe memory impairment) Jaffe and Katz (1975) first confirmed that appropriate cueing could enhance the recall of previ-ously learned material. They then used the partial information cue of initial letters to teach this subject the names of staff members on the hospital ward. He had failed to acquire these over a period of five years in the hospital. The subject was given the staff members' names and asked to recall them with the initial letters as a cue. The cues were then faded. The patient was then able spontaneously to greet these staff members using their names. Although this technique does not yet appear to have been attempted with elderly people who have memory disorders its potential deserves to be explored.

It is also likely that variations in learning procedures that enhance acquisition and retention in normal subjects would also be effective in handicapped groups. For example, it is well established in normal adult subjects that, given equivalent amounts of time, spaced learning results in better acquisition than massed practice. Again there has been little or no attempt to seriously examine this type of finding in any patient group with memory problems let alone the elderly. An almost solitary exception is Lewinsohn *et al*. (1977) who looked at subjects with brain injury. They had brain injured patients using visual imagery as an aid in the remembering of lists of words and demonstrated that it had a similar beneficial effect with this group to that extensively reported in normal subjects) e.g. Paivio, 1971). Again such approaches are wide open for exploitation with the elderly.

Although psychologists have not so far been very forthcoming in trying to apply their skills and knowledge to the amelioration of the disturbances in memory and other functions that occur in the elderly there have been a few innovations. One technique designed particularly for the elderly is "Reality orientation" (see: Barns *et al*., 1973; Folsom, 1968). In essence reality orientation tries to ensure that the patient relearns if necessary, and then continually rehearses, essential information relating to his orientation for time, place and person. In practice, knowing the names and uses of commonly encountered objects and environmental features are usually included. Reality orientation is promulgaged in two main ways. There are formal classes which are designed to go over the basic information that reality orientation stresses. In addition all staff working on the unit are required to emphasize information about orientation in all their interactions with patients. For example the nurse giving out medication would say "Here are your midday tablets, Mrs Smith" to show who is involved and the time rather than just "Here are your pills".

There is developing interest in reality orientation with many poorly controlled or anecdotal reports. One of the few well-conducted trials is that of Brook, *et al*. (1975) who examined the effects of daily reality orientation classes. Introduction of subjects to the special reality orientation room with its materials had an initial benefit but this soon declined. Only when patients were required to actively participate in reality orientation sessions was sustained improvement ensured. Amongst other things this report suggests that any beneficial effects of reality orientation are over and above those arising from just increasing the general level of stimulation on the ward.

It was once assumed that the mentally disturbed or impaired elderly were a uniformly hopeless group. Important clinical studies, such as that of Roth (1955), then showed that it was wrong to lump all such patients together as a single category of psychiatric disorder. Subgroups, such as those with depression, could be distinguished which did not have the bad prognosis associated with the blanket term of "senile psychosis". This still left those with dementia who in turn were then assumed to have a poor outcome and to be unresponsive to any form of therapeutic intervention.

Today, the general opinion is changing even further. Although the demented elderly person is unlikely to recover (unless he has one of the rare, treatable forms of dementia) this is not to say that those with dementia are not responsive to environmental manipulations and that it is not worthwhile making the effort to preserve their functional capacities as long as possible. Preliminary results offer some encouragement and some of these have been cited above (for a more detailed discussion see Miller, 1977a, b; Woods and Britton, 1977). It appears that psychological techniques will have an increasing part to play in the management of the mentally disturbed elderly. With regard to the specific problem of impaired memory in old age there appear to be some things that can be done providing that we are content with limited goals. Although these goals may be very limited in terms of making an impact upon the memory disturbance as such, it can happen that an achievement such as the acquisition or reacquisition of a simple skill or piece of information can have a major effect on the quality of life for the aged individual.

V. Conclusions

Understanding the memory changes that occur with age is hampered by two major problems. The first is methodological. The sole reliance on experimental designs which use the cross-sectional comparison of old and young groups leaves a situation in which it is not possible to judge the extent or time course of any decline in memory that occurs with ageing. A large amount of evidence exists which could be related to elucidating the nature of the memory changes in normal ageing. This is difficult to interpret, partly because of methodological difficulties, but particularly because of the lack of an adequate general model of memory on which any interpretation could be based. Study of the common memory impairment that occurs in the aged, that associated with dementia, is less well advanced but again understanding may founder on the same difficulties as those involved in the interpretation of normal age changes. Nevertheless there are signs that something can be done to ameliorate the drastic consequences of memory impairment in the aged. In terms of the practical benefit that might accrue it is this latter opportunity that needs to be explored in greater detail.

References

✝ Ankus, M. and Quarrington, B. (1972). Operant behavior in the memory disordered. *J. Geront.* **27**, 500–510.

Baddleley, A. D. and Hitch, G. (1974). Working memory. *In* "The Psychology of Learning and Motivation" (G. H. Bower, Ed.). Vol. 8, pp. 47–90. Academic Press, London and New York.

Barns, E. K., Sack, A. and Shore, H. (1973). Guidelines to treatment approaches: modalities and methods for use with the aged. *Gerontologist* **13**, 513–527.

Belbin, E. (1958). Methods of training older workers. *Ergonomics* **1**, 207–221.

Belbin, E. and Downs, S. (1964). Activity learning and the older worker. *Ergonomics* **7**, 429–438.

→ Birren, J. E. (1964). "The Psychology of Aging". Prentice Hall, New Jersey.

Botwinick, J., Brinley, J. F. and Birren, J. E. (1958). The effect of motivation by electric shock on reaction time in relation to age. *Am. J. Psychol.* **71**, 408–411.

Broadbent, D. E. (1971). "Decision and Stress". Academic Press, London and New York.

Brook, P., Degun, G. and Mather, M. (1975). Reality orientation, a therapy for psychogeriatric patients: a controlled study. *Br. J. Psychiat.* **127**, 42–45.

✝ Clark, L. E. and Knowles J. B. (1973). Age differences in dichotic listening performance. *J. Geront.* **28**, 173–178.

Craik, F. I. M. (1968). Short-term memory and the aging process. *In* "Human Aging and Behavior" (G. A. Talland, Ed.). Academic Press, New York and London.

Craik, F. I. M. (1977). Age difference in human memory. *In* "Handbook of the Psychology of Aging" (J. E. Birren and K. W. Schaie, Eds). Van Norstrand, New York.

— Craik, F. I. M. and Lockhart, R. S. (1972). Levels of processing: a framework for memory research. *J. Verb. Learn. Verb. Behav.* **11**, 671–684.

Davies, G., Hamilton, S., Hendrickson, E., Levy, R. and Post, F. (1977). The effect of cyclandelate in depressed and demented patients: a controlled study in psychogeriatric patients. *Age and Ageing* **6**, 156–162.

✓— Drachman, D. A. and Leavitt, J. (1972). Memory impairment in the aged: storage versus retrieval deficits. *J. exp. Psychol.* **93**, 302–308.

Erber, J. T. (1974). Age differences in recognition memory. *J. Geront.* **29**, 177–189.

Eysenck, M. W. (1974). Age differences in incidental learning. *Develop. Psychol.*
    10, 936–941.
Folsom, J. C. (1968). Reality orientation for the elderly patient. *J. geriat.
    Psychiat.* **1**, 291–307.
Ganzler, H. (1964). Motivation as a factor in the psychological deficit of aging.
    J. Geront. **19**, 425–429.
Hoyer, W. J. (1973). Applications of operant techniques to the modification of
    elderly behavior. *Gerontologist* **13**, 18–22.
Hoyer, W. J., Kafer, R. A., Simpson, S. C. and Hoyer, F. W. (1974). Re-
    instatement of verbal behavior in elderly patients using operant procedures.
    Gerontologist **14**, 149–152.
Husen, T. (1951). The influence of schooling upon IQ. *Theoria* **17**, 61–88.
Inglis, J. (1970). Memory disorder. *In* "Symptoms of Psychopathology"
    (C. Costello, Ed.).' Wiley, New York.
Inglis, J., Sykes, D. H. and Ankus, M. N. (1968). Age differences in short-term
    memory. *In* "Psychological Functioning in Normal Aging and Senile Aged"
    (S. M. Chown and R. F. Riegel, Eds). S. Karger, Basel.
Jaffe, P. G. and Katz, A. N. (1975). Attenuating anterograde amnesia in
    Korsakoff's psychosis. *J. abnorm. Psychol.* **84**, 559–562.
Kline, D. W. and Szafran, J. (1975). Age differences in backward monoptic
    visual noise masking. *J. Geront.* **30**, 307–311.
Kriauchiunas, R. (1968). The relationship of age and retention interval activ-
    ity in short-term memory. *J. Geront.* **23**, 169–73.
Laurence, M. W. (1967). Memory loss with age: a test of two strategies for its
    retardation. *Psychonomic Sci.* **9**, 209–210.
Lewinsohn, P. M., Danaher, B. G. and Kikel, S. (1977). Visual imagery
    as a mnemonic aid for brain injured persons. *J. consult. clin. Psychol.* **45**,
    717–723.
McGhie, A., Chapman, J. and Lawson, J. S. (1965). Changes in immediate
    memory with age. *Br. J. Psychol.* **56**, 69–75.
MacKay, H. A. (1965). Operant techniques applied to disorders of the
    senium. Unpublished Ph.D. Thesis, Queen's University, Kingston,
    Ontario.
Marcer, D. (1974). Ageing and memory loss—role of experimental psychol-
    ogy. *Gerontol. Clin.* **16**, 118–125.
Miller, E. (1971). On the nature of the memory disorder in presenile dementia.
    Neuropsychologia, **9**, 75–78.
Miller, E. (1973). Short- and long-term memory in presenile dementia
    (Alzheimer's disease). *Psychol. Med.* **3**, 221–224.
Miller, E. (1974). Retrieval from long-term memory in presenile dementia.
    Bull. Br. Psychol. Soc. **27**, 173–174.
Miller, E. (1975). Impaired recall and the memory disturbance in presenile
    dementia. *Br. J. Soc. Clin. Psychol.* **14**, 73–79.
Miller, E. (1977a). "Abnormal Ageing." Wiley, Chichester.
Miller, E. (1977b). A note on visual information processing in presenile
    dementia. *Br. J. Soc. Clin. Psychol.* **16**, 99–100.

148   E. Miller

Miller, E. (1977c). The management of dementia: a review of some possibilities. *Br. J. Soc. Clin. Psychol.* **16**, 77–83.

Miller, E. (1978). Retrieval from long-term memory in presenile dementia: two tests of an hypothesis. *Br. J. Soc. Clin. Psychol.* **17**, 143–148.

Mistler-Lachman, J. L. (1977). Spontaneous shift in encoding dimensions among elderly subjects. *J. Geront.* **32**, 68–72.

Mueller, D. J. and Atlas, L. (1972). Resocialization of regressed elderly residents: a behavioral management approach. *J. Geront.* **27**, 390–392.

Murdock, B. B. (1967). Recent developments in short-term memory. *Br. J. Psychol.* **58**, 421–433.

Naylor, G. and Harwood, E. (1975). Old dogs, new tricks: age and ability. *Psychol. Today* (English Edn) **1**, 29–33.

Owens, W. A. (1966). Age and mental abilities: a second adult follow-up. *J. educ. Psychol.* **57**, 311–325.

Paivio, A. (1971). "Imagery and Verbal Processes." Holt, Rinehart and Winston, New York.

Pearce, J. and Miller, E. (1973). "Clinical Aspects of Dementia." Bailliere Tindall, London.

Peterson, L. R. and Peterson, M. J. (1959). Short-term retention of individual verbal items. *J. exp. Psychol.* **58**, 193–198.

Raymond, B. (1971). Free recall among the aged. *Psychol. Reports* **29**, 1179–1182.

Roth, M. (1955). The natural history of mental disorder in old age. *J. Ment. Sci.* **101**, 281–301.

Savage, R. D. (1973). Old age. *In* "Handbook of Abnormal Psychology" (H. J. Eysenck, Ed.). (second edn). Pitman, London.

Schaie, K. W. and Gribbin, K. (1975). Adult Development and ageing. *Ann. Rev. Psychol.* **26**, 65–96.

Schaie, K. W. and Strother, C. R. (1968a). The effect of time and cohort differences upon age changes in cognitive behavior. *Multivar. Behav. Res.* **3**, 259–294.

Schaie, K. W. and Strother, C. R. (1968b). A cross-sequential study of age changes in cognitive behavior. *Psychol. Bull.* **70**, 671–680.

Schonfield, D. and Robertson, B. (1966). Memory storage and ageing. *Can. J. Psychol.* **20**, 228–236.

Schonfield, D., Trueman, V. and Kline, D. (1972). Recognition tests of dichotic listening and the age variable. *J. Gerontol.* **27**, 487–493.

Schonfield, D. and Wenger, L. (1975). Age limitation of perceptual span. *Nature* **253**, 377–378.

Taub, H. A. (1975). Mode of presentation, age, and short-term memory. *J. Gerontol.* **30**, 56–59.

Walsh, D. A. and Thompson, L. W. (1978). Age differences in visual sensory memory. *J. Gerontol.* **33**, 383–387.

Warrington, E. K. and Weiskrantz, L. (1970). Amnesic syndrome: consolidation of retrieval? *Nature* **228**, 628–630.

Watkins, M. J. (1974). Concept and measurement of primary memory. *Psychol. Bull.* **81**, 695–711.

Wickens, D. D. (1970). Encoding categories of words: an empirical approach to meaning. *Psychol. Rev.* **77**, 1–15.

Woods, R. T. and Britton, P. G. (1977). Psychological approaches to treatment of the elderly. *Age and Ageing* **6**, 104–112.

Woods, R. T. and Piercy, M. (1974). A similarity between amnesic memory and normal forgetting. *Neuropsychologia* **12**, 437–445.

6. Eyewitness Memory

R. BULL AND B. CLIFFORD

Department of Psychology,
North East London Polytechnic,
London, UK

I. Introduction

In 1973 Doob and Kirshenbaum reported a criminal incident in which two men stole seven thousand dollars from a Canadian supermarket. The only description of the criminals that the female cashier was able to provide was that one of them "was rather good-looking". This poor description by an eyewitness of a clearly visible criminal is not such an infrequent nor inexplicable occurrence as the layman might believe. Witnesses's cognitive processes, their stereotypic conceptions and their individual differences all contribute to the final memory accuracy as do the methods used of gathering information from witnesses.

In this chapter we shall attempt to show that psychology can, and is, making a practical contribution to the understanding of eyewitness memory. Contrary to what is common belief, and to what the 1976 Devlin Committee on law and procedures in criminal identification thought to be the case, psychologists are able to offer advice and explanation on this topic. However, until fairly recently psychologists had failed to make widely known their knowledge in this area and the appearance of a book such as this one, which is concerned with a great variety of real-life memory phenomena, is in our opinion long overdue.

We believe that psychology needs *to be seen* to be relevant to real life, and indeed it may well be that by attempting to have more ecological validity we may now make our greatest steps forward. In this chapter we shall offer explanations of why eyewitness memory appears to be fairly poor. We shall see how memory is affected by witnesses's stereotypic conceptions about what they think they saw (or are seeing) and by the questions that are asked. Individual differences in eyewitness memory are examined and some suggestions for present, real-world, practices of using eyewitness memory are offered.

II. Cognitive Processes in Eyewitness Memory

The view which the layman or the juror holds of a witness's ability to report accurately the details of an observed event or to identify an observed criminal differs markedly from that of experimental psychologists. While Marshall (1969) believes that "The life of the courts, the trial process, is based upon the fiction that witnesses see and hear correctly and so testify", and while the legal concept of testimony or identification seems to imply that perception and memory are single, simple processes, experimental memory research argues that such cognitive processes are characterized by inbuilt structural and processing limitations. As a result of these structural and functional shortcomings sense data is held to be fallible, recall to be idiosyncratic and memory to be inherently unreliable.

Thus, as Buckhout (1974) indicates, when a person is asked to identify someone after seeing them briefly, he or she is being asked to do something that the normal human is not created to do. Human memory and perception are selective, generative, decision-making processes: to view them as copying processes is both wrong and dangerous. Additionally, as Clifford and Bull (1978) have argued, many aspects of eyewitness behaviour are inexplicable unless we take into account what the person is, what he is trying to do and the ways his beliefs, values and motivations act not only at the time of perception but also during the period of storage and especially at the time of recall. Put succinctly, as Buckhout (1974) said "memory and perception are social systems."

From this it follows that many of the implicit assumptions of laymen concerning testimony may be wrong. Specifically, all witnesses will not be equally good or bad, and secondly, we cannot decouple memory from either other cognitive sub-systems, such as language, or from more socially-based processes such as stereotyping. The remainder of this chapter will be concerned to document these linguistic and social influences but we will begin by looking at the information processing limitations in man's testimony behaviour.

It is clear that memory errors are of two types: errors of omission and errors of commission. The first type of error, generally speaking, stems from inherent limitations in processing structure and capacity; the latter from the fact that memory is reconstructive (e.g. Bartlett, 1932) or constructive (e.g. Cofer, 1973; Gomulicki, 1956; Zangwill, 1972) rather than literal. To take information processing limitations first, Bruner (1958) has suggested that because the "organism has a highly limited span of attention, and a highly limited span of immediate memory selectivity is forced upon us". This selectivity operates in attention, in perception and in memory.

A great deal of evidence is available that man exhibits selective attention (e.g. Broadbent, 1971; Cherry, 1953; Norman, 1969; Treisman, 1964) and while controversy rages over just how much of the unattended message gets through to consciousness (see Forster and Govier, 1978), and how this is achieved, all agree that there is little or no *memory* for the content of unattended messages. This strongly suggests that in real-life we should be careful of equating duration of exposure to a crime with probability of accurate identification of perpetrator because in such situations victims or potential witnesses may be focusing all their attention on aspects of the situation relevant to escape rather than stimuli useful for later identification. Over and above inappropriate selection, emotion also is known to have a disruptive effect upon attention and perception (e.g. Laughery, 1971; Scott, 1977). Buckhout (1974) reported that air crews progressively decreased monitoring instruments as anxiety increased, and both Berrien (1955) and Kobler (cited in Whipple, 1915) showed that excitement and stress interfered with observational ability and subsequent reporting of a criminal event. (See Chapter 7).

Perception also is limited, not so much in terms of actual registration, but rather in the conversion of these sensory inputs into more durable, veridical, memory formats. This is the so-called encoding problem. Sperling's (1960, 1967) "partial report" technique exhibits this clearly. When subjects are cued (immediately *after* stimulus off-set) to recall only certain parts of a visual display, recall is almost perfect, unlike the situation when they are cued to recall all the display ("whole report"). These two findings, taken together, suggest that all stimuli are registered but an irreducible time is necessary for encoding into more durable storage.

Using stimuli more akin to the eyewitness situation Potter (1976; Potter and Levy, 1969) presented evidence that a picture of a scene could be recognized (i.e. processed and matched to an internal representation) within one-eighth of a second but that a further one-third of a second was required for storage of that scene in memory. If this further time was not available, or not utilized for encoding, then no memory remained of what had been perceived.

Perception is limited also by being selective, this selectivity being primed by pre-existing epistemic structures. This interaction of perceptual strategy and stored category is shown in a study by Ellis et al. (1975) in which they demonstrated that black and white subjects used different patterns of reference in description of black and white faces and, by inference, that they also employed different perceptual scanning patterns when processing these different faces.

The limitations and selectivity found in attentional and perceptual processes are also found in memory. Memory is known to be fallible due to such factors as passive decay (e.g. Brown, 1957), systematic distortion of the memory traces (e.g. Wulf, 1922), interference between traces such that similar memories cannot be distinguished (e.g. Postman, 1972), motivated forgetting, retrieval failure (e.g. Tulving, 1969), and displacement of existing memories by incoming material (e.g. Waugh and Norman, 1965). Additionally, physical trauma, drug abuse and senility are other causes of forgetting. While all these psychological factors have some validity no one theory explains all the facts of eyewitness testimony and in addition few if any of the theories in and of themselves explain the errors of commission found in testimony. Processes of distortion are crucial features of human memory in general and eyewitness testimony in particular. Fortunately, recent research has begun to investigate this distortion process—regarding inbuilt system-limitations as necessary but not sufficient conditions for its explanation.

While a somewhat sterile debate has developed around the issue of whether memory errors occur at input (constructive memory errors) or at output (reconstructive memory errors) the facts of distortion are not at issue, and the main explanatory mechanism—inference drawing—has been shown to be a robust effect (Baggett, 1975; Bransford et al., 1972; Frederiksen, 1975; Keenan and Kintsch, 1974; Kintsch, 1977). Thus, there is little reason to doubt that such processes also go on in eyewitness testimony, and there is a good deal of evidence that they do (Clifford and Hollin, in preparation, d; Marshall, 1966; Trankell, 1972; Wall, 1965). To paraphase C. S. Morgan (1917), we fill up the lowlands of our memories from the highlands of our imagination, or at least from our knowledge of spatial, temporal, logical and personal relationships. The important point to grasp in terms of assessing eyewitness accuracy is that it is almost impossible for the subjects to differentiate between factual memories and inferential memories. However, there seems to be a paradox between what we have said above and what visual memory data suggest. If we address the question "How good is witness memory?" by making recourse to picture memory research we would have to argue that it is about 90% accurate (e.g. Nickerson, 1965; Shepard, 1967; Standing, 1973; Standing *et al.*, 1970). If we make deductions from face photograph research we would have to estimate witness accuracy as somewhere between 90% + (Hochberg and Galper, 1974; Yin, 1969), 80% + (Shepherd and Ellis, 1973) and 70% + (Chance *et al.*, 1975; Elliott *et al.*, 1973; Goldstein and Chance, 1971; Malpass and Kravitz, 1969; Scapinello and Yarmey, 1970). Thus recognition rates with visual material can be phenomenally high. In addition, there is an apparent absence of a delay effect with face photographs at lags of 20 minutes to 35 days (e.g. Goldstein and Chance, 1971; Laughery *et al.*, 1974; Scapinello and Yarmey, 1970; Shepherd and Ellis, 1973).

However, the paradox is more apparent than real because in the laboratory Goldstein and Chance (1971) have given clear evidence of very poor picture memory, and Jenkins *et al.* (1969) found 7-year-old childrens' memory was no better for pictures than for words, while Ducharme and Fraisse (1965) likewise found no difference in recall of pictures and name stimuli among children aged 8–10 years. Also, the estimate of just how good face memory can be varies with the methodology employed. Clifford (1979a,b; Clifford and Hollin, in preparation, e) has argued that face photograph research lacks ecological validity and both experimental and mundane realism. Thus when we ask how good witness memory can be, and use event, or mock crime methodology estimates (based on paradigms high on both the latter realisms) we find accuracy to be about 12–13% for identification (Buckhout, 1974; Dent, 1977; Dent and Gray, 1975) and between 25% for recall of details in civilians (Buckhout, 1974) and about 47·5% for policemen in very simple static, but live, situations (Clifford and Richards, 1977).

III. Stereotypic Effects in Eyewitness Memory

In 1974 Deputy Assistant Commissioner David Powis was reported to have advised policemen to observe in court persons in custody for the theft or unlawful taking of motor vehicles to "see to which category they belong. This will help you to slant your mind to the general type of

persons you must watch for when patrolling". It is certainly not possible to say that such advice is worthless but it may be that such advice
can be misguided and productive of errors of commission. The important thing is to be able to gauge how useful it is and similarly to be able
to know to what extent stereotypic notions play a role in person
recognition situations. Bruner *et al.* (1958) have reminded us that:

> It is a truism that the acts performed by people are not independent of one
> another—a man who steals is likely to lie as well. The fact of consistency
> of behaviour, the backbone of personality theories, is represented in the
> language by which people are commonly described. It is characteristic of
> words like "honest" or "clever" that they do more than denote specific
> acts of a person. Indeed, they summarize or package certain consistencies
> of behaviour.

If witnesses believe in these alleged consistencies of behaviour then
such beliefs may influence their memory performance. One apparently
widely held belief is the "what is beautiful is good" stereotype. For
example, Jones and Hirschberg (1975) found that an individual's facial
attractiveness had an effect on how threatening other people judged
that person to be. They observed that the more attractive a person's
face the less threatening the individual was believed to be.

In this section we shall attempt to illustrate briefly the extent to
which people's expectancies concerning how certain types of individuals behave can influence their perception of these individuals and their
ability to recognize them. Though many studies in this area have found
that observers frequently agree upon the attributes they assign to
people solely on the basis of their appearance, the validity or truth of
these observations has rarely been examined.

Hurwitz *et al.* (1975) found that personality traits are readily attributed to facial photographs in a consistent manner and Hochberg and
Galper (1974) showed how intention can be attributed as a function of
physiognomy. The latter authors concluded that, "physiognomy does
affect the attribution of behavioural intentions". Secord *et al.* (1954)
found observers to agree largely upon the personality characteristics
they expected photographed individuals to possess but they noted that
the observers were frequently unable to verbalize the bases for their
ratings of personality. Landy and Aronson (1969) found, in a simulated
setting, that the appearance of the defendant had a significant effect
upon decisions of "jurors" about the length of prison sentence that
should be given. The unattractive defendant was sentenced far more
severely for a given crime than a defendant with an attractive character
and appearance. Efran (1974) also examined the effect of physical

appearance on the judgment of guilt and the severity of recommended punishment in a simulated jury task. Over 100 people filled in a questionnaire and this survey revealed that (a) only 21% believed that a defendant's character and previous history should not influence juror's decision, whereas (b) over 93% believed that the defendant's physical appearance should not bias these decisions. A further 66 students received written details of an example of alleged cheating during an examination and they were required to rate how likely it was that the person mentioned had been cheating and the extent of the punishment that should be given. Two-thirds of the "jurors" also received a photograph of the defendant and these were also required, as their last task, to rate the defendant for physical attractiveness. For each of these "jurors" the photograph was of an opposite sexed individual. Efran found for female defendants that the more physically attractive individuals were judged to be significantly less guilty and to merit milder punishment than the unattractive female defendants.

Space does not permit discussion of the possible reasons for the existence of such effects (see Clifford and Bull, 1978), however if they exist in the real world they could well be present in settings in which a witness is unsure and yet is being pressed either explicitly or implicitly to act. It seems likely to be a widely held stereotype that physically attractive individuals are not so inclined to do unpleasant or anti-social things. Thus, when in doubt we might hesitate to pick such a person out from an identification parade, from mugshots, etc. In such cases the attractive criminal may be less likely to be punished for the crime. The converse may also be true. Do we tend at a later date to recognize only the attractive (or outstanding) strangers who were at the party a few weeks ago though at the time we saw the faces of all who were present? In the Doob and Kirshenbaum (1973) case described earlier, the witness could remember little about the robber except that he was "rather good looking".

If a witness did get a good view of someone whom he was later required to recognize then it has been found that attractive faces are sometimes recognized better than unattractive ones (Cross *et al.*, 1971). Shepherd and Ellis (1973) found that faces both high and low on attractiveness were better recognized than those of medium attractiveness and they suggest that the findings of Cross *et al.* may merely have been a function of the fact that in the study by Cross *et al.* there was no control over the time that the subjects initially spent looking at each face. Shepherd and Ellis argue that if the subjects spent a greater time viewing the more attractive faces then the superior recognition of these faces is not at all surprising. However, Cross *et al.* (1971) comment that if anything their observers spent the least time looking at the attractive faces. Kleck and Rubinstein (1975) found, after an interval of two to four weeks, a tendency for the clothing of a female confederate to be more accurately remembered by those observers (all male) who had seen her with make-up than by those who saw her without make-up. Conversely, Hamid (1972) found that male observers' descriptive accuracy was lower when the female target wore make-up than when she did not. (If make-up = attractive, then Hamid's finding implies higher attraction = lower accuracy.) The relationship between physical attraction and witness memory is one which would benefit from more research to unearth the factors involved.

The implication of research on stereotypic conceptions is that observers' recall of individuals will be a function not only of what they actually perceived at the time of the relevant incident but also of what their stereotypic notions suggest to them. Furthermore, some researchers believe that stereotypes can have an influence not only at the time of recall but also at the time of perception. Stritch and Secord (1956) stated that their "results suggest that personality impressions formed from the photographs act as organizing factors in the perception of physiognomic traits". More research is certainly needed on this particular hypothesis but it does seem likely that when the sighting of an individual is incomplete (or memory fades) the observer will add factors, and these probably will be a function of his stereotypes and expectancies. The publication "Science and the Police" (from the British Association for the Advancement of Science) stated that: "There is a tendency to fill in gaps in remembrance, even of those parts of a happening where what actually occurred has been forgotten". Freedman and Haber (1974) have suggested that: "The organizational properties of perceptual memory are important determinants of the adequacy of that memory", and that their study provided "evidence that recognition memory is aided by perceiver-elicited organizations imposed on the material to be remembered". These perceiver-elicited organizations may arise from many sources. "Modern criminologists do not believe that criminals belong to a single physical or psychological type" (Liggett, 1974), but does the general public? Casting directors of cinema and TV films frequently select actors to play parts for which they look "right".

In 1962 Kozeny obtained photographs of 730 convicted criminals which he then divided into 16 categories depending upon the type of crime which had been committed. From each of these 16 groups of photographs a composite portrait was made and these "demonstrated statistically significant dependence of the resultant physiognomic character upon the respective category of crime from which the criminal's pictures had been taken". Should it therefore be concluded that the people who commit crimes are of similar appearance? To some observers this might seem an unlikely state of affairs; but think of a situation in which you had a poor and brief view of a mugging. When attending an identification parade would you expect the line-up to consist of young and scruffy men, or older men in pin-stripe suits or women in bikinis?

Shoemaker et al. (1973) found evidence that we do have stereotypic notions about the appearance criminals have. They concluded that, "on the basis of our findings it would be plausible to assume that stereotypic conceptions of what a particular suspect should look like could influence the selection of "the one who did it" by an eyewitness of a crime, particularly when that eyewitness did not have a good, clear look at the offender". In 1958 Secord gave a brief verbal personality account of two imaginary characters to a group of subjects. One of the characters was described as "warmhearted and honest", the other "ruthless and brutal". The subjects were required to give some indication of the appearance they expected the characters to have by rating on seven-point scales each of 32 facial (and hair) characteristics. For 25 of these 32 features the ratings were found to be significantly different as a function of the personality accounts. Secord noted that for the majority of those characteristics which differentiated between the two descriptions the "warmhearted and honest" person was rated as being average (e.g. average width of nose) whereas the "ruthless and brutal" individual was judged as having abnormal features (for example, the observers accorded to him either an extremely narrow nose or an extremely wide one). It seems that the observers in Secord's study were employing a stereotype that has frequently come to Bull's notice in his study of the psychological significance of facial deformity, namely that the general public take abnormality of appearance to be indicative of abnormality of personality and likely behaviour. It has been found (Bull, 1979) that the more scars (0, 1 or 2) a face has the more dishonest is that person judged to be. Cavior et al. (1975) suggest that, "low physical attractiveness contributes to careers of deviancy" and in 1941 Monahan noted that, "even social workers accustomed to dealing with all types often find it difficult to think of a normal, pretty girl as being guilty of a crime. Most people, for some inexplicable reason, think of crime in terms of abnormality of appearance and I must say that beautiful women are not often convicted". Psychologists could (and do?) address themselves to the problem of making Monahan's "inexplicable reason" explicable.

In a series of experiments conducted in our department by Clive Hollin, some evidence has been found to support Wall's (1965) observations that witnesses often infer the presence of one physical feature from their recall of the observed person's possession of another. A person entered a lecture to search for a briefcase and after walking around the room the lecturer asked him to leave. In the first of such incidents the "target" person was blond, with green eyes and a fair complexion. The eyewitnesses' descriptions of the target person were very accurate for hair colour, 93% of the witnesses reported that the hair was blond. However, of this 93% almost half described the person as having blue eyes, whereas only 7% correctly said green. (Fourteen percent incorrectly reported other colours and the remainder did not mention eye colour at all.) Of those who reported blond hair 75% correctly reported the target person as having a fair complexion. Thus the proportion of the observers which indicated that the target person had blond hair, a fair complexion and blue eyes was 36%. In the second incident, with a different audience, the target person had dark hair, grey eyes and a light complexion. All the observers in this part of the study described correctly the target person's hair colour. However, over half of them incorrectly reported the eye colour as being brown and none of them correctly reported it as being grey. Forty-four percent correctly reported a fair complexion whereas 56% reported the target person as having a dark complexion. Thus the proportion of the observers who reported that the target person had dark hair, brown eyes and a dark complexion was 44%. Hollin takes these effects of blond hair incorrectly implying blue eyes and dark hair suggesting brown eyes and a dark complexion, to indicate that witnesses fill in gaps in their recall by employing stereotypes or known population norms. Sometimes such confabulation will be correct (perhaps even on most occasions if the stereotype has validity) but on some occasions it will lead to inaccurate descriptions.

IV. Individual Differences in Eyewitness Memory

Individual difference factors are perhaps one of the most important considerations in memory research, yet for too long they have been "relegated to the error term" in experimentation (M. W. Eysenck, 1977). Although eyewitness research tends to follow this tradition, here we shall outline what is currently known about individual and group difference factors in testimony research.

Age has consistently been shown to be an important factor in testimony, with both earlier research (e.g. Binet, 1900; Stern, 1939) and more modern research suggesting that children are poorer witnesses than adults. Ellis *et al.* (1973) found 17-year-olds to be much better than 12-year-olds at face recognition. Goldstein and Chance (1964) also showed clear improvement in face recognition over the age range 5 to 15 years. A study by Cross *et al.* (1971), which at first sight appeared not to support the general proposition of age-related accuracy, on further analysis using signal detection measures (by Ellis, 1975) did reveal that recognition accuracy increased from 7 years through 12 and 17 years to adulthood. There is, however, some suggestion of a peak age beyond which memory does not improve and may decrease. Diamond and Carey (1977) found face memory improved from 6 to 10 years but little thereafter, and Harwood and Naylor (1969) found young adults to be significantly better on delayed recall and recognition than elderly subjects. However, in a detection-of-targets task (in a film sequence) Tickner and Poulton (1975) found older subjects (mean age 50 years) were not significantly different from younger subjects (mean age 20 years).

Sex differences in witness memory was one of the first variables to be examined in testimony research and from the onset conflicting evidence was produced. While Stern (1939) reported that men were 20–30% more accurate than women this conflicted with Gross (1897) Borst (1904) and Wreschner (1905). More recent research is likewise divided with Howells (1938), Schill (1966) and McKelvie (1972) showing no sex differences in overall recognition of faces, but Cross *et al.* (1971), Ellis *et al.* (1973) and Goldstein and Chance (1971) all suggesting that females are more accurate than males, at least with female stimuli. Witryol and Kaess (1957) observed that females were more accurate with faces of either sex. Conflict also exists with videotaped violent incidents with Clifford and Scott (1978) indicating that females were poorer than males in recalling details of violent incidents, and Lipton (1977) suggesting that females were better. In real life, while Levine and Tapp (1973) found police preferred female witnesses, Kuehn (1974) observed that female victims gave less complete descriptions of their assailants than did male victims. These conflicting findings must be resolved in the very near future and a pattern discerned.

Given that cognitive style has been defined as characteristic ways of apprehending, storing, transforming and utilizing information (Kogan, 1970) it would seem that this individual difference factor would have direct application to testimony research. However Clifford and Bull (1978) have argued that this potential has remained unrealized. One cognitive style which has been fairly well researched, although the evidence is conflicting, is that of field dependence/field independence (Witkin *et al.*, 1974). Earlier research found field dependent subjects to be better than field independent subjects at face recognition tasks (e.g. Crutchfield *et al.*, 1958; Messick and Damarin, 1964). The explanation for these findings was basically that faces were socially relevant stimuli and thus especially important for field dependent subjects. However it could be argued that faces are also complex perceptual patterns and thus field independent subjects should perform better. Baker (1967), using identikit facsimile representation of human faces, did find that field independent subjects out-performed their dependent counterparts, and Lavrakas *et al.* (1976) found that independent subjects were better than dependent subjects on recognition of other-race faces—a facial configuration best construed as a complex pattern (Hake, 1975). There is also the suggestion (Hoffman and Kagan, 1977) that the type of learning situation (incidental or intentional) importantly determines which class of subject will perform better. However, while Beijk-Docter and Elshout (1969), using an incidental learning test of face recognition, found field independent subjects were better than field dependent subjects, Adcock and Webberly (1971) also found field independent subjects were better at face recognition in an *intentional* paradigm. Thus while this cognitive style is obviously relevant to witness memory the evidence is conflicting. Clarification in more realistic situations is urgently required.

Like cognitive style, personality may be an individual difference factor with either predictive or explanatory power in the field of eyewitness testimony. Only a few personality differences have been studied under this rubric. Persons high in need for approval (n-App) may be sensitive to faces. Schill (1966) tested this by comparing males and females high or low on n-App in an incidental memory for faces task. High n-App subjects performed significantly better than low n-App subjects. People also differ in need for affiliation (n-Aff) and this again could increase perceptual sensitivity to faces as social stimuli. Atkinson and Walker (1955) tested the allied assumption that motives sensitize perception for motive-related stimuli—in this case faces. These researchers presented slides divided into 4 quadrants in one of which face-related stimuli always appeared. All quadrant content was presented below threshold and subjects were asked to indicate which quadrant "stood out" or was the clearest. High n-Aff subjects selected the face quadrant significantly more frequently than did low n-Aff subjects.

While the personality dimension of introversion and extraversion has been extensively researched within the verbal learning tradition little work has been conducted in visual memory generally or in eyewitness memory specifically. However Gilliland and Burke (1926) found that extraverts were significantly better than introverts on immediate recall of faces and Hunt (1928) found a positive correlation (+0·55) between extraversion and memory for names and faces. On the other hand, in several studies conducted by Clifford and Hollin (in preparation, b, c, d), employing the event methodology or videotaped recordings of staged incidents, there was a constant failure to find any relationship between extraversion/introversion and either recall of criminal details or identification of "criminal" targets. Similarly Clifford and Scott (1978) failed to obtain any significant correlation between extraversion/introversion and recall of either physical actions or descriptions in either violent or non-violent videotaped incidents.

Another dimension of personality described by H. J. Eysenck (1967) is that of neuroticism-stability. Research with this dimension has hardly begun but Clifford and Hollin (in preparation, b) suggests a weak relationship between neuroticism and accuracy of recall, and Zanni and Offermann (1978) found that the subject's level of neuroticism interacted with question wording, especially of the indefinite article type (see the section on questioning procedures in this chapter).

The last individual or group difference we will look at is that of race. The generally accepted finding is that one race has difficulty remembering and identifying faces of another race. Explanations of this finding fall under three main headings: the "inherently more difficult" hypothesis; the "differential experience or familiarity" hypothesis; and the "attitudinal component" hypothesis. The findings by Malpass and Kravitz (1969) and Cross et al. (1971) that both black and white observers recognized white targets better than black targets support the inherently more difficult hypothesis. However, Goldstein and Chance (1976, 1978) have argued against certain race faces being more difficult to process, store or retrieve than others by showing that when subjects are asked to judge whether two faces presented on slides are of the same person or not, no significant difference in either latency of response or correctness is found with white subjects and white or Japanese faces presented for judgement. Galper (1973) presented evidence against the inherently more difficult hypothesis and for the familiarity or attitudinal hypotheses by showing that both black and white subjects were better at recognizing their own race faces. While strong support for the familiarity hypothesis comes from the finding of Chance et al. (1975), that for white and black subjects recognition was best for their own race, next best for familiar other races and least good for unfamiliar other races, unfortunately Luce (1974) found quite the opposite. In this latter study blacks and whites had mutual experience

of each other but not of Asian-Americans, who in turn had equal
familiarity with both blacks and whites. All subjects gave best own-race
recognition but whites recognized Asians much better than blacks,
blacks recognized whites and Asians with very low accuracy and Asians
gave medium recognition scores for blacks and very low accuracy
scores for whites. Luce explains this by "perceptual blanking". Thus
while overall no one theory has overwhelming support, and all
hypotheses have some truth, the applied point is that eyewitness memory is not simply a function of intact sense organs. Testimony will be of
doubtful validity if and when the race of the witness and the suspect
differ.

V. Linguistic Influences on Eyewitness Memory

Evidence has been accumulated which suggests that language can
"bewitch" eyewitness memory for seen people and events, and that law
enforcement agents must be careful not only that they ask the right
questions, but that they ask the right questions in the right way. This
section will focus on the use of language by the "witness", in the form of
labels and the use of language by those who are concerned to elicit an
identification, a recall or a description. Finally we will look at the effect
of overall style of questioning.

The basic question of interest is; does language in any way influence
memory for visual material? This question, seen in its broadest perspective is part of the "linguistic relativity hypothesis" which suggests
that language is a powerful determinent of perception and thought.
The basic suggestion is that we dissect and interpret nature along lines
laid down by our native languages. Slobin (1971) has suggested that
there are currently two forms of this Whorf-Sapir linguistic relativity
hypothesis: a strong form which states that aspects of language can
determine thought, perception and memory, and a weak form which
states that language can predispose people to think or act or perceive in
one way rather than another. As Carroll (1964) points out, the linguistic relativity hypothesis has received little convincing support, and at
best only the weak form carries any kind of conviction. However, what
is certain is that memory can be affected by linguistic factors.

A number of studies have shown a correlation between verbal codability and visual memory, though correlation does not imply causality.
Rather stronger, better, evidence comes from experiments on the
influence of labelling on memory for visual forms. For example, Ellis
(1968) and Santa and Ranken (1972) have shown that providing verbal

labels aids recognition of nonsense (meaningless) shapes, when they are later presented for recognition, at least if the shapes are complicated and/or numerous. There is however, some doubt over whether labelling can in fact aid long-term retention: Daniel and Ellis (1972) say that it can, but Santa and Ranken (1972) suggest that it does not. As possible explanations of the beneficial effect of labels in visual perception and memory, Ellis (1972) suggested that verbal labels have their beneficial effect by focusing attention on distinctive stimulus features at the encoding stage while Santa and Baker (1975) suggest that verbal labels aid retrieval. Ellis's (1972) "conceptual coding hypothesis" would suggest that labels may have their effect by influencing the subject's encoding or scanning strategy, in such a way as to make him attend to specific features of the face at time of viewing. This view of labels has affinity to Gibson's (1969) predifferentiation hypothesis of perceptual learning. The opposite view of the labelling effect comes from research based on Miller and Dollard's (1941) "acquired distinctiveness of cues" hypothesis. This argument contends that labels make memory codes for different stimuli more distinct from each other by being part of the memory representation. In this case labels function mainly to aid retrieval by (1) increasing the distinctiveness of each stored trace, and (2) providing more retrieval routes. This obviously has affinity with Paivio's (1971, 1976) dual coding hypothesis.

While the theoretical locus of the labelling effect is both important and interesting a more immediate problem is whether, in fact, labelling goes on with meaningful material. There is rather good evidence that it does. In 1932 Carmichael et al. presented a series of 12 ambiguous forms to two groups. To one of the groups, as they were being presented with these ambiguous forms, the experimenter presented a label, e.g. "bottle" while to the other group the experimenter presented the label "stirrup". When subsequently required to reproduce the forms, subjects tended to distort their drawings in the direction of the appropriate label. This would seem to have direct relevance to the case where the witness is presented with a crime which, because of its speed, dynamism and inherent emotionality, can be likened quite easily to an "ambiguous" situation. The label then attached to it, either by the perceiver himself, or by other witnesses, could very importantly distort the memory of the actual event. A study by Prentice (1954) throws some light on the locus of this effect. He showed that the effect of labelling was not present with recognition testing, suggesting that the labels did not affect storage of the visual trace but rather produced distortion at retrieval, recognition being held not to involve retrieval in the same way as does recall. Further support for the argument of labels having their effect at retrieval comes from Hanawalt and Demarest (1939) who showed that labelling distortions can be produced when unlabelled figures are learned and subsequently cued by means of a label, e.g. "Draw the figure that looked like a stirrup". More recent research consolidates the effect verbal labels can have on visual memory. Cohen (1966, 1967) studied the effect of labels at recognition and found that when subjects were presented with an ambiguous figure (a circle with a 90° gap) and a label suggesting it was a clock with the hands at "five to seven" or "ten to eight", both subsequent reproductions and recognitions (from a set of circles with gaps at different sizes) reflected the suggestion given during viewing of the initial circle. Thus subjects produce or "recognize" larger gaps resulting from the label "five to seven" being given. This reproduces the Carmichael *et al.* (1932) finding. Cohen argued that in recognition as in reproduction, subjects use the labels to retrieve features from the representation of the stimulus in memory.

In the above studies "reproduction" and "recognition" have been used as if they are measuring the same type of memory. *A priori*, it would seem that recall to a policeman taking down a statement or description, or a photo-fit constructor, because it uses verbalizations, ought to contain a greater possibility of a labelling effect than recognition which merely involves a perceptual matching. Cohen and Granstrom (1970) tested reproduction (recall) and recognition of irregular geometric visual forms after an interval of seven seconds, which was either filled with a visual distractor task (remembering sets of three faces) or with a verbal distraction task (remembering three names). The verbal distractor task interfered with the reproduction memory but not with the recognition memory, while the visual intereference produced poorer recognition, but not poorer reproduction memory. Baddeley (1976) interpreted these results as showing that the recall of visual material depends on verbal coding whereas visual recognition is not dependent on verbal factors. However, this is at odds with the findings of Cohen (1966, 1967) and with the study by Doob and Kirshenbaum (1973). Real-life experiences and some experimental evidence do strongly suggest that verbal labelling occurs with visual experience and that these labels reappear at the time of trying to recognize the earlier seen object.

In the light of what has been discussed above a safe summary may be the one proposed by Santa and Baker (1976) that, "language in the form of labelling exerts a strong influence on the organization and retrieval of nonverbal representations". Now it may be the case that labels are only beneficial with abstract shapes, and when used with meaningful material they may become less useful (e.g. Davies, 1969;

Kurtz and Hovland, 1953) or positively harmful (Bahrick and Boucher, 1968). This would have serious implications for face recognition if it were the case.

Work with multi-dimensional scaling shows that subjects can readily ascribe adjectives (labels) to seen faces. The important question is whether such labelling aids memory for faces? McKelvie (1976) investigated the effects of labelling on the encoding and recognition of schematic faces. He presented easy-to-label and hard-to-label schematic faces and he found that giving a label to a hard-to-label face produced better recognition than merely observing the hard-to-label face, and when sufficient care was taken experimentally, labels also aided recognition of easy-to-label faces. Thus labelling faces might improve later recognition, at least with schematic faces. McKelvie showed that labels have their main effect by focusing attention on specific facial features during viewing, and that the labels may be stored along with the visual trace to be used at output. He concluded that "The major conclusion emerging (from this experiment) is that verbal labels appear to serve a dual role in recognition memory . . . they guide the subjects examination and encoding of the stimulus during viewing and serve as mediators in the memory representation". Also important is the fact that some results show that labels will only be effective if actively generated by the subject.

Chance and Goldstein (1976) made some comment on the type of labelling that went on in their study. They said that they "are struck by the undifferentiated nature of labels". Responses like "dark hair", "looks studious", "seems mean" might seem unlikely to possess sufficient uniqueness to provide the subject with much advantage in later recognition. However, in crime episodes it may be a single, stereotypic, verbal response which is stored with a poorly perceived and therefore poorly registered face (e.g. Doob and Kirshenbaum, 1973). Witnesses usually have to give descriptions of seen criminals before they are actually asked to recognize or identify him. Now, following the work by Kay (1955), it would seem that if a witness says, "Was rather attractive" then he will remember this description and feel committed to it. At recognition he will try to pick out the person who best fits this publicly given description. Thus what we have is a visual sighting, a verbal labelling and then a later visual recognition based on the remembered verbal label. The label can be the same but the two visualized people can be different. The composition of a line-up predisposes witnesses to this type of error.

If it can be accepted, with qualification, that subject-generated verbal input can affect, either positively or negatively, accuracy of recognition then it ought to follow that linguistic input from outsiders could also affect memory for seen events and people. The input from outsiders is usually in the form of questions. The interesting possibility then becomes whether such questions will influence memory for the event. Harris (1973) asked the simple question, "How tall was the basketball player?" or "How short was the basketball player?" Subjects asked the former question gave an answer whose average was 79 inches, while the second group gave an answer whose average was 69 inches. In a replication experiment Harris asked subjects either, "How long was the movie?" or "How short was the movie?" He got back average answers of 130 minutes and 100 minutes respectively. This shows rather clearly that the changing of one word in a question can have a large effect on the answer given.

Loftus (1974) had 100 students view a short film sequence depicting a multi-car accident. Immediately after viewing the film the subjects were given a 22-item questionnaire which contained six critical questions, three referring to items present in the film, and three referring to items not present. For half the subjects all the six critical questions began with the words, "Did you see a . . .?", for the remainder of the subjects all the questions began with, "Did you see the . . .?" "The" presupposes the presence of something, "A" does not. "The" questions produced a greater number of perceptions of non-present items than did the "A" questions.

In 1974 Loftus and Palmer presented a video film of a car crash and asked viewers questions about it. The questions used were shown to influence the numerical estimate of speed of the colliding cars. The questions were identical in form except for the verb. All sentences comprised the following form: "What speed were the cars going when they ———— (into) each other?" The dash was filled by different verbs for different subjects. The verbs used were "smashed", "collided", "bumped", "hit" and "contacted". The numerical estimates of speed increased with the increased "violence" of the verb.

These studies serve to show that the form and wording of an outsider's question can bias the way in which subjects access their stored visual memory. Can it also be shown that the type of question asked can actually alter the storage of memory traces? Loftus is again the chief experimentalist here. Her interest is in the influence of language on memory for fast moving, fairly complex events. The basic paradigm is to present a video film, then ask a series of questions and then, at a later date, ask another series of questions and compare answers to the second set of questions given by groups of subjects given different initial questions. The crucial manipulation is the first questionnaire which contains presuppositional type questions. The rationale is that if the subjects treat the first set of questions as new information then they will introduce this into their already stored memories, and so change this initial memory.

In one study a ten-item questionnaire was administered. The first question asked about the speed of a car in one of two ways:

1 (a) "How fast was the car going when it ran (past) the stop sign?"

or

2 (b) "How fast was the car going when it turned right?"

The last question was identical for all subjects:

10   "Did you see a stop sign for the car?"

Subjects responded to question (10) by circling Yes or No. Fifty-three percent of the group who received question 1 (a) said they had seen a stop sign, while 35% of those subjects who had been given question 1 (b) answered "yes", they had seen a stop sign. It is important to note in this experiment that the stop sign was actually present on film, and thus the differential rates of saying "yes", they had seen a stop sign, for the two groups given different forms of question 1 admits of a number of explanations. Loftus (1975) argues that it could be the case that the persons who answered "yes" had seen the stop sign and stored it, and question 1 (a) merely served to strengthen this storage. Alternatively, it could be argued that the person did not see the stop sign and thus had no stored memory of it, but when the question 1 (a) was asked the subject revisualized or constructed the scene as it must have been, and thus stored a stop sign as a trace. Thus when he answered question (10) he was reading off from a stored trace which was not the product of a visualization or perception, but was rather the outcome of a verbal input and the question which involved a stop sign. The way to sort out these two possible alternatives is to use presuppositional questions which refer to something *not* present in the film.

This was done by Loftus and Palmer (1974) in the study which varied the verb used in the questions about the speed of cars. These questions were used as "priming" or "distorting" questions, because one week later the subjects were brought back and, among other questions were asked: "Did you see any broken glass?" The number of sightings of broken glass increased with the vigour of the verbs used one week earlier. No broken glass appeared in the film! This strongly argues for the second alternative argument advanced above. The subjects could not have had an initial memory of broken glass because none appeared in the film. Thus a "new" memory for a supposed visual event was laid down by a verbal question. This shows clearly the role of inferential processes in human memory because there is more chance of broken glass occurring as the severity of the car collisions increase. Space does not permit much mention of further studies by Loftus (e.g. 1977) but it is worthy of note that in one of her most recent publications (Loftus *et al.*, 1978) she found that when subjects were exposed to either consistent, misleading or irrelevant information, the misleading information produced less accurate responding. The misleading information had a stronger effect if introduced just prior to final test rather than immediately after the initial event. Loftus *et al.* concluded that, "information to which a witness is exposed after an event is integrated into the witness's memory of the event".

This research shows clearly that subtlety with which we are dealing in person and event identification: memory is no simple affair! It seems beyond doubt that the use of presuppositional questions can cause faulty memory. Presuppositional questions are all too easy to ask if one is dealing with a question of fact about which you have some theory—precisely the position Trankell (1972) argues characterizes the police interrogation of witness and suspect.

So far then we have looked at language as labels and found it to be both a positive and a negative force. We then looked at language as questions and found it to be predominantly negative. A third important area is the overall style of questioning: whether it is better to allow people to freely construct their own accounts (narrative reports) or for a list of questions to be produced which they have to fill in (interrogative reports).

These two basic types of report structure can be assessed under at least three headings (Hunter, 1964): (1) range—the number of items measured; (2) accuracy—factual correctness; (3) assurance—degree of confidence by the witness that his recall is accurate and correct. Research has concluded that narrative reports are more accurate but less complete, while interrogative reports or depositions are more complete but less accurate. This has been reported by, among others, Gardner (1933), Marquis *et al.* (1972), Marston (1924) and Whipple (1909). Several investigators have sought possible interactive effects typically employing both narrative and interrogative reports but changing the order for different groups of subjects. Thus when one group received narrative and then interrogative questioning while the other group received them in the opposite order, Cady (1924) found more accurate testimony when the narrative report was given first. Snee and Lush (1941) supported Cady's findings and also indicated that a narrative-interrogative order produced more correct responses, fewer "don't knows", but no appreciable change in the frequency of incorrect responses. Whitely and McGeoch (1927) investigated the delay between completing one set of reports and then another, where delays were at least 30 days. They concluded that the narrative-interrogative order had a facilitative effect upon subsequent narrative recalls at delays of 30, 60, 90 and 120 day intervals.

Generally speaking an interrogative report produces greater range but less accuracy. The proportion of inaccurate items is something like a tenth for narrative reports and a quarter for interrogative. Why should this be so? In free report the subjects will report only what he remembers and is sure of, while under interrogative report he will be asked questions about which he has no relevant memory, but because he is being asked by an authority figure an answer is likely to be given; also, by the very fact of being asked a question the implication is that he ought to know the answer, and is considered capable of giving it. When an answer has been given, however uncertainly and haltingly, it becomes a "fact" and the witness leaves all doubts behind and accepts his output as the outcome of genuine recall, and this is especially the case if the interrogator seems pleased with the answer, and goes on to ask further, consecutive or follow-up questions. It seems to be the case that children are inferior to adults in both the range and accuracy of their testimony, i.e. they give fewer items and what they do give is more likely to be inaccurate.

Thus to summarize early research it seems as if errors of testimony are almost unavoidable and that while interrogative measures are excellent means of filling out gaps in spontaneous report, they have their dangers. They lead witnesses, especially children and unsophisticated adults, into false depositions. However, closer inspection of the data cast several doubts on these implications. The use of semi-structured or very structured questioning procedures can result in only a small increase in the amount of error obtained while at the same time significantly increasing the amount of material covered by testimony. The earlier findings of large increases in reported error resulting from the employment of specific questions can be explained by the failure to distinguish between the type of question asked and the difficulty of the information being sought (Marquis et al., 1972). Marshall (1966) examined this possibility by looking at the effect of questioning on the accuracy of reporting three items. Specific questions increased the amount of testimony error for two items. These items were held to be difficult in the sense that they were seldom mentioned spontaneously in narrative testimony. An item which was reported by most people initially was answered correctly in response to specific questions.

Thus the possibility exists that it is not the form of the question itself which produces the inaccurate memory but rather the difficulty of the material being remembered. Therefore recent research has used a more intensive approach to the simple question of whether narrative or interrogative approaches are better for eliciting accurate memory. Such a study is one by Marquis *et al.* (1972). They at one and the same time sought to compare the accuracy and completeness of testimony under supportive and challenging atmospheres: to determine whether specific or more general questions were productive of greater accuracy; to see whether leading or non-leading questions influenced accuracy; and lastly they examined the interactive effect of these various factors. A number of the general findings are interesting. (1) Witnesses who were challenged by the questioner ("challenging atmosphere") were slightly more likely to think that the questioners wanted biased answers. (2) Those who were asked leading questions were more likely to expect that the questioner wanted them to distort their testimony. (3) In terms of the effect of the different types of questions greatest accuracy was found under free report, least accurate testimony being found under leading question conditions. (4) The type of atmosphere had little effect on accuracy or completeness of testimony. The main effect, however, of the type of question on accuracy was mediated by item difficulty, such that the question type effect was greatest for difficult-to-remember items and weakest for easy material. Thus for free report, accuracy is high for both easy and difficult items but for structured questions (e.g. leading) accuracy is high for easy items but very low (about 50%, chance level) for difficult items. Thus the conclusion from the earlier research on eyewitness testimony may need some qualification: structured questions introduce greater amounts of error but only for difficult items. Leading questions for difficult items produce much greater completeness than non-structured questions. The suggestion then in this research is that law enforcement agencies ought to be aware of the trade-off between accuracy and completeness which is a function of both the degree of specificity of the question and the difficulty of the to-be-recalled information. Similarly, they and jurors ought to be aware that a witness's confidence or assurance in the accuracy of his testimony has repeatedly been found *not* to be related to the true accuracy of his testimony (for a review of such studies see Deffenbacher, 1978).

VI. Present Practices of Using Eyewitness Memory

There are a number of ways in which witness memory plays a role in real life. Three major areas for the psychologist are (1) the giving of verbal descriptions by the witness; (2) the witness's construction of "photo-fit" resemblances; (3) the witness's performance at identification parades. The first of these has already been discussed in this chapter.

Ellis *et al.* (1977) conducted a comprehensive study of the efficiency of the photo-fit system of reconstructing faces. They found that there was no effect on reconstruction accuracy of either the delay interval between seeing a face and later trying to reconstruct it nor the initial face inspection times. They also found that subjects "who made a special effort to remember the face" were no better than those not so instructed, and that reconstructing a photo-fit did not affect witnesses's subsequent recognition accuracy. Additionally, the individual differences of sex, imagery, field dependence and the witnesses's confidence in their reconstructions all failed to relate meaningfully to accuracy of photo-fit reconstruction. They did find white subjects to reconstruct more accurately white faces than black faces and that the presence of feature boundary lines on photo-fit composites can impair their memorability. However, the main conclusion which Ellis *et al.* arrived at was that the photo-fit aid to eyewitness memory was, in fact, a very insensitive instrument which frequently led to poor resemblances being constructed.

The validity of identification parades has been much discussed recently and a government committee of inquiry was set up (for a criticism of its findings see Bull and Clifford, 1976; Clifford and Bull, 1978). This Devlin Committee recognized that the differences between visual and verbal processes that were discussed earlier are relevant to criminal identification when it noted that, "recognition depends upon the human ability to memorise a face, even when it cannot be described with any accuracy". As Devlin put it, the problem in legal settings at the moment is that, "Evidence of recognition if accepted, proves identity, it can be attacked as false or mistaken, but if the attack fails it is enough by itself to constitute proof". The Committee suggested that if a witness could be no surer of identification than that the suspect resembled the wanted person then such evidence is not as strong as that of recognition. This distinction has some merit but it glosses over the problem that there is little evidence that a witness's confidence in his identification (high confidence often being taken as synonymous with correct recognition) is of any use when judging the true accuracy of the identification. Devlin noted that, "Psychological studies of the processes of memory and recall underline the need to approach evidence of eye-witness identification with great caution".

In the vast majority of real-life episodes the witness has only a partial memory of what took place and of who perpetrated the crime. This partial memory is a source of bias. Before a line-up takes place, the witness has almost certainly given a verbal description of the criminal to the police. The problem with this is that once a person makes a public commitment (official statement) that person will adhere rigidly to it (Brehm and Cohen, 1962; Kiesler, 1971), and we have already indicated the perverting effect that this can have.

This finding leads to a crucially important procedural point made by Bytheway and Clark (1976). They point out that the composition of a line-up based on the Home Office recommendations of "persons who are as far as possible the same age, height, general appearance (including standard of dress and grooming) and position in life" could be positively harmful, because it could eventuate in a line-up which would be markedly different from a line-up based on the witness's verbal description. The Home Office line-up composition stems from the suspect the police have, a better line-up composition could stem from the witnesses' initial descriptions.

The first requirement for a satisfactory appraisal of identification parades is to get clear just how accurate eyewitnesses are, and how their behaviour can be assessed. In the absence of any information from actual cases we have to rely on experimental estimates, because at real identification parades the guilt or innocence of the suspect is not generally known. However, by the use of controlled experimentation the variables present in real-life situations can be partially separated out to isolate the most relevant ones and their effect upon accuracy determined. Estimates of identification accuracy vary—but the estimations are uniformly low.

A suggestion that we have put forward elsewhere (Bull and Clifford, 1976) is that two parades be used, only one of which contains the suspect. As far back as 1929 the Royal Commission on Police Powers and Procedures noted that some witnesses, "may unconsciously tend to identify the person who most resembled their recollection of the culprit disregarding, apparently the alternative that he may not be present at all". Buckhout (1974) employed two line-ups and found that half the subjects who appeared to have good memories (by positively identifying the criminal) went on to impeach themselves by selecting an innocent person from the line-up in which the criminal was not present. Thus a double parade has the dual effect of indicating unreliable witnesses and cutting down on the "social set" or pressure on a witness to pick someone out of a parade which he (the witness) "knows" contains a criminal suspect. Thus the main argument for a two-parade situation is that the witness is informed that in fact one of the parades does not contain a suspect.

Since recognition and identification are always the result of an approximate match between initial memory and subsequent perceptions of an individual and since a witness may be cognizant of the possibility that the culprit's appearance may have changed somewhat since initial perception there is value in Dent and Gray's (1975) point that, "whether or not the witness decides to identify someone depends not only on how closely that person resembles his memory of the criminal, but also on how close he thinks the resemblance ought to be before he makes a positive identification". It is precisely here that social psychological factors such as stereotypes can have a profound effect.

Patterson (1978) has examined the effects of purposely changing aspects of an individual's appearance between initial perception and subsequent attempts at recognition (a change which any intelligent criminal might make). She found that the disguise of adding or removing a wig, or a beard, or both, significantly reduced recognition performance compared with the case in which no change of appearance occurred. Further, she noted that changing the method by which the targets were presented (photo vs film) from initial viewing to later recognition caused a similar significant decrease in performance. Patterson pointed out that witnesses often see a criminal in the way portrayed in her film, yet they are often required by the police to try to pick that person out from photographs. Thus, an identification parade which required all the participants to be seen to be moving might prove to be an improvement.

Dent and Gray (1975) found some evidence that colour photographs of the individuals in a parade lead to a greater proportion of correct identifications than did a conventional parade. However, these authors wisely noted that all participants were aware that the situation was merely an experimental one. In this study the photographs were examined one at a time and their results may have some bearing on the suggestion that identification parades be replaced by a system in which each person who would have been a member of a traditional parade enters in turn a room where the witness is present. Thus the witness would see the people one at a time and each would leave before the next enters. The witness would not be told how many people are available for viewing and a court could note if the witness needed a second run through this sort of "parade". If such a system as this were adopted (and here research is needed) it would prevent non-suspects from conveying to the witness who the real suspect was and it would provide information on how readily the witness made his choice. Furthermore, since the witness would not know how many people were going to be in this "parade" it might reduce the number of occasions upon which the witness picks out the "best resemblance" as in a traditional parade. Also, since the "parading" people would be seen walking this would help get over the problem of present line-ups in which the witness is asked to identify a static person, who may originally have been seen in motion at the time of the crime.

It is our view that if society wishes to convict persons who commit crimes, and in some cases the only evidence against them is that of identification, then identification parades as presently conducted (or preferably modified in line with the suggestions which we have made) are perhaps the most efficient way of achieving this. It is worth stressing again that no type of conviction can ever be certain. As Samuel Butler said, "Life is the art of drawing sufficient conclusions from insufficient data", and this certainly applies to psychology.

References

Adcock, C. and Webberley, M. (1971). Primary mental abilities. *J. gen. Psychol.* **84**, 229–243.

Atkinson, J. and Walker, E. (1955). The affiliation motive and perceptual sensitivity to faces. *J. abnorm. soc. Psychol.* **53**, 38–41.

Baddeley, A. D. (1976). "The Psychology of Memory". Harper and Row, New York.

Baggett, P. (1975). Memory for implicit and explicit information in pictures. *J. Verb. Learn. Verb. Behav.* **14**, 538–548.

Bahrick, H. and Boucher, B. (1968). Retention of visual and verbal codes of the same stimuli. *J. exp. Psychol.* **78**, 417–422.

Baker, E. (1967). Perceiver variables involved in the recognition of faces. Unpublished Ph.D. thesis, University of London.

Bartlett, F. (1932). "Remembering: a Study in Experimental and Social Psychology". Cambridge University Press, Cambridge.

Beijk-Docter, M. and Elshout, J. (1969). Valdafhan kelij kheid en geheugen met betrekking tot sociaal relevant en sociaal niet-relevant materiaal. *Nederlands Tijdschrift voor de Psychologie enhaar Grensgebieden* **24**, 267–279.

Berrien, F. (1955). Psychology and the Court. *In* "Psychology for Law Enforcement Officials" (G. Dudycha, Ed.). C. C. Thomas, Springfield, Illinois.

Binet, A. (1900). "La Suggestibilitie". Schleicher Freres, Paris.

Borst, M. (1904). Recherches experimentalles sur l'educabilite et la fidelite du temoignage. *Archives de Psychologie* **111**, 1–30.

Bransford, J. D., Barclay, J. R. and Franks, J. J. (1972). Sentence memory: a constructive vs. interpretive approach. *Cognitive Psychol.* **3**, 193–209.

Brehm, J. and Cohen, A. (1962). "Explorations in Cognitive Dissonance". Wiley, New York.

British Association for the Advancement of Science (1974). "Science and the Police". B.A.A.S., London.

Broadbent, D. E. (1971). "Decision and Stress". Academic Press, London and New York.

Brown, J. (1958). Some tests of the decay theory of immediate memory. *Q. J. exp. Psychol.* **10**, 12–21.

Bruner, J. (1958). Social psychology and perception. *In* "Readings in Social Psychology" (E. Maccoby, T. Newcombe and E. Hartley, Eds). Henry Holt, New York.

Bruner, J., Shapiro, D. and Tagiuri, R. (1958). The meaning of traits in isolation and in combination. *In* "Person Perception and Interpersonal Behaviour" (R. Tagiuri and L. Petrullo, Eds.) Stanford University Press.

Buckhout, R. (1974). Eyewitness testimony. *Scient. Am.* **231**, 23–31.

Bull, R. (1979). The influence of stereotypes on person identification. *In* "Psychology, Law and Legal Processes" (D. Farrington, K. Hawkins and and S. Lloyd-Bostock, Eds). Macmillan (in press).

Bull, R. and Clifford, B. R. (1976). Identification: the Devlin Report. *N. Scient.* **70**, 307–308.

Bytheway, W. and Clark, M. (1976). The conduct and uses of identification parades. *J. Crim. Law*, July.

Cady, H. (1924). On the psychology of testimony. *Am. J. Psychol.* **35**, 110–112.

Carmichael, L., Hogan, H. and Walter, A. (1932). An experimental study of the effect of language on the reproduction of visually perceived form. *J. exp. Psychol.* **15**, 73–86.

Carroll, J. (1964). "Language and Thought". Prentice-Hall, Englewood Cliffs.

Cavior, H., Hayes, S. and Cavior, N. (1975). Physical attractiveness of female offenders. *In* "The Female Offender" (A. Brodsky, Ed.). Sage Publications, London.

Chance, J. and Goldstein, A. (1976). Recognition of faces and verbal labels. *Bull. Psychonomic Soc.* **7**, 384–387.

+Chance, J., Goldstein, A. and McBride, L. (1975). Differential experience and recognition memory for faces. *J. soc. Psychol.* **97**, 243–253.

Cherry, E. C. (1953). Some experiments on the recognition of speech, with one and with two ears. *J. Acoust. Soc. Am.* **25**, 975–979.

Clifford, B. R. (1978). A Critique of Eyewitness Research. *In* "Practical Aspects of Memory" (M. M. Gruneberg, P. E. Morris and R. W. Sykes, Eds). Academic Press, London and New York.

Clifford, B. R. (1979). Eyewitness testimony: The bridging of a credibility gap. *In* "Psychology, Law and Legal Processes" (D. Farrington, K. Hawkins and S. Lloyd-Bostock, Eds). Macmillan (in press).

Clifford, B. R. and Bull, R. (1978). "The Psychology of Person Identification". Routledge and Kegan Paul, London.

Clifford, B. R. and Hollin, C. (in preparation, a). The effect of number of targets on eyewitness recall and recognition.

Clifford, B. R. and Hollin, C. (in preparation, b). Experimentally manipulated arousal and eyewitness testimony.

Clifford, B. R. and Hollin, C. (in preparation, c). Testimony accuracy as a function of questioner status.

Clifford, B. R. and Hollin, C. (in preparation, d). Conformity effects in eyewitness testimony.

Clifford, B. R. and Hollin, C. (in preparation, e). eyewitness testimony: A review of theory, data and paradigms.

Clifford, B. R. and Richards, G. (1977). Comparison of recall by policemen and civilians under conditions of long and short durations of exposure. *Percept. Mot. Skills* **45**, 39–45.

Clifford, B. R. and Scott, J. (1978). Individual and situational factors in eyewitness testimony. *J. appl. Psychol.* **63**, 352–259.

Cofer, C. N. (1973). Constructive processes in memory. *Am. Psychol.* **61**, 537–543.

Cohen, R. (1966). Effect of verbal labels on the recall of a visually perceived simple figure: recognition vs. reproduction. *Percept. Mot. Skills* **23**, 859–862.

Cohen, R. (1967). Interaction between a visually perceived simple figure and an appropriate verbal label in recall. *Percept. Mot. Skills* **24**, 287–292.

Cohen, R. and Granstrom, K. (1970). Reproduction and recognition in short-term visual memory. *Q. J. exp. Psychol.* **22**, 450–457.

Cross, J., Cross, J. and Daly, J. (1971). Sex, race, age and beauty as factors in recognition of faces. *Percept. Psychophsyics* **10**, 393–396.

Crutchfield, R., Woodworth, D. and Albrecht, R. (1958). Perceptual performance and the effective person USAF WADC. *Tech. Note* Nos 58–60.

Daniel, T. and Ellis, H. C. (1972). Stimulus codability and long term recognition memory for visual form. *J. exp. Psychol.* **93**, 83–89.

Davies, G. (1969). Recognition memory for pictured and named objects. *J. exp. Child Psychol.* **7**, 448–458.

Deffenbacher, K. (1978). Some predictors of eyewitness memory accuracy. *In* "Practical Aspects of Memory" (M. M. Gruneberg, P. E. Morris and R. N. Sykes, Eds). Academic Press, London and New York.

Dent, H. (1977). Stress as a factor influencing person recognition in identification parades. *Bull. Br. Psychol. Soc.* **30**, 339–340.

Dent, H. and Gray, F. (1975). Identification on parade. *N. Behav.* **I**, 366–369.

Devlin Report (1976). "Report to the Secretary of State for the Home Department of the Departmental Committee on Evidence of Identification in Criminal Cases". HMSO, London.

Diamond, R. and Carey, S. (1977). Developmental changes in the representation of faces. *J. exp. Child Psychol.* **23**, 1–22.

Doob, A. and Kirshenbaum, H. (1973). Bias in police line-ups—partial remembering. *J. Police Sci. Admin.* **I**, 287–293.

Ducharme, R. and Fraisse, P. (1965). Etude genetique de la memorisation de mots et d'images. *Can. J. Psychol.* **19**, 253–261.

Efran, L. (1974). The effect of physical appearance on the judgement of guilt, interpersonal attraction, and severity of recommended punishment in a simulated jury task. *J. Res. Person.* **8**, 45–54.

†Elliott, E., Wills, E. and Goldstein, A. (1973). The effect of discrimination training on the recognition of white and oriental faces. *Bull. Psychonomic Soc.* **2**, 71–73.

Ellis, H. C. (1968). Transfer of stimulus predifferentiation to shape recognition and identification learning: the role of properties of verbal labels. *J. exp. Psychol.* **78**, 401–409.

Ellis, H. C. (1972). Verbal processes in the encoding of visual pattern information: an approach to language, perception and memory. *In* "Third Western Symposium on Learning: Cognitive Learning" (M. Meyer, Ed.). Western Washington State College, Bellingham.

Ellis, H. D. (1975). Recognizing faces. *Br. J. Psychol.* **66**, 409–426.

Ellis, H. D., Shepherd, J. and Bruce, A. (1973). The effect of age and sex upon adolescents' recognition of faces. *J. genet. Psychol.* **123**, 173–174.

Ellis, H. D., Deregowski, J. and Shepherd, J. (1975). Descriptions of white and black faces by white and black subjects. *Int. J. Psychol.* **10**, 119–123.

Ellis, H. D., Davies, G. with Shepherd, J. (1977). An investigation of the photo-fit system for recalling faces. Report to the Social Science Research Council. Psychology Department, Aberdeen University.

Eysenck, H. J. (1967). "The Biological Basis of personality". Charles C. Thomas, Springfield, Illinois.

Eysenck, M. W. (1977). "Human Memory: Theory, research and individual differences". Pergamon Press, Oxford and London.

Forster, P. M. and Govier, E. (1978). Discrimination without awareness? *Q. J. exp. Psychol.* **30**, 282–295.

Frederiksen, C. H. (1975). Acquisition of semantic information from discourse: Effects of repeated exposures. *J. Verb. Learn. Verb. Behav.* **14**, 158–169.

Freedman, J. and Haber, R. (1974). One reason why we rarely forget a face. *Bull. Psychonomic Sci.* **3**, 107–109.

Galper, R. (1973). "Functional Race Membership" and recognition of faces. *Percept. Mot. Skills* **37**, 455–462.

Gardner, D. (1933). The perception and memory of witnesses. *Cornell Law. Q.* **18**, 391–409.

Gibson, E. J. (1969). "Principles of Perceptual Learning and Development". Appleton-Century-Crofts, New York.

Gilliland, A. and Burke, R. (1926). A measure of sociability. *J. Appl. Psychol.* **10**, 315–326.

Goldstein, A. and Chance, J. (1964). Recognition of children's faces. *Child Devel.* **35**, 129–136.

Goldstein, A. and Chance, J. (1971). Visual recognition memory for complex configurations. *Percept. Psychophysics* **9**, 237–241.

† Goldstein, A. and Chance, J. (1976). Measuring psychological similarity of faces. *Bull. Psychonomic Soc.* **7**, 407–408.

Goldstein, A. and Chance, J. (1978). Judging face similarity in own and other races. *J. Psychol.* **98**, 185–193.

Gomulicki, B. G. (1956). Recall as an abstractive process. *Acta Psychol.* **12**, 77–94.

Gross, H. (1897). "Criminal Psychology". Leipzig.

Hake, H. (1975). Discussant in J. Chance (Chair), "Faces: How do we perceive and remember them?" Symposium presented at the meeting of the Midwestern Psychological Association, Chicago.

Hamid, P. (1972). Some effects of dress cues on observational accuracy, a perceptual estimate and impression formation. *J. soc. Psychol.* **86**, 279–289.

Hanawalt, N. and Demarest, I. (1939). The effects of verbal suggestion in the recall period upon the reproduction of visually perceived forms. *J. exp. Psychol.* **25**, 159–174.

Harris, R. (1973). Answering questions containing marked and unmarked adjectives and adverbs. *J. exp. Psychol.* **97**, 399–401.

Harwood, E. and Naylor, G. (1969). Recall and recognition in elderly and young subjects. *Aust. J. Psychol.* **21**, 251–257.

+Hochberg, J. and Galper, R. (1974). Attribution of intentions as a function of physiognomy. *Memory and Cognition* **2**, 39–42.

Hoffman, C. and Kagan, S. (1977). Field dependence and facial recognition. *Percept. Mot. Skills* **44**, 119–124.

Howells, T. (1938). A study of ability to recognize faces. *J. abnorm. soc. Psychol.* **33**, 124–127.

Hunt, T. (1928). The measurement of social intelligence. *J. appl. Psychol.* **12**, 317–333.

Hunter, I. M. L. (1964). "Memory". Penguin Books, Harmondsworth.

Hurwitz, D., Wiggins, N. and Jones, L. (1975). Semantic differential for facial attributions: the face differential. *Bull. Psychonomic Soc.* **6**, 370–372.

Jenkins, J., Stack, W. and Deno, S. (1969). Children's recognition and recall of picture and word stimuli. *Audio Visual Communication Rev.* **17**, 265–271.

Jones, L. and Hirschberg, N. (1975). "What's in a face? Individual differences in facial perception". Paper presented at the 83rd Annual Convention of the American Psychological Association.

Kay, H. (1955). Learning and retaining verbal material. *Br. J. Psychol.* **46**, 81–100.

Keenan, J. M. and Kintsch, W. (1974). The identification of explicitly and implicitly presented information. *In* "The Representation of Meaning in Memory". (W. Kintsch, Ed.). Erlbaum Associates, Hillsdale, New York.

Kiesler, C. (1971). "The Psychology of Commitment". Academic Press, London and New York.

Kintsch, W. (1977). "Memory and Cognition". John Wiley and Sons, New York.

Kleck, R. and Rubenstein, C. (1975). Physical attractiveness, perceived attitude similarity and interpersonal attraction in an opposite-sex encounter. *J. Personal. soc. Psychol.* **31**, 107–114.

Kobler, G. (1915). Cited in G. Whipple Psychology of testimony. *Psychol. Bull.* **12**, 221–224.

Kogan, N. (1970). Educational aspects of cognitive style. *In* "Psychology and Educational Practice" (G. Lessor, Ed.). Scott Foresman, London.

Kozeny, E. (1962). Experimentelle untersuchungen zur ausdruckshkunde mittel photographisch-statistischer Methode (Experimental investigation of physiognomy utilizing a photographic-statistical method). *Archiv fur die Gesamte Psychologie* **114**, 55–71.

Kuehn, L. (1974). Looking down a gun barrel: person perception and violent crime. *Percept. Mot. Skills* **39**, 1159–1164.

Kurtz, K. and Hovland, C. (1953). The effect of verbalization during observation of stimulus objects upon accuracy of recognition and recall. *J. exp. Psychol.* **45**, 157–164.

Landy, D. and Aronson, E. (1969). The influence of the character of the criminal and his victim on the decisions of simulated jurors. *J. exp. soc. Psychol.* **5**, 141–152.

Laughery, K. (1971). "Human Memory and the Identification Process". Technical Report from the State University of New York at Buffalo, Department of Psychology, September, 1971.

Laughery, K., Fessler, P. Lenorogitz, D. and Yoblick, D. (1974). Time delay and similarity effects in facial recognition. *J. appl. Psychol.* **59**, 490–496.

Lavrakas, P., Buri, J. and Mayzner, M. (1976). A perspective on the recognition of other-race faces. *Percept. Psychophysics* **20**, 475–481.

Levine, F. and Tapp, J. (1973). Cited in F. Levine and J. Tapp "The psychology of criminal identification: the gap from Wade to Kirby". *Univ. Pennsylvania Law Rev.* **121**, 1079–1132.

Liggett, J. (1974). "The Human Face". Constable, London.

Lipton, J. (1977). On the psychology of eyewitness testimony. *J. appl. Psychol.* **62**, 90–95.

Loftus, E. F. (1974). Reconstructing memory: the incredible eyewitness. *Psychol. Today* **8**, 116–119.

Loftus, E. F. (1975). Leading questions and the eyewitness report. *Cognitive Psychol.* **7**, 560–572.

Loftus, E. F. (1977). Shifting human color memory. *Memory and Cognition* **5**, 696–699.

Loftus, E. F. and Palmer, J. (1974). Reconstruction of automobile destruction: an example of the interaction between language and memory. *J. Verb. Learn. Verb. Behav.* **13**, 585–589.

Loftus, E. F., Miller, D. and Burns H. (1978). Semantic integration of verbal information into visual memory. *J. exp. Psychol.* **4**, 19–31.

Luce, T. (1974). Blacks, whites and yellows: they all look alike to me. *Psychol. Today* **8**, 107–108.

McKelvie, S. (1972). Strategies of encoding in memory for faces. Ph.D. thesis, McGill University.

McKelvie, S. (1976). The effect of verbal labelling on recognition memory for schematic faces. *Q. J. exp. Psychol.* **28**, 459–474.

+Malpass, R. and Kravitz, J. (1969). Recognition for faces of own and other race. *J. Personal. soc. Psychol.* **13**, 330–335.

Marquis, K., Marshall, J. and Oskamp, S. (1972). Testimony validity as a function of question form, atmosphere, and item difficulty. *J. appl. soc. Psychol.* **2**, 167–186.

Marshall, J. (1966). "Law and Psychology in Conflict". Anchor Books, New York.

Marshall, J. (1969). The evidence: Do we see and hear what is? Or do our senses lie? *Psychol. Today* **2**, 49–52.

Marston, W. (1924). Studies in testimony. *J. Am. Inst. Crim. Law* **15**, 5–31.

Messick, S. and Damarin, F. (1964). Cognitive styles and memory for faces. *J. abnorm. soc. Psychol.* **69**, 313–318.

Miller, N. and Dollard, J. (1941). "Social Learning and Imitation". Yale University Press, New Haven.

Monahan, F. (1941). "Women in Crime". Ives Washburn, New York.

Morgan, C. S. (1917). A study in the psychology of testimony. *J. Am. Inst. Crim. Law* **8**, 222.

– Nickerson, R. (1965). Short term memory for complex, meaningful visual configurations: a demonstration of capacity. *Can. J. Psychol.* **19**, 155–160.

Norman, D. A. (1969). "Memory and Attention". Wiley, New York.

Paivio, A. (1971). "Imagery and Verbal Processes". Holt, Rinehart Winston, New York.

Paivio, A. (1976). Imagery in recall and recognition. *In* "Recall and Recognition" (J. Brown, Ed.). Wiley, New York.

Patterson, K. (1978). Face recognition: more than a pretty face. *In* "Practical Aspects of Memory" (M. M. Gruneberg, P. E. Morris and R. N. Sykes, Eds). Academic Press, London and New York.

Postman, L. (1972). A pragmatic view of organisation theory. *In* "Organisation of Memory" (E. Tulving and W. Donaldson, Eds). Academic Press, New York and London.

Potter, M. (1976). Short term conceptual memory for pictures. *J. exp. Psychol. Human Learning and Memory* **2**, 509–522.

Potter, M. and Levy, E. (1969). Recognition memory for a rapid sequence of pictures. *J. exp. Psychol.* **81**, 10–15.

Powis, D. (1974). A booklet "Thieves on Wheels" cited in Peter Evans, "The Police Revolution". Allen and Unwin, London.

Prentice, W. (1954). Visual recognition of verbally labelled figures. *Am. J. Psychol.* **67**, 315–320.

Santa, J. and Baker, L. (1975). Linguistic influences on visual memory. *Memory and Cognition* **3**, 445–450.

Santa, J. and Ranken, H. (1972). Effects of verbal coding on recognition memory. *J. exp. Psychol.* **93**, 268–278.

+Scapinello, K. and Yarmey, D. (1970). The role of familiarity and orientation in immediate and delayed recognition of pictorial stimuli. *Psychonomic Sci.* **21**, 329–330.

Schill, T. (1966). Effects of approval motivation and varying conditions of verbal reinforcement on incidental memory for faces. *Psychol. Reports* **19**, 55–60.

Scott, B. (1977). "The role of attentional processes in eyewitness behaviour". Paper presented at the meeting of the American Psychological Association, San Francisco, August, 1977.

Secord, P. (1958). Facial features and inference processes in interpersonal perception. *In* "Person Perception and Interpersonal Behaviour" (R. Tagiuri and L. Petrullo, Eds). Stanford University Press.

Secord, P., Dukes, W. and Bevan, W. (1954). Personalities in faces: I. An experiment in social perceiving. *Gent. Psychol. Monogr.* **49**, 231–279.

—Shepard, R. (1967). Recognition memory for words, sentences and pictures. *J. Verb. Learn. Verb. Behav.* **6**, 156–163.

†Shepherd J. and Ellis, H. D. (1973). The effect of attractiveness on recognition memory for faces. *Am. J. Psychol.* **86**, 627–633.

Shoemaker, D., South, D. and Lowe, J. (1973). Facial stereotypes of deviants and judgments of guilt or innocence. *Soc. Forces* **51**, 427–433.

Slobin, D. (1971). "Psycholinguistics". Scott, Foresman, New York.

Snee, T. and Lush, D. (1941). Interaction of the narrative and interrogatory methods of obtaining testimony. *J. Psychol.* **11**, 229–336.

Sperling, G. (1960). The information available in brief visual presentations. *Psychol. Monogr.* **74**, whole No. 498.

Sperling, G. (1967). Successive approximations to a model of short-term memory. *Acta Psychol.* **27**, 285–292.

—Standing, L. (1973). Learning 10,000 pictures. *Q. J. exp. Psychol.* **25**, 207–222.

—Standing, L., Conezio, J. and Haber, R. (1970). Perception and memory for pictures: single trial learning of 2560 visual stimuli. *Psychonomic Sci.* **19**, 73–74.

Stern, L. W. (1939). The psychology of testimony. *J. abnorm. soc. Psychol.* **34**, 3–20.

Stritch, T. and Secord, P. (1956). Interaction effects in the perception of faces. *J. Personal.* **24**, 272–284.

Tickner, A. and Poulton, E. (1975). Watching for people and actions. *Ergonomics* **18**, 35–51.

Trankell, A. (1972). "Reliability of Evidence". Beckmans, Stockholm.

Triesmann, A. (1964). Monitoring and storage of irrelevant messages in selective attention. *J. Verb. Learn. Verb. Behav.* **3**, 449–459.

Tulving, E. (1969). Forgetting: another look at an old problem. Paper presented at the XIX International Congress of Psychology, London.

Wall, P. (1965). "Eyewitness Identification in Criminal Cases". Thomas, New York.

Waugh, N. C. and Norman, D. (1965). Primary Memory. *Psychol. Rev.* **72**, 89–104.

Whipple, G. (1909). The observer as reporter: a survey of the "psychology of testimony". *Psychol. Bull.* **6**, 153–170.

Whitely, R. and McGeoch, J. (1927). The Effect of one form of report upon another. *Am. J. Psychol.* **38**, 280.

Witkin, H., Dyk, R., Faterson, H., Goodenough, D. and Karp, S. (1974). "Psychological Differentiation: Studies in Development". Lawrence Erlbaum, Potomac, Maryland (reprint).

Witryol, S. and Kaess, W. (1957). Sex differences in social memory tasks. *J. abnorm. soc. Psychol.* **54**, 343–346.

Wreschner, A. (1905). Zur psychologie der aussage. *Archiv. fur die gesemate psychologie* **1**, 148–183.

Wulf, F. (1922). Uber die Veranderumg von Vorstellungen. *Psychologisch Forschung* **I**, 333–373.

✛Yin, R. (1969). Looking at upside-down faces. *J. exp. Psychol.* **81**, 141–145.

Zangwill, O. L. (1972). Remembering revisited. *Q. J. exp. Psychol.* **24**, 123–138.

Zanni, G. R. and Offermann, J. T. (1978). Eyewitness testimony: an exploration of question wording upon recall as a function of neuroticism. *Percept. Mot. Skills* **46**, 163–166.

7. Stress and Memory

D. M. JONES

Department of Applied Psychology,
University of Wales Institute of Science and Technology,
Cardiff, UK

I. Introduction

The study of "stress" covers a broad spectrum of human activity. Within its compass are factors such as divorce, illness, heat, marriage, fear, retirement, battle fatigue, anger, noise, commuting . . . The list is well nigh endless. Instead of considering the whole range of stresses, the chapter focuses on those situations which are likely to influence memory performance, particularly as they apply to a practical setting.

The study of stress and memory is of obvious practical importance. The vulnerability of memory to disruption by extreme stress has been tacitly recognized down the ages. Military forces in particular have long realized that memory for skills breaks down under the stress of battle. Soldiers have been drilled in preparation for warfare, not only to instil discipline and obedience, but also to produce well learned "automatized" skills which are assumed to be immune to breakdown. The rote learning of military skills is a direct attempt to ensure that performance will not break down under stress. Such extremes of stress are seldom found in civilian life; though rare, when crises do occur, undisrupted correcting action is vital. In an age when industrial and aviation accidents approach the magnitude of military catastrophes, high level skills need to be exercised to avoid heavy loss of life.

Moreover these modern-day skills are ones which cannot usually be acquired by rote-learning; they often involve the acquisition and up-dating of information, thereby increasing the memory load on an operator. The effects of these extremes of stress will be the subject of the first section of the review of empirical work.

Another section will deal with less extreme forms of stress, often found in everyday life: on the shop floor, in the office and in the home. Noise is perhaps the most obvious example of this kind of insidious and ubiquitous stress. Interest has focused on stresses like noise, not only because they increase annoyance or discomfort, but because they are also likely to impair efficiency. Aside from an interest in the effect of stressful environments on memory, this chapter is also concerned with information which is intrinsically arousing or stressful. The best practical example here arises out of the use of "shock" or "horror" appeals in advertising, for example, when road safety information is presented with photographs of road accidents.

Before embarking on a detailed discussion of each of these three areas, a discussion of the conceptual and methodological issues provoked by the study of stress and memory is necessary.

Conceptual Issues

In this chapter "stress" will apply to conditions outside the normal range of experience. "Arousal" on the other hand will refer to the change in the state of the organism exposed to stress. This state of the organism can be viewed at either psychological or physiological level, that is, responses to stress can be considered to arise from behavioural arousal or be manifested in a physiological response.

The word "stress" enjoys popular usage, but in the process has gained a pejorative meaning and is now used to denote any seemingly undesirable aspect of life. Indeed, modern man is seen as the arch-victim of stress. Little heed has been paid to the beneficial effect of the stress which we all experience at one time or another. There is general agreement that part of the response to stress is the recognition of a discrepancy between an actual and desired state of affairs: an imbalance between demand and capacity. What usually follows is a process of adaptation during which this discrepancy is resolved. Naturally, stress will be perpetuated where the response is inadequate or maladaptive. In most cases adaptation is the expected sequel to a stressful episode. Indeed, this very flexibility is the key to survival in a changing world. Whether the stress is successfully resolved or not, this kind of formulation implies that stress results from the disruption of a state of psychological equilibrium. The idea that organisms have a quiescent state of this sort has its roots in an analogous view of physiological function embodied in the concept of homeostasis. Physiological systems have a natural tendency to restore themselves to a steady-state in response to externally induced disturbances. Implicit in the psychological formulation of homeostasis is the idea that response to stress is non-linear. Competence may decrease in states which are either above or below the optimum. Individuals seem to function best in conditions where demands are neither too high nor too low. In turn, reactions to stress are seen as attempts to secure an optimum level of arousal.

Hebb (1955) proposed that behavioural arousal and performance were related by an inverted-U function. Performance is best at intermediate levels of arousal; when arousal is too high (hyperarousal) the organism is disorganized and overreactive, whereas in conditions of low arousal it is lethargic and insensitive. This notion is intuitively plausible, and documented instances of stress in war support those changes predicted for the middle and upper range of the continuum. For example, Mira (1944), in his account of reactions to bombing in the Spanish Civil War, found a progressive deterioration in performance above the optimal level of stress. Mild degrees of fear were beneficial, producing a more vigilant and better organized response in the civilian population. Slightly greater levels of fear led to disorganized activity. Extremes of fear resulted in hysteria often accompanied by loss of memory. As expected from the inverted-U relationship, intermediate levels of stress had a beneficial effect and eventually competence declined at high levels of stress.

Many laboratory findings using milder degrees of stress corroborate those found by observation. Most fit the inverted-U function, with performance being poor at the ends of the stress continuum. However these functions are inevitably derived *post hoc*; it is usually difficult to specify the optimum point in advance. As a further complication it appears that different tasks have different optimal levels. This makes the predictive power of the inverted-U relationship notoriously weak.

There is also general agreement that stress not only brings about quantitative changes in performance but also qualitative ones. Easterbrook (1959) for example, proposed that in over-aroused subjects attention tends to be concentrated on the dominant and obvious aspects of the situation. This leads to the expectation that some aspects of performance may be unaffected by stress but that performance on other, less important, aspects of the task may be impaired. Recent modifications to this view have further emphasized that stress also increases the lability of attention and interferes with the capacity to discriminate relevant from irrelevant aspects of a task (cf. Kahneman, 1973). Here, the distinction is made between breadth and stability of attention. Stress tends both to narrow the breadth and disrupt the stability of attention. In essence, what seems to happen is that stress produces strategic changes, rather than a straightforward depression of performance.

There are also conceptual problems in restricting discussion to the effects of stress on memory. Although the focus on memory is in keeping with the objectives of the book, the distinction between memory and other types of performance is largely artificial. Memory processes cannot be studied in isolation, they do not represent the action of a separate faculty as distinct from, for example, perception. The advent of the information processing approach has highlighted this issue by advocating that memory systems are intimately involved in processes that have been conventionally labelled as "perception" and "response" (Haber, 1969). True, the qualitative and quantitative attributes of storage may differ in each case, but what should be recognized is that memory plays a role in every psychological activity. It follows that there is no such thing as a non-memory task; tasks differ in their reliance on the various mechanisms of storage and retrieval. What psychologists mean when they refer to memory tasks are paradigms where the role of memory is pronounced.

In assessing the effects of stress on memory, the main aim is to locate the particular stage or level of processing where the stress-induced change takes place. The usual approach is to systematically vary the demands made on a particular functional stage in memory and to study the outcome when a stress is applied. However, the result cannot always be unambiguously interpreted as the result of a change in memory function. For example, if it is hypothesized that a stress, like noise, exerts its influence on the retrieval mechanism, the usual approach is to vary the demands made on retrieval (by, for instance, comparing recall and recognition) during exposure to noise. If the hypothesis is correct then noise will produce its greatest effect in that condition where retrieval demands are greatest (in recall). This conclusion may be unsound since the manipulation of retrieval also changes the difficulty of the task. Since stress is primarily a motivational concept, there is always the possibility that arousal increases with the difficulty of the task which will augment the stress-induced arousal. Thus stress can have an effect arising out of the motivational demands of the task rather than form its effects on a stage of processing. There is good reason to believe that memory tasks offer a combination of task-demand characteristics which are quite different to those found in so-called non-memory tasks. Memory tasks usually require a higher rate of response, are more paced and contain more intrinsic knowledge of failure than their non-memory counterparts. There appears to be a distinction between effects of stress arising out of memory tasks and those arising out of memory systems, although it is well nigh impossible to separate out these effects (cf. Jones *et al.*, 1978a).

Methodological Issues

Three techniques are available for the study of stress: anecdotal, observational and experimental. Anecdotal accounts abound, but unfortunately they suffer from inevitable distortion with the passage of time and by their nature are difficult to verify. Observational data are often more reliable and offer a slightly more detached view, but they too tend to be distorted. Despite being selective and descriptive these two techniques offer some insight into the more extreme forms of stress which are not easily simulated.

The experimental approach can be used in either the field or in the laboratory. The major asset of field studies is the realism that can be achieved, since situations can be devised which mimic all but the most intense stresses. Even so, subjects seldom show extreme responses in such simulations: the circumstances never quite seem to be completely convincing. For example, a study of Berkun *et al.* (1962) attempted to study the stress reaction of soldiers in what was apparently a realistic setting. These investigators were surprised to find relatively low levels of stress even in those parts of the study where live ammunition was used. In interviews which followed the experiment the soldiers rationalized their plight by assuming that they were in no real peril. They reasoned that the Army would simply not allow them to be exposed to danger.

Aside from the problem of fidelity, a major difficulty with field studies is the problem of response measurement. Those tasks which are appropriate to the field setting are not amenable to the same sophisticated analysis which is expected from tasks specially developed for the laboratory. Realistic tasks are usually complex, where the memory component is at best obscure and at worst contaminated. Moreover, tasks developed for laboratory use appear contrived when used in the field, thus reducing the sense of realism. This point is particularly germane when an investigation attempts to focus on one particular aspect of performance such as memory. The study of memory immediately suggests a set of paradigms which would appear completely out of place in a realistic setting.

Laboratory studies offer tight control over stress induction and response measurement. Their main drawback is one of low fidelity. The experimental subject is exposed to a completely contrived situation. It cannot be assumed safely that the artificiality of the laboratory setting leads only to a diminution in the magnitude of the response which, in all other respects, resembles that found in the field. Laboratory responses to stress may be both qualitatively and quantitatively different from those found in real life. Recent work in social psychology tends to support this contention. Orne (1962) has argued that experiments constitute a distinctive social situation, in which subjects try to guess the hypothesis behind the experiment, so that the subject may either comply with the experimenter's wishes or may try to sabotage the experiment (see Weber and Cook, 1972, for a review). It seems likely that these changes, arising out of what Orne calls demand characteristics, will be heightened in laboratory studies of stress where a subject's competence at a task will be threatened by aversive stimuli.

In summary, although the conceptual issues in stress research at first appear straightforward, they are of little predictive value. Methodologically, the solutions are no clearer. Field and laboratory studies each have their merits. Most of what follows is in fact drawn from laboratory studies, due simply to their relative numerousness. The problems of generalizing from these findings are apparent and the results reviewed below can only be suggestive of the effects to be found in a realistic setting. In the section that follows findings from anecdotal reports and simulations of extreme stress will be reviewed to see if there is a prima facie case for supposing that memory is easily disrupted by stress.

II. Extremes of Stress

Naturally, the soldier in combat is unlikely to perform as well as he did in training. Even an overlearned skill, like rifle loading, may deteriorate under stress. Soldiers in battle during the American Civil War were found to have repeatedly reloaded their rifles without firing them. One rifle was found to have been reloaded twenty-one times without being fired once (Walker and Burkhart, 1965 cited by Baddeley, 1972). As stress is increased above the norm, skills may become disorganized or components of the skill may be forgotten. Contemporary accounts also indicate that well-learned actions may be forgotten in an emergency. For instance, a large proportion of fatalities in underwater diving are a result of the failure to perform simple and usually well-learned escape procedures. Even in the inexperienced diver who has not undergone training the most obvious course of action is often ignored. Norman (1976) quotes an example of a diver who drowned while recovering golf balls from a tank: the diver had surfaced in panic, but was later found to be wearing a jettisonable weight belt and clutching a heavy bag of golf balls.

These observations about the vulnerability of memory to disruption by stress are bolstered by similar findings from field simulation. For example, Berkun (1964), reports a study of retention during a simulated aircraft ditching exercise. Before taking-off all the subjects were asked to read a manual on ditching procedure. During their flight an experimental group was led to believe that the aircraft was in imminent danger of making a forced landing. Before ditching, they were asked to fill out two ostensibly routine questionnaires. One required the subjects to give an inventory of their personal possessions, where the instructions on the form were deliberately difficult to follow. A second questionnaire tested their retention of the ditching procedures which were learned just before the flight. The control group were given an uneventful flight and asked to fill out the same questionnaire as a matter of course. Scores on the complex inventory task were some 10% lower in the stressed group. In the memory-for-ditching-procedure task the deficit was much greater: subjects in the experimental group recalled nearly 30% fewer items than their unstressed counterparts. This finding suggests that memory for recently learned items is especially sensitive to disruption by stress. However the information that was to be recalled had obvious survival value and this may have produced an especially large effect. It seems quite probable that the stress of ditching was exacerbated by the stress of having to recall information necessary for the preservation of life.

This conclusion is supported by data from another part of the Berkun study where memory was tested for material that had no survival value. In this case soldiers were led to believe that they had seriously injured a comrade by their ineptitude in wiring up explosive charges. During the ensuing melée the subject had to perform a number of duties. Among his tasks was one requiring the backward recall of strings of digits which was given to him over an intercom. In this case subjects were only marginally worse than the control group: a difference of only one digit in recall. So, the type of material to be recalled does seem to be an important factor. Nevertheless, this must be considered to be a tentative conclusion in view of the differences in the way that stress was induced in these two cases.

Memory seems just as liable to disruption as any other complex cognitive function. Trying to remember information which may be of special use in escaping from a dangerous environment may not unnaturally be especially vulnerable to disruption. Adequate practice of safety procedures would help to overcome this difficulty but, as the observational studies show, this is by no means a panacea. In cases where no safety drill can be given, system designers should capitalize on the well-established habits and expectations of the population. For example, in the design of escape routes from buildings every effort should be made to reduce memory load, both long and short term. This can be achieved by capitalizing on factors such as direction-of-motion stereotypes: door handles should operate in the expected direction and emergency doors should open outwards not inwards, and so on.

Thus far the emphasis has been on the disruptive effects of stress on memory. In the next part of this section the emphasis is on training *for* stress. This involves a familiarity with both the skills which have to be deployed and the stress environment.

Learning usually takes place in the relative calm of the classroom or simulator. In contrast these skills are often implemented in stressful situations approaching bedlam. If material is learned in one context and retrieval takes place in another, quite different context, then performance usually suffers. Tulving and Thompson (1973) have proposed that failure to retrieve is largely due to this contrast between conditions of encoding at acquisition and those at retrieval. In their terms, the contrasting conditions encompass both intra-list and extra-list cues which may be present during the initial learning but absent or different at the time of testing. Of particular interest to the study of stress is the way in which extra-list cues determine the level of performance. Learning which is dependent on extra-list cues of this sort can be said to be context-dependent or state-dependent. The view that learning is context-dependent proposes that adequate retrieval depends on the presence of the whole ensemble of physical cues which were present at acquisition. Greenspoon and Ranyard (1957) were able to show context effects by simply changing the type of room in which testing took place. They found that if the recall context was different from that of the original learning, performance was much poorer than if both contexts were the same. Furthermore, if learning and recall took place in the same environment, the interfering power of an interpolated list was reduced when it was presented in a contrasting context. This so-called context-dependent effect may have arisen from one of a number of possible confounding sources: the mere distraction of moving from one room to another or the social effects of additional involvement with the experimenter in changing the test environment. More recent evidence by Godden and Baddeley (1975) suggests that context-dependent learning is not entirely due to distraction effects. They were interested in comparing context-dependent effects in learning or recalling on land and underwater. As expected from context-dependent learning, lists of unrelated words were best recalled in their learned context. As a control for distraction effects these investigators compared learning and recall on land with either: no interpolated activity, or a short dive between the two tests. No differences were found between these two conditions showing that their results arise not from distraction, but from true context-dependent learning. The results of these experiments suggest that if tasks are to be used in stressful environments, where a whole plethora of additional extrinsic cues may be present, then the fidelity of simulation during training must be high. Simulations of low fidelity may give comparable results to complex, realistic and expensive ones, when the circumstances are undemanding, but it may be that the latter type give more immunity to disruption by stress.

In state-dependent learning it is the internal organismic cues which change from one occasion to the next. Learning which takes place in one physiological state may be best recalled in the same physiological state. Studies of this type have customarily used drugs to manipulate subject-state, for example marijuana (Eich *et al.*, 1975) or alcohol (Weingartner *et al.*, 1976). Usually, these state-dependent effects occur most strongly when the demands made on retrieval are high, in for example, recall rather than recognition (Baddeley, 1976; Eich *et al.*, 1976). No evidence exists of a comparable effect with stress states. Despite this lack of data it seems reasonable to conclude that part of training should involve conditions which mimic any stressful circumstances with which the operator may be faced. Whether any benefit derived from such a regime arises from state-dependent and context-dependent effects or simply out of acquaintance with the stress is open to question. Familiarity with a stress (such as parachute jumping) usually produces a diminished or displaced stress response (Epstein and Fenz, 1965; Hammerton and Tickner, 1968) but adequate training of this sort allows individuals to gain experience both in coping with their own stress response and with the host of extraneous events thrust upon them during an emergency.

In the sections that follow stresses of lower magnitude are described. To begin there is a discussion of memory for emotive events: the effects of so-called item-arousal.

III. Memory for Arousing Events

Much of the research on propaganda has centred on the effectiveness of fear or shock appeals in areas such as road safety or preventive medicine. Unfortunately for our present purpose, these studies have emphasized changes in attitude following fear appeals rather than on the straightforward retention of items in the message (for a review of attitude change, see Sternthal and Craig, 1974). Of the studies that follow, only one has been specifically addressed to the issue of retention in a practical framework. Nevertheless, there are several laboratory studies which have dealt with the effects of spontaneous arousal to items within lists and these are also reviewed in view of the paucity of evidence from practical settings.

All the studies on item arousal employ a common strategy: the magnitude of physiological arousal accompanying an item is linked to the probability of recall. Several different types of physiological measures have been used in this way and all claim to be indices of behavioural arousal. The discussion will focus on Electrodermal Activity (EDA), although those studies using either the Electroencephalogram (EEG) or pupil size are also mentioned.

EDA reflects the action of sweating, and in this way acts as an indicant of autonomic nervous system arousal. This view must be considered as barely adequate: the complexity of the control centres and their interconnections had led one writer to conclude that, ". . . the common utilization of EDA as a relatively monolithic arousal indicator is a gross and erroneous oversimplification" (Edelberg, 1972, p. 394). Nevertheless for the purpose of this chapter the discussion makes the simplifying assumptions that arousal is an unitary concept and that EDA is a valid and reliable measure of arousal.

Only one study has used material that can in any way be said to be of practical origin. Levonian (1967, 1968) studied the retention of arousing items in a road safety film. The subjects were school children who were shown the film as part of a driver education course. Fifteen events in the film were chosen for study. The children were given a recognition test immediately after the film and again a week later. Arousal to each of the items in the film was measured by EDA. Within each subject's EDA responses to the 15 items, arousals were ranked and dichotomized, yielding groups of higher- and lower-arousal items. The number of items retained was plotted in four conditions: for high- and low-arousal items, at both long- and short-term recall. Levonian found a significant interaction between arousal and retention interval. In the short term high-arousal items show poorer recall than low-arousal items. Long-term recall shows the reverse of this trend with low-arousal items being worse than high-arousal items. This particular form of results is not without precedent (see below), but the novel aspect of the Levonian study is that he used realistic material which was presented continuously. In the studies that follow, which are laboratory based, items have been presented discretely within a list.

In a seminal series of studies Kleinsmith and Kaplan (1963, 1964) attempted to plot the time course of the retention of items which were accompanied by either high or low EDA arousal during acquisition. Skin Resistance (SR) was measured during the presentation of items in a paired-associate task. In the first experiment, subjects were given a single learning trial involving the presentation of word-digit pairs. The list was composed of four high-arousal words (e.g. vomit, rape) and four low-arousal words (e.g. dance, swim), coupled with one of eight single-digit numbers. Since the EDA response has a relatively long latency, periods of colour naming were interspersed between the presentation of each pair of associates which allowed the response to return to its baseline before the onset of the next word-digit pair. Subjects were asked to concentrate carefully on the word-digit pairs during presentation, but no mention was made of their recall. Within each subject the words with the three highest reductions in SR at presentation were designated as high-arousal items and the three items showing the smallest change were designated as low-arousal items. The retention of each of these two types of material was assessed after intervals of 2, 20, 45 minutes, 1 day and 1 week. Kleinsmith and Kaplan found that the digit responses to low-arousal words were better recalled after short intervals but thereafter were poorly recalled. Recall of high-arousal items showed the reverse of this trend, being low after short retention intervals with a marked improvement as the retention interval increased. These effects of arousal on recall were extremely large, at the shortest interval the recall of low-arousal items was four times higher than that for high-arousal items.

These findings, like those of Levonian, can be interpreted in terms of Walker's (1958, 1967) theory of preservative consolidation. According to this view, arousal at input produces an increase in reverberation of a trace which determines its retrievability. The very fast reverberation of high-arousal traces decreases the accessibility of an item. At the same time, diminished access ensures that the trace in question will not be disrupted by any other activity in the nervous system. With slow reverberation, which is a characteristic of low-arousal traces, the trace is readily accessible, but at the same time the possibility that the trace can be disrupted is high. Reverberation diminishes in both high- and low-arousal traces as the period of retention increases. Taken together these notions are seen as a complete account of the arousal-retention interval interaction. High-arousal items are poorly recalled in the short term because of the *caisson* of reverberatory activity surrounding the trace. At longer retention intervals, after reverberatory activity has diminished, the high-arousal items become more accessible, and by virtue of the early protection afforded by the reverberation, the items are intact. The lack of reverberatory activity surrounding the low-arousal items means that in the short term, access is easy and hence retrievability is high. Poor long-term recall of low-arousal traces results from both disruption by other on-going neural activity and by dissipation of the reverberatory activity as the retention interval increases. Consequently, after short periods of retention recall is high for low-arousal items, but recall declines as the retention interval increases. This apparently neat account of the data is beset with interpretative difficulties. Preservative consolidation invokes neurophysiological notions which are, at best, highly speculative. For example, there seems to be no firm support for the notion that long- or short-term storage is undertaken by reverberating circuits. Moreover, the proposition that high arousal leads to an increase in the rate of reverberation has yet to be supported by neurophysiological evidence.

Strangely, the classification of words by EDA arousal and *a priori* ratings of arousal did not agree. The emotive material in the list need not have been classed as being of high arousal on the basis of the EDA. Indeed, a study by Maltzman *et al*. (1966) which employed an *a priori* designation of high- and low-arousal items, based solely on the rated emotionality of the words, failed to find an arousal-retention interval interaction: high-arousal words were better recalled throughout. In a later experiment, Kleinsmith and Kaplan (1964) employed nonsense syllables as stimuli and replicated the massive effect they had found with emotive words. In fact there is no indication of how these spontaneous arousals arise, they are not obviously related to any manipulable stimulus variable.

The absence of any clear account of these changes points to the possibility that some confounding factor may have been at work. Craik and Blankstein (1974) offer what is perhaps the most attractive explanation for the arousal-retention interval interaction. They suggest that the effect of habituation of EDA within a list may have led to those items early in the list being classed as high-arousal words, and those items appearing late in the list being classed as low-arousal words. There is ample evidence that as the retention interval increases correct items tend to be predominantly from the first few items in the list, while at short retention intervals most items tend to be from the last few items. When taken together these facts suggest that the items late in the list tend to be classed as low-arousal words and are well recalled in the short term, the influence of recency diminishing as the retention interval increases. Items early in the list tend to be inferior to late items at short intervals, but this position is reversed as the retention interval increases. Such a view harmonizes well with data provided by Walker (1967). However, several studies (Kaplan and Kaplan, 1968; Butter, 1970) have failed to find systematic relationships between EDA and serial position which weakens any view like that of Craik and Blankstein's. It seems that unless item-arousal can be anchored to observable and manipulable variables, conclusive statements about the relationship between arousal and retention are impossible to formulate. Finally, as Craik and Blankstein (1974) point out, the theory of preservative consolidation is maladaptive: it would be more useful for an organism to remember an emotive event than to forget it.

In view of the empirical and theoretical confusion arising from these studies the practical recommendations for advertisers and propagandists are unclear. Although potentially useful, the arousal-retention interval interaction found with EDA fails to be both empirically robust and intuitively satisfying. In the remaining parts of this section there is a discussion of those studies using pupil size and electrical activity of the brain as indices of arousal. Although falling into the same general class as the EDA studies, they are primarily concerned with gaining insight into effort and anxiety as concomitants of acquisition, rehearsal and recall.

Studies employing pupil size (cf. Hess, 1972) and the EEG have typically used digit strings rather than lists of words. These studies show that memory tasks have high levels of intrinsic arousal with large swings in arousal being exhibited during the presentation of the strings. Using the EEG, Jones et al. (1979) have shown that arousal progressively increases during digit presentation and extends into the early stages of recall. They also found that when EEG arousal was high, immediate recall was poor. This finding is in line with that of Kleinsmith and Kaplan for short-term recall. However, Jones et al. prefer an interpretation based on effort and anxiety to one based on preservative consolidation. Two features of their findings inclined them toward this view. First the phenomenological description of the process of rehearsal and recall: subjects reported that as the list is heard, increasing effort is expended in rehearsing the digits. Near the end of the list the subject becomes aware of some failure to recollect an item (cf. Jones and Rhodes, in press). As a result of this retrieval failure, anxiety is increased which in turn disrupts the acquisition of later items. Second, within- and between-subject analyses suggested that the EEG reflects a subject's mastery of the task. For instance, good performers showed a smaller increase in arousal during string presentation than poor performers. Similarly, as the subjects gained more experience of the task their EEG showed a less marked increase in arousal during digit presentation.

Studies by Kahneman and his co-workers using pupil size also conclude that effort is a factor producing changes in arousal they found in short-term memory tasks (see, Kahneman, 1973, for a general review). However Kahneman suggests that in his studies the effects of task-induced anxiety are slight in comparison with those of effort. However, several studies have found anticipatory pupil responses prior to the commencement of list-learning, an effect which cannot easily be incorporated into an effort model and implicates at least some effects of anxiety (Johnson, 1971; Kahneman and Beatty, 1966; Kahneman and Wright, 1971; Kahneman et al., 1969).

In summary, studies of the psychophysiology of memory fall into two interpretative camps. The first, represented by EDA studies, relies on neurophysiological notions, where arousal is viewed as a physiological response to emotive events. The second camp is cognitive; the studies involving pupil size and EEG typify this approach with arousal being seen to arise from active engagement in the task. Findings from this latter group serve to throw into relief the special task-demand characteristics of memory tasks. Moreover they suggest that memory tasks are in themselves highly arousing. This task induced arousal may augment arousal arising from extrinsic influences, such as those from a stressful environment.

It is to these external influences that we now turn; the next section deals with arousal arising, not from the material that is being remembered, but from influences of a stressful environment.

IV. Environmental Stress

Included in this discussion are those factors which, subsumed under the heading of arousal, are particularly likely to influence efficiency at work. Again, most of the evidence is drawn from laboratory studies. This section will cover the effects of noise, heat, time of day and sleeplessness. According to Broadbent (1971) each of these factors owes its effect to its place on the arousal continuum. The direction of the effect depends on the inverted-U relationship between arousal and performance. For example, noise and sleeplessness can be placed at the two ends of the continuum: poor performance resulting from under-arousal in the case of sleeplessness and hyperarousal in the case of noise. When present in combination the deleterious effects of these two stresses is cancelled out (Wilkinson, 1963), and because their individual action is opposite, their concurrence brings the overall level of arousal to the middle of the continuum at the optimal portion of the inverted-U function. Although the precise details of the action of heat and time of day differ from those already mentioned, the underlying rationale is the same: that their effects are brought about by changes in arousal.

Noise

Noise is defined as "any unwanted sound" (Rodda, 1967). This definition is useful in that it places emphasis on the psychological nature of response to noise. A noise need not necessarily be loud for it to be annoying or distracting. However, research on the effects of noise on performance has been concentrated on the effects of loudness, and in particular on the loudness of white noise. This type of noise contains equal quantities of energy from the whole of the audible spectrum. Although white noise is not often encountered outside the laboratory, it has been employed because of its supposedly arousing properties.

Owing possibly to the ease with which noise can be applied, and no doubt due to the ecological importance of noise as a stress, research on the effects of noise on performance has blossomed in recent years with effects of noise on memory receiving a good deal of attention. Three areas of interest can be delineated. The first concerns whether noise has its effect on long- or short-term memory, or both. The second centres on the effects of noise on allocation of attention in short-term memory (STM). Finally, there is a group of studies which has examined the effects of noise on retrieval.

Results from the first of these areas have been equivocal. Some studies have suggested that noise improves immediate retention (Archer and Margolin, 1970) while others have shown an impairment (McLean, 1969) and still others have suggested that noise has no effect on immediate retention (Sloboda and Smith, 1968). Studies of long-term memory (LTM), though fewer in number, have been consistent in showing that LTM is improved by the presence of noise during the presentation of the material to be learned (Berlyne *et al.*, 1966; McLean, 1959).

Results from the second area of interest, on the allocation of attention in STM, suggest that both the beneficial and deleterious effects of noise can be reconciled by considering the subtle shifts in allocation policy within the task. Hockey and Hamilton (1970) were among the first to point out that components of a STM task can be differentially affected by noise. They studied the changes in allocation of attention to relevant and irrelevant task components. During their exposure to either noise (80dB) or quiet (55dB) subjects were shown a list of eight words, projected one at a time onto a screen. The words were presented in different corners of the screen. Subjects were initially asked to recall the words on the screen. It was only after the words were recalled that subjects were asked to indicate their appropriate location. Ordered recall scores for words of the group working in noise were superior to those of the quiet group. However, recall of locations was significantly worse in noise. These findings were interpreted as evidence for Easterbrook's (1959) view that stress produces a shift in the allocation of attention, with a move toward the high priority component of the task (word order) and away from the low priority component (locations) in noise. Similar results for STM by Davies and Jones (1975), by Fowler and Wilding (in press) and by Hockey (1970) in a non-memory task suggest that this is a general finding.

However, at least one study has shown that capacity may increase in noise. Hamilton *et al.* (1972) compared the effects of a fixed and a random recall order in a paired associate task. Subjects were presented with lists in either loud noise (85dB) or quiet (55dB). Loud noise improved recall but only when the order of items was fixed, that is, when items on the test trial were in the same order as those on the learning trial. This suggests that more order information is stored in noise and that information about links between items remains undisrupted. Daee and Wilding (1977) also found that white noise during the presentation of a word list tended to improve the recall of the original sequence. However, this was only true when the learning of position was incidental, if the learning of position was intentional there was no effect of noise. The results were complicated by the fact that the effects of noise on sequence was non-monotonic, that is, 75dB of noise produced better recall of the original sequence than either conditions of quiet, or 85dB of noise. In spite of this additional difficulty of the particular level of noise at presentation, it does seem clear that noise can produce an increase or decrease in capacity. Furthermore both types of experiment suggest that noise increases the reliance on order cues.

This predilection for order cues in noise may overall produce either beneficial or deleterious effects depending on the particular task demands. For example, Daee and Wilding found that the recall of words in categories decreased when recall in sequence increased. So, investment in order cues may detract from the categorization of material. Several studies have shown that the recall of categories is worse in noise, although it is not clear whether these effects arise from a shift to the use of order cues. For example, Hormmann and Osterkamp (1966) employed lists of words containing several categories of meaning (animals, trees, musical instruments, tools, containers and vegetables). When randomly dispersed in a list, category members tend to be recalled together in clusters (cf. Bousfield, 1953). They found that these clusters were more fragmented and poorly organized when noise was present during the task. However, these effects were limited to subjects who showed high interference scores on the Stroop test (cf. Stroop, 1935; Jensen and Rowher, 1966). More recently Smith *et al.* (in preparation) found poor clustering for the whole group of individuals which they studied. Poor categorical recall in noise may be a result of an increased tendency to favour recall in the order presented. Alternatively, increasing the investment of resources in remembering order information may also detract from deeper levels of processing which would aid clustered recall. This last view is compatible with that of Dornic (1973) who proposed that noise, like any other method of increasing task difficulty, increases the chances that subjects "parrot back" lists and forego a deeper level of analysis. These various suggestions, particularly the one which speculates that increased use of order cues disrupts categorical recall, obviously require further testing.

So far this section has largely dealt with the effects of noise at input, but there are a number of studies which show that noise can produce effects at retrieval. One study by Schwartz (1973) suggests that noise may affect retrieval strategies. In this experiment subjects listened to short stories each containing four characters, two of whose names were common while the other two were rare. Subjects heard the stories either with no added noise, with low noise (65dB), or with loud noise (85dB). The results were analysed in a decision theory framework: d' giving an index of the sensitivity and β as a measure of the decision criterion (cf. Swets, 1964). Under the no-noise condition subjects employed a cautious criterion for the recall of rare names and a more risky criterion for the recall of common names. Criteria for both rare and common names moved more closely together as the noise level increased. Accompanying this shift in criterion was an increase in sensitivity (d'), with common names being better recalled in noise. While the results of this study suggest that noise may influence retrieval through changes in both sensitivity and criterion placement, a recent replication suggests that noise only produces effects in criterion placement. Part of Schwartz's (1974) procedure involved the auditory presentation of material in noise and it is possible that the d' changes that he found were due to masking of the passage by loud noise. In the replication reported by Thomas (1978) visual presentation was used, with the result that the convergence of values was again found, but this time without a corresponding effect on d'.

Noise induced arousal may produce an effect at either acquisition or retrieval. A detailed examination of noise effects has shown that arousal may produce subtle shifts in processing. Depending on the demands of the task, noise can produce beneficial or deleterious effects. A consistent finding is that memory for order is improved in noise and it may be that this shift toward ordered recall detracts from higher-level memory coding. In any case, these effects occur at relatively low levels of noise, in the region of 80dB.

Heat

Heat ranks second only to noise in its prevalence as an environmental factor producing psychological effects. The human operator is often exposed to extremes of heat arising from some industrial process (such as smelting) or heat produced as an inevitable byproduct of the activity of machines. Factors such as inadequately ventilated buildings, poorly governed heating systems and radiation from sunlight, also conspire to produce mild forms of heat stress.

Two factors lead to discomfort by heat: dry air temperature and humidity. A recent study by Allen and Fischer (1978) on the effects of warmth on paired-associate learning suggests that it is the level of humidity alone that impairs memory. On the other hand, in a study where humidity was held constant, Wing and Touchstone (1965) found effects of temperature, with levels above 32 °C producing a significant impairment in the learning of word lists. Clearly a careful empirical comparison of humidity and air temperature as they affect memory is required.

The picture of the action of heat is further complicated by the fact that duration of exposure is a vital factor in shaping the effects of heat on performance. Poulton and Kerslake (1965) propose that subjects go through a series of stages in their physiological response to heat which are reflected in performance. There is an initial stimulating effect of warmth producing an increase in arousal level which accounts for the improved efficiency they found in a perceptual task. A second stage corresponds to the time at which body temperature rises. Here arousal level falls, with a consequent deterioration in performance. The third and fourth stages of response to heat occur as a result of marked increases in body temperature. In the third stage arousal increases, producing improved performance, while in the fourth stage perform- ance deteriorates before giving way to a state of collapse.

In an unpublished study, Jones and Irving attempted to plot the course of memory changes due to heat as a function of exposure. They employed two levels of environmental warmth, 21°C and 30°C, in combination with two lengths of exposure, 5 minutes and 40 minutes. The exposure durations were designed to tap the first two stages delineated by Poulton and Kerslake. The task involved the free recall of lists containing categorizable words. This task offers two indices of the efficiency of memory: first, an index of retention (in the form of the number of words recalled) and second, an index of organization in memory (in the form of the cohesiveness of categorical recall). In order to check on the subjects' state of arousal, Jones and Irving required subjects to fill out a mood-adjective check-list (cf. Nowlis, 1966). After short exposures, high temperatures adversely affected performance in the form of the number of items recalled from a list. Long exposures to high temperatures produced a beneficial effect, in this case on the organization of categories in recall. Data from mood ratings show that short exposures to heat produce an increase in arousal and that long exposures are de-arousing.

Poor performance at short arousing exposures and improved per- formance at the long de-arousing exposures fits neatly with the Kleinsmith and Kaplan data for short-term recall. However the data for heat are not consistent with those of Poulton and Kerslake, who used a perceptual task. They found that performance was improved by short exposures to heat and that long exposures made performance worse. In other words, the effects for memory are in the opposite direction to those for non-memory tasks.

Like noise, heat can produce positive or negative effects on retention. Detrimental effects on memory have been found above 30°C although this effect may be restricted to exposures of less than 40 minutes.

Time of Day and Shift Work

Ebbinghaus (1885) was among the first to provide empirical data about memory performance as a function of time of day. He found that his performance was better in the morning, which led him to conclude that:

"in the later hours of the day mental receptivity and vigour are less" (p. 66). The evidence gathered since that time has tended to confirm Ebbinghaus' empirical evidence but not his interpretation.

Early studies of time of day effects were concerned with the practical question of which time of day was best for the retention of material in a classroom setting. For example, Winch (1912a,b) found consistent evidence of morning superiority, but these studies are characterized by relatively small groups of subjects, with infrequent sampling, and inadequate controls for practice effects. Over half a century passed before the next substantial study of memory and time of day by Blake (1967). In this study subjects performed a battery of tasks at five times between 8 a.m. and 9 p.m. Of the eight tasks which Blake employed the five which showed a general *improvement* over the day were non-memory tasks. In contrast, STM for digits was found to be better in the morning than in the evening. Blake regards this paradoxical effect of time of day on memory as being due to either an inverse relationship between memory and arousal, with arousal being greater in the evening, or a direct effect of body temperature on the process of consolidation. Recent evidence by Jones *et al.* (in press, Experiment 3) indicates that the former explanation may be true. They found that memory performance was best in the morning when EEG arousal was at its lowest.

Studies since Blake's have tended to confirm the trend of morning superiority in memory tasks. For example, Baddeley *et al.* (1970) using a digit span task assessed STM performance twice a day: between 9 a.m. and 11 a.m. and between 3 p.m. and 5 p.m. Immediate retention of the digit sequences was superior in the morning. Thus memory performance is best in the morning when arousal is low. High arousal in the evening brings about better non-memory performance when short-term retention is at its nadir.

Folkard *et al.* (1977) returned to the educational setting used by the early workers and investigated both immediate and delayed recall of a story learned at either 9 a.m. or 3 p.m. They, too, found data consistent with those of Blake: children who listened to a story at 9 a.m. obtained higher immediate memory scores than those who listened to the story at 3 p.m. Folkard *et al.*, in examining the effect of the delayed task, took care not to confound the time of presentation with the time of recall. The design allowed the comparison of delayed recall to be made at the same or different time of day to the presentation. The data from delayed recall showed that children who were read the story at 3 p.m. exhibited better recall performance than those who read it at 9 a.m. This afternoon superiority of delayed recall was unaffected by the time of day at which recall was made, which suggests that time of day influences the acquisition of material rather than its retrieval.

In one of the few studies which has examined the effects of shift systems on STM, Folkard *et al.* (1976) systematically varied the memory load during an extensive study of the periodicity of memory function in two individuals. The subjects lived in the laboratory for some 18 days where they were subjected to a rapidly rotating 2–2–2 shift system which entailed an initial 2-day rest period, 2 days on a morning shift, 2 days on an evening shift and 2 days on a night shift. This cycle of events was repeated twice with the last 2 days of the experiment being rest days. The direction of the time-of-day effects was crucially dependent on the memory loading. With a low memory load, performance was at a minimum early in the day reaching a maximum at approximately 8 p.m. However, with a high memory load this trend was reversed, showing a maximum at 4 a.m. and a minimum at 4 p.m. Again, these data harmonize with those of Blake (1967) in finding that as memory load increases there is a tendency towards morning superiority.

Despite instances to the contrary (Adams; 1973) Jones *et al.*, 1978b) the weight of the evidence indicates that morning superiority is the usual trend for STM tasks. Blake's approach of employing a battery of psychological tasks has been particularly illuminating by showing that memory tasks tend to show the opposite effect to non-memory tasks. It is tempting to conclude that memory is inversely related to arousal, with arousal increasing throughout the day, while the performance of non-memory tasks is directly related to arousal. This temptation should be resited on two counts: firstly, mental arithmetic, though showing evening superiority, contains a major memory component; secondly, the memory task employed by Blake was shorter, more paced and contained more intrinsic knowledge of results than any of the non-memory tasks employed. Similarly, any study, like that of Folkard *et al.* (1976), which attempts to vary the memory load in a task, runs the risk of confounding load with task difficulty.

Aside from these interpretative difficulties it is clear that in practical terms memory is better early in the day. Furthermore, memory performance is best at a time when other tasks are performed badly. This last trend also appeared in the effects of heat and is in line with some of the effects to be reviewed in the next section.

Sleep Deprivation

Allied to the effects of time of day are those of sleep deprivation. If the individual is deprived of sleep it is often at a time of day when the normal level of arousal is low. The study of sleep deprivation is of outstanding practical importance since the loss of sleep is usually encountered in occupations where critical tasks have to be performed (in hospitals, for example) and alertness is thus at a premium (see Poulton *et al.*, 1968). Wilkinson (1964) notes that for a task to be vulnerable to sleeplessness they must be both complex and uninteresting. From what follows it seems that experimenters have unerringly aimed to fulfil these criteria.

The effects of sleeplessness have been studied in two ways. First, the retroactive effect of sleep: initial learning is the same for all groups, the main variable of interest being the degree of wakefulness between initial learning and retrieval. Second, the proactive effect of sleep: learning and retrieval take place after some sleep loss.

Studies falling into the first class have examined whether sleep aids recall by effectively removing the subject from interfering activity. Events experienced in the waking state, between learning and recall, are thought to interfere with information held in storage (cf. Postman and Underwood, 1973). Interference is less during sleep therefore forgetting should be diminished. Several studies have demonstrated that there is less forgetting over a period of sleep than after wakefulness (e.g. Jenkins and Dallenbach, 1924; Lovatt and Warr, 1968), which has been generally taken as support for the view that forgetting is due to interference. However, there are several alternative interpretations of these data which have yet to be dismissed, one possibility is that deprivation of sleep lowers arousal, which in turn produces a retrieval deficit.

Not withstanding this interpretative dilemma, it is well established that sleep has a beneficial effect on recall. This only appears to be true for night-time sleep; daytime sleep does not confer the same advantage (Hockey *et al.*, 1972). Moreover, the beneficial effects depend on the qualitative nature of sleep. Interest has centred on two types of sleep: Stage 4 (or slow-wave sleep), predominating in the early part of the night, and REM sleep (usually accompanied on waking by reports of dreaming). Empson and Clarke (1970), selectively deprived subjects of REM sleep (with the consequence that the amount of stage 4 sleep increased) and found recall to be poorer than for controls. This contrasts with the results of Yaroush *et al.* (1971) who found *reduced* forgetting after sleep in the first half of the night where stage 4 predominated. No reduction in forgetting was found after sleep in the second half of the night where REM sleep is usually prevalent. Unfortunately this study confounds sleep loss with the time of night when recall took place, and in addition, no clear distinction can be made between explanations relying on interference and arousal.

Usually, the proactive effects of sleep are also beneficial. Williams *et al.* (1959) found that in a task requiring subjects to remember the answers to a list of questions produced ten minutes earlier, recall declined progressively after 28 hours of sleeplessness. They propose that the effects of sleeplessness can be attributed to attentional lapses. This view gains support from a later study by Williams *et al.* (1966) who found that a picture recognition task showed no effect of 24 hours of sleeplessness when the initial learning took place under normal conditions. There remains the possibility that in requiring long-term recognition, this task might be qualitatively different to the other studies. However, recent data tends to confirm the lapse hypothesis: Polzella (1975) for instance, viewed the deficits he found in a probe recognition task as being consistent with: ". . . periods of lowered reactive capacity, which prevent the encoding of items in short term memory" (p. 194).

Results of another type of experiment within the class of proactive studies suggest that the capacity to learn and remember is *reduced* in the period shortly after awaking. Again the extent of this deficit appears to depend on the stage of sleep from which the subject is awakened. Stones (1977) compared retention in subjects who had either no prior sleep or were awoken from non-REM (stage 2 or deeper) sleep or REM sleep. Measures of retention were taken at both immediate and delayed (20 min) test, in a task involving categorical recall. In the REM and non-REM groups subjects slept for less than two hours in all. Subjects in the non-REM group produced poorer performance, in terms of the number of categories recalled, than the other two groups. This effect appeared at both times of testing. The no-prior-sleep and REM-awakened groups were strikingly similar in showing almost perfect performance at both retention intervals. This high level of performance may have produced a ceiling effect, concealing a real difference between the two groups. Recall in terms of the mean number of items per category was near the maximum, but again scores in the non-REM groups were worse. However, this time the deleterious effect of non-REM sleep was restricted to delayed recall.

The form of these data suggests some qualitative differences in the effect of non-REM awakening between times of test: the immediate test shows that categories are adequately recalled, but category instances are not, implicating an encoding deficit; in the delayed condition, recall of both categories and category instances show an effect, which suggests a retrieval deficit. Stones (1977) suggests that non-REM awakening has a direct and specific effect on memory in immediate recall, and that at delayed recall, performance is a function of the subject's low level of arousal. While the first point needs more empirical verification, the second is in conflict with the findings already reviewed. Evidence from conditions of low arousal (such as long exposures to heat) suggests that categorical recall is improved by low arousal. Furthermore, deficits in categorical recall, like the one found by Stones, are usually a result of heightened arousal as is the case with noise. However these data, along with others (e.g. Stones, 1973) suggest that short periods of sleep can be damaging to retention.

One study, in which subjects were deprived of sleep by delaying retirement, found that quite long periods of sleeplessness have a beneficial effect on memory. Hamilton *et al.* (1972) investigated the effects of sleep deprivation on three tasks: vigilance for tones, mental arithmetic and a running digit-span test. Sleep deprivation was brought about by delaying retirement, a technique which avoids the confounding of time of day with sleep deprivation. In addition Hamilton *et al.* observed the cumulative effect of sleep loss over 4 days. Subjects who slept for $7\frac{1}{2}$ hours showed a gradual improvement of the parameter d' (used as an index of detection efficiency) over the 4 days. The result of 4 hours' sleep was to diminish the rate of improvement of detection efficiency. In the calculations test, the effects of sleep deprivation were cumulative, with the 4 hours' sleep condition showing a progressively larger deficit as the days passed. The digit-span task showed the opposite effect to that found for calculations. They found that 4 hours' sleep gave *best* performance. In this case the magnitude of the difference between deprivation conditions, though modest, was significant. Moreover, there seemed to be no cumulative effect of sleep deprivation on memory performance as a result of successive days of deprivation.

Thus far there have been several instances where arousal produces opposite effects in memory tasks to those found on "non-memory" tasks. This trend appeared for heat, time of day and sleep deprivation. It is far from clear why memory is related to arousal in this way. One possibility is that memory tasks produce high levels of intrinsic arousal, and that this source of arousal augments arousal from environmental sources. Memory tasks tend to involve more pacing and contain more intrinsic knowledge of failure than "non-memory" tasks. In normal circumstances, these factors may produce a heightened state of arousal which may be above the optimum level on the inverted-U curve. The beneficial effect of sleep deprivation on memory can be explained by supposing that the subjects' state of low arousal, is augmented by task-induced arousal, bringing the *overall* level of arousal up to an optimum. States of low arousal (such as those found in the morning or after long exposures to heat) benefit from arousal added by the task. Environmental conditions producing high arousal, in conjunction with task-induced arousal, produce hyperarousal with a consequent deterioration in performance. This may go some way to explaining why, for example, memory performance can be disrupted by low levels of noise. This view is obviously speculative and has some difficulty in encompassing the detailed effects of environmental sources of arousal on recall in, for instance, noise.

V. Conclusions

Memory is easily disrupted by extremes of stress. This is particularly true when the material to be remembered forms part of an escape procedure or an essential correcting action.

The memory load should be reduced to a minimum in tasks which may have to be performed under extremes of stress. This can be achieved in two ways: first, by overlearning or "automatizing" the skill, and second, by capitalizing on the well-learned habits and expectations of the relevant population. Immunity to stress may be achieved by training, using adequate simulation. Ideally, simulation should attempt to mimic all aspects of a stressfull environment.

Evidence on the retention of arousing *material* is equivocal. There is some indication that recall of highly arousing material, though worse in the short term, may be significantly improved in the long term. However, more research is needed on this topic, particularly with materials that are ecologically representative. Environmental influences, inducing relatively small changes in arousal, may bring about changes in memory performance. There is some evidence (particularly from the case of noise) that memory is particularly susceptible to disruption at quite modest levels. It is unclear whether this sensitivity is due to the effect of stress on memory tasks or on memory systems. Stress may bring about quite subtle changes in the allocation of attention. Thus, effects may be beneficial or deleterious depending on the demands of the task.

Stressful environments may produce specific effects: (a) Noise produces effects at acquisition and retrieval, with the consistent finding that memory for order is improved by noise. Effects may be found at levels as low as 75dB. (b) The effect of heat depends on the duration of exposure; short exposures are arousing, producing poor recall, whereas long exposures have a soporific effect which improves some aspects of retention. (c) The effect of time of day is crucially dependent on memory loading. Memory performance appears to be best in the morning. (d) Sleep loss acts retroactively and proactively. In the retroactive mode sleep is beneficial. The proactive effects depend on the length of sleep deprivation. Short periods of sleeplessness can have beneficial effects. However, long periods of sleep loss can be damaging, possibly by increasing the frequency of attentional lapses.

Acknowledgement

Thanks are due to Hugh Foot and Tony Chapman for useful discussions on this chapter.

References

Adams, A. H. (1973). Time of day effects of short-term memory. *Royal Aircraft Establishment Technical Memorandum.* HFG 122.

Allen, M. A. and Fischer, G. J. (1978). Ambient temperature effects on paired associate learning. *Ergonomics* **21**, 95–102.

Archer, B. U. and Margolin, R. R. (1970). Arousal effects in intentional recall and forgetting. *J. exp. Psychol.* **86**, 8–12.

Baddeley, A. D. (1972). Selective attention and performance in dangerous environments. *Br. J. Psychol.* **63**, 537–546.

Baddeley, A. D. (1976). "The Psychology of Memory." Academic Press, London and New York.

Baddeley, A. D., Hatter, J. E., Scott, D. and Snashall, A. (1970). Memory and time of day. *Br. J. Psychol.* **22**, 605–609.

Berkun, M. M. (1964). Performance decrement under psychological stress. *Human Factors* **6**, 21–30.

Berkun, M. M., Bialek, H. M., Kern, R. P. and Yagi, K. (1962). Experimental studies of psychological stress in man. *Psychol. Monogr.* **76**, Whole number 534.

Berlyne, D. E., Borsa, D. M., Hamacher, J. H. and Koenig, I. D. V. (1966). Paired associate learning and the timing of arousal. *J. exp. Psychol.* **72**, 1–6.

Blake, M. J. F. (1967). Time of day effects on performance in a range of tasks. *Psychonomic Sci.* **9**, 349–350.

Bousfield, W. A. (1953). The occurrence of clustering in recall of randomly arranged associates. *J. gen. Psychol.* **49**, 229–240.

Broadbent, D. E. (1971). "Decision and Stress." Academic Press, London and New York.

Butter, M. J. (1970). Differential recall of paired associates as a function of arousal and concreteness—imagery levels. *J. exp. Psychol.* **84**, 252–256.

Craik, F. I. M. and Blankstein, K. R. (1974). Psychophysiology and Human Memory. *In* "Research in Psychophysiology" (P. H. Venables and M. J. Christie, Eds). Wiley, London.

Daee, S. and Wilding, J. M. (1977). Effects of high intensity white noise on short-term memory for position in a list and sequence. *Br. J. Psychol.* **68**, 335–349.

Davies, D. R. and Jones, D. M. (1975). The effects of noise and incentive upon attention in short-term memory. *Br. J. Psychol.* **66**, 61–68.

Dornic, S. (1973). Order error in attended and unattended tasks. *In* "Attention and Performance" (P. M. A. Rabbitt and S. Dornic, Eds). Vol. 5. pp. 119–125. Academic Press, London, and New York.

Easterbrook, J. A. (1959). The effect of emotion on cue utilization and the organization of behaviour. *Psychol. Rev.* **66**, 183–201.

Ebbinghaus, H. (1885). "Memory." Republished in translation (1964). Dover, New York.

Edelberg, R. (1972). Electrical activity of the skin: its measurement and uses in psychophysiology. *In* "Handbook of Psychophysiology" (N. S. Greenfield and R. A. Sternbach, Eds). pp. 367–409. Holt, Rinehart and Winston, London.

Eich, J. E., Weingartner, H., Stillman, R. C. and Gillin, J. C. (1975). State-dependent accessibility of retrieval cues in the retention of categorized lists. *J. Verb. Learn. Verb. Behav.* **14**, 408–417.

Empson, J. A. C. and Clarke, P. R. F. (1970). Rapid eye movements and remembering. *Nature* **227**, 287–288.

Epstein, S. and Fenz, W. D. (1965). Steepness of approach and avoidance gradients in humans as a function of experience: theory and experiment. *J. exp. Psychol.* **70**, 1–13.

Folkard, S., Knauth, P., Monk, T. H. and Rutenfranz, J. (1976). The effect of memory load on the circadian variation in performance under a rapidly rotating shift system. *Ergonomics* **19**, 479–488.

Folkard, S., Monk, T. H., Bradbury, R. and Rosenthall, J. (1977). Time of day effects in school children's immediate and delayed recall of meaningful material. *Br. J. Psychol.* **68**, 45–50.

Fowler, D. J. H. and Wilding, J. M. Differential effects of noise and incentives on learning. *Br. J. Psychol.* (in press.)

Godden, D. R. and Baddeley, A. D. (1975). Context-dependent memory in two natural environments: on land and underwater. *Br. J. Psychol.* **66**, 325–332.

Greenspoon, J. and Ranyard, R. (1957). Stimulus conditions and retroactive inhibition. *J. exp. Psychol.* **53**, 55–59.

Haber, R. N. (1969). "Information-Processing Approaches to Visual Perception." Holt, Rinehart and Winston, London.

Hamilton, P., Hockey, G. R. J. and Quinn, J. G. (1972). Information selection, arousal and memory. *Br. J. Psychol.* **63**, 181–189.

Hamilton, P., Wilkinson, R. T. and Edwards, R. S. (1972). A study of four days partial sleep deprivation. *In* "Aspects of Human Efficiency: Diurnal Rhythm and low of sleep" (W. P. Colquhoun, Ed.). English Universities Press, London.

Hammerton, M. and Tickner, A. H. (1968). An investigation into the effects of stress upon skilled performance. *Ergonomics* **12**, 851–855.

Hebb, D. O. (1955). Drives and the CNS (Conceptual Nervous System). *Psychol. Rev.* **62**, 243–254.

Hess, E. H. (1972). Pupillometrics: A method of studying mental, emotional, and sensory processes. *In* "Handbook of Psychophysiology" (N. S. Greenfield and R. A. Sternbach, Eds). pp. 491–527. Holt, Rinehart and Winston, London.

Hockey, G. R. J. (1970). Signal probability and spatial location as possible bases for increased selectivity in noise. *Q. J. exp. Psychol.* **22**, 37–42.

Hockey, G. R. J. and Hamilton, P. (1970). Arousal and information selection in short-term memory. *Nature* **226**, 866–867.

Hockey, G. R. J., Davies, S. and Gray, M. M. (1972). Forgetting as a function of sleep at different times of day. *Q. J. exp. Psychol.* **24**, 386–393.

Hormann, H. and Osterkamp, V. (1966). Uber den einfluss von kontinuier-lichem larm auf die organisation von gedachtnisinhalten. *Zeitschrift fuer Experimentelle und Angewandte Psychologie* **13**, 31–38.

Jenkins, J. G. and Dallenbach, K. M. (1924). Obliviscence during sleep and waking. *Am. J. Psychol.* **35**, 605–612.

Jensen, A. R. and Rowher, W. D. (1966). The Stroop colour-word test: A review. *Acta Psychol.* **25**, 36–93.

Johnson, D. A. (1971). Pupillary responses during a short-term memory task. *J. exp. Psychol.* **90**, 311–318.

Jones, D. M. and Irving, M. (In preparation). Effects of length of exposure to environmental warmth upon category clustering and subjective estimates of mood.

Jones, D. M. and Rhodes, R. (In press). Short-term memory and the EEG: effects of instructions to rehearse. *Biol. Psychol.*

Jones, D. M., Davies, D. R., Hogan, K. M., Patrick, J. and Cumberbatch, W. G. (1978a). Short-term memory during the normal working day. *In* "Practical Aspects of Memory" (M. M. Gruneberg, P. E. Morris and R. N. Sykes, Eds). Academic Press, London and New York.

Jones, D. M., Lewis, M. J. and Spriggs, B. (1978b). The effects of low doses of diazepam on human performance in group administered tasks. *Br. J. Clin. Pharmac.* **6**, 333–337.

Jones, D. M., Gale, M. A. and Smallbone, A. (1979). Short-term recall of 9-digit strings and the EEG. *Br. J. Psychol.* **70**, 97–119.

Kahneman, D. (1973). "Attention and Effort." Prentice Hall, London.

Kahneman, D. and Beatty, J. (1966). Pupil diameter and load on memory. *Science* **154**, 1583–1585.

Kahneman, D., Tursky, B., Shapiro, D. and Crider, A. (1969). Pupillary strategies in a short-term memory task. *Q. J. exp. Psychol.* **23**, 187–196.

Kahneman, D., Tursky, B., Shapiro, D. and Crider, A. (1969). Pupillary, heart rate, and skin resistance changes during a mental task. *J. exp. Psychol.* **79**, 164–167.

Kaplan, S. and Kaplan, R. (1968). Arousal and memory: a comment. *Psychonomic Sci.* **10**, 291–292.

Kleinsmith, L. J. and Kaplan, S. (1963). Paired-associate learning as a function of arousal and interpolated interval. *J. exp. Psychol.* **65**, 190–193.

Kleinsmith, L. J. and Kaplan, S. (1964). Interaction of arousal and recall interval in nonsense syllable paired-associate learning. *J. exp. Psychol.* **67**, 124–126.

Levonian, E. (1967). Retention of information in relation to arousal during continuously presented material. *Am. educ. Res.* **4**, 103–116.

Levonian, E. (1968). Short-term retention in relation to arousal. *Psychophysiology* **4**, 284–293.

Lovatt, D. J. and Warr, P. B. (1968). Recall after sleep. *Am. J. Psychol.* **81**, 253–257.

Maltzman, I., Kantor, W. and Langdon, B. (1966). Immediate and delayed retention, arousal, and the orienting and defensive reflex. *Psychonomic Sci.* **6**, 445–446.

McLean, P. D. (1969). Induced arousal and time of recall as determinants of paired-associate recall. *Br. J. Psychol.* **60**, 57–62.

Mira, E. (1944). "Psychiatry in War." Chapman and Hall, London.

Norman, D. A. (1976). "Memory and Attention." Wiley, London.

Nowlis, V. (1966). Research with the Mood Adjective Check List. *In* "Affect, Cognition, and Personality" (S. S. Tomkins and C. E. Izard, Eds). Tavistock, London.

Orne, M. T. (1962). On the social psychology of the psychological experiment: with particular reference to demand characteristics and their implications. *Am. Psychol.* **17**, 776–783.

Polzella, D. J. (1975). Effects of sleep deprivation on short-term recognition memory. *J. exp. Psychol: Human Learning and Memory* **104**, 194–200.

Postman, L. and Underwood, B. J. (1973). Critical issues in interference theory. *Memory and Cognition* **1**, 19–40.

Poulton, E. C. and Kerslake, D. Mck. (1965). Initial stimulating effect of warmth upon perceptual efficiency. *Aerospace Med.* **36**, 29–32.

Poulton, E. C., Hunt, G. M., Carpenter, A. and Edwards, R. S. (1978). The performance of junior hospital doctors following reduced sleep and long hours of work. *Ergonomics* **21**, 279–295.

Rodda, M. (1967). "Noise in Society." Oliver and Boyd, London.

Schwartz, S. (1974). Arousal and recall: effects of noise on two retrieval strategies. *J. exp. Psychol.* **102**, 896–899.

Sloboda, W. and Smith, E. E. (1968). Disruption effects in human short-term memory: some negative findings. *Percept. Mot. Skills* **27**, 575–582.

Sternthal, B. and Craig, C. S. (1974). Fear appeals: revisited and revised. *J. Consum. Res.* **1**, 22–34.

Stones, M. J. (1973). The effect of prior sleep on rehearsal, recoding and memory. *Br. J. Psychol.* **64**, 537–543.

Stones, M. J. (1977). Memory performance after arousal from different sleep stages. *Br. J. Psychol.* **68**, 177–181.

Stroop, J. R. (1935). Studies of interference in serial verbal reactions. *J. exp. Psychol.* **18**, 643–662.

Swets, J. A. (Eds) (1964). "Signal Detection and Recognition by Human Observers." Wiley, London.

Thomas, R. (1978). Memory in noise. *In* "Practical Aspects of Memory" (M. M. Gruneberg, P. E. Morris and R. N. Sykes, Eds). Academic Press, London and New York.

Tulving, E. and Thompson, D. M. (1973). Encoding specificity and retrieval processes in episodic memory. *Psychol. Rev.* **80**, 352–373.

Walker, E. L. (1958). Action decrement and its relation to learning. *Psychol. Rev.* **65**, 129–142.

Walker, E. L. (1967). Arousal and the memory trace. *In* "The Organisation of Recall" (D. Kimble, Ed.). Academy of Sciences, New York.

Walker, N. K. and Burkhart, J. F. (1965). The combat effectiveness of various human operator controlled systems. *Proc. 17th Military Operations Research Symposium.*

Weber, S. J. and Cook, T. D. (1972). Subject effects in laboratory research: an examination of subject roles, demand characteristics, and valid inference. *Psychol. Bull.* **77**, 273–295.

Weingartner, H., Adefris, W., Eich, J. E. and Murphy, D. L. (1976). Encoding-imagery specificity in alcohol state-dependent learning. *J. exp. Psychol: Human Learning and Memory* **2**, 83–87.

Wilkinson, R. T. (1963). Aftereffect of sleep deprivation. *J. exp. Psychol.* **66**, 439–442.

Wilkinson, R. T. (1964). Effects of up to 60 hours' sleep deprivation on different types of work. *Ergonomics* **7**, 175–186.

Williams, H. L., Lubin, A. and Goodnow, J. J. (1959). Impaired performance and acute sleep loss. *Psychol. Monogr.* **73**, Whole number 484.

Williams, H. L., Gieseking, C. G. and Lubin, A. (1966). Some effects of sleep loss on memory. *Percept. Mot. Skills* **23**, 1287–1293.

Winch, W. H. (1912a). Mental fatigue in day school children as measured by immediate memory. Part 1. *J. educ. Psychol.* **3**, 18–23.

Winch, W. H. (1912b). Mental fatigue in day school children as measured by immediate memory. Part 2. *J. educ. Psychol.* **3**, 75–82.

Wing, J. F. and Touchstone, R. M. (1965). The effects of high ambient temperature on short-term memory. *Aerospace Medical Research Labs Report* Wright Patterson AFB, Report: AMRL-TR-65-103.

Yaroush, R., Sullivan, M. J. and Ekstrand, B. R. (1971). Effect of sleep on memory, II: Differential effect of the first and second half of the night. *J. exp. Psychol.* **88**, 361–366.

8. Memory for Skill

J. ANNETT

*Department of Psychology,
University of Warwick, UK*

I. Introduction

It is a commonsense observation that, having once learned, one never forgets how to swim. The same generalization would seem to fit everyday experience with a whole range of motor skills such as riding a bicycle, playing games and performing on musical instruments. One might at first be a shade "rusty" but with a little practice the old skill returns. Whether memory for motor skills is better than memory for words, scenes or events is a question to which we shall return shortly but since most of the literature on memory concerns verbal memory some of the similarities and differences must be noted. It is true to say that until fairly recently there was very little cross-referring between the fields of verbal and motor learning and the two research traditions have developed almost independently working with their own characteristic experimental methods.

Many of the basic techniques for studying memory were established by Ebbinghaus in 1885 and only a few years later (Woodworth, 1899, Bryan and Harter, 1897, 1899) some of the first systematic studies of motor skills were carried out. Although the acquisition and retention of motor skills has received only a fraction of the attention accorded to "ideational" learning a steady trickle of work, swelled by the occasional burst of interest in particular tasks and problems, has accumulated into a substantial, if occasionally murky, pool of empirical findings. Bourdin (1901) was reported by Swift (1905) to have found very high levels of retention for motor skills and Swift (1905, 1906, 1910) in a classic series of studies with juggling and typewriting showed apparently very little loss of skill over a year without practice. Figures 1 and 2 show Swift's results with typewriting and juggling respectively. In Fig. 1 the right-hand curve shows the original learning which was completed on Christmas Day, 1903, whilst the steeper curve to the left shows the relearning trials which began just over two years later in January, 1906.

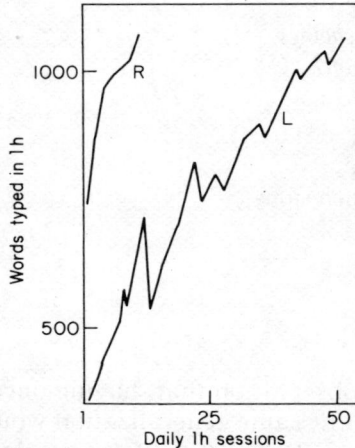

Fig. 1. Learning (L) and relearning (R) curves for typewriting. After Swift, 1906.

The juggling consisted of "Keeping two balls going with one hand, one being caught while the other was in the air". The score in Fig. 2 is the number of catches per ten misses. The lower curve shows the original learning in 1902 over 45 daily trials whilst the steeply rising curve shows the relearning beginning 6 years and 17 days later in 1907. The obvious feature of both sets of data is that the original skill is very rapidly relearned and even surpassed after long periods without practice. Hill (1914) followed up Swift's work with studies of mirror drawing and letter substitution confirming both Swift's findings and Thorndike's expectations of "the superiority of sensori-motor functions for permanence". The implied comparison with verbal learning became the principal matter of theoretical interest in the 1920s and 1930s (see for example Irion's review, 1969). By 1951 Hovland reviewing learning and retention, reported that motor skills are (1) retained with little loss but (2) that the source of this superior retention was unknown and (3) that not enough studies had been done to permit the specification of reliable retention curves. The 1950s brought increased activity in the field of skills, particularly due to the number of studies of military training and partly because of the pursuit rotor which turned out to be a convenient vehicle for studying some important aspects of C. L. Hull's theory of learning.

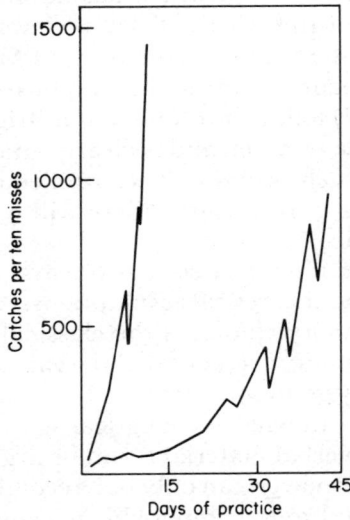

Fig. 2. Learning (L) and relearning (R) curves for juggling. Labelling of curves as in Fig. 1. After Swift, 1910.

The first systematic review devoted exclusively to the retention of skill was carried out by J. C. Naylor and G. E. Briggs for the Aerospace Medical Laboratories of the USAF at Dayton, Ohio, in 1961. This was the era of the "Sputnik scare" and the beginning of the race to the moon when research on training in the sophisticated aerospace technologies received a sudden boost. The Naylor and Briggs review was critical of the general quality of earlier work but as well as repeating the more obvious generalizations proposed "task organization" as a major basic variable underlying differences in retention. This same variable was suggested by Naylor (1962) as relevant to the part/whole learning controversy (see Chapter 2).

Adams (1967) included a whole chapter on motor response recall in his text on "Human Memory" and found the early work conceptually impoverished. He too recorded the classical findings of good motor retention and suggested that motor responses may be less susceptible to interference than verbal responses. Bilodeau's (1969) review, commenting on the lack of a generally valid forgetting curve (because motor skills are not readily forgotten) went on to produce a two-stage theory of motor forgetting following the work by Bilodeau and Levy (1964) on the basis of single learning trials with a simple lever positioning response.

Among the more recent reviews, Schmidt (1972) and Stelmach (1974) exemplify a new interest which has developed in recent years amongst physical educationalists. Their reviews, which are mainly concerned with short-term motor memory (STMM), concentrate on the acquisition of elementary positioning responses. A review by Gardlin and Sitterley (1972) follows up Naylor and Briggs but with a strong emphasis on aerospace research and is clearly aimed at the problem of the retention of skills such as manually controlled re-entry at the end of extended space flights during which there will have been little or no opportunity for practice.

The literature, spreading over so many years, encompasses a wide range of techniques and theoretical assumptions. A basic design in both verbal and motor memory studies is the classical three phase experiment of initial learning, retention interval and retention test. Experimenters usually go to some lengths to ensure that their subjects are naive with respect to what is being learned, and although this is difficult enough with verbal material it can be argued that, at least for adults, no motor skill is new, it can only be a recombination of sub-skills which already exist and so it is impossible to establish a true baseline for learning. This is important when it comes to the study of retention, for Jost's law states that if two associations are of equal strength but of different ages, the older will lose strength more slowly with the further passage of time. In practice most experimenters have just ignored this problem, but in comparing verbal and motor memory the degree or the "age" of the initial learning should be controlled.

The retention interval can vary from seconds to years and may be filled with specified or unspecified activities. In most experiments the best that can be hoped for is that subjects will not have rehearsed the specific skills involved in the experiment. Some experiments deliberately introduce interpolated training. If this is intended to promote learning it is usually termed rehearsal but in some experiments tasks or material are introduced with the aim of interfering with retention, that is to produce retroactive interference with the original learning. Measures of retention can take many forms. In most studies the task and the method of scoring are identical to that employed in the original learning but in transfer studies, for example, where training is given on a simulator which may not perfectly mimic the final task, there could be discrepancies even in the method of scoring.

Obviously, if retention interval duration is to be a variable in the experiment, separate groups of subjects will have to be used for different intervals since almost any form of retesting is likely to involve an unknown degree of relearning. This naturally increases the problems associated with sample size and the matching of groups. Furthermore, it means that retention curves are composite with different subjects at different intervals. As in most learning experiments, independent group designs are to be preferred to the more economical repeated measures designs, often resulting in the need for large numbers of subjects.

In verbal memory studies generally one has a choice of recognition or recall tests but in motor skills one is clearly confined to recall or, more properly, reconstruction, which is attempting to perform the task under standard conditions. Assuming the measurement technique remains constant the simplest measure of retention is the absolute or relative performance difference between the last trial of original learning and the first post-retention-interval trial. However, if the trials are short, scores tend to be statistically unreliable whilst if they are long, then additional learning will take place during the retention trials. For this reason most investigations involve relearning and, if this relearning is carried to the same criterion as the original learning a percent savings score can be calculated, $\frac{OL - RL}{OL} \times 100$ where OL = time or number of trials to criterion on the original learning and RL = time or number of trials to the same criterion on relearning.

In the review that follows it would be tedious to spell out for each study all the methodological details. "Retention" will often be mentioned without specifying how it was measured, though *savings* is the most commonly used method. The non-specialist reader will, I hope, appreciate that confidence in the results of a particular study and comparisons between studies involving many different variables will often be stated as a matter of the reviewer's opinion. To include all the supporting detail would make this review excessively long.

Most of the studies reviewed in the following sections are concerned with long-term memory (LTM) in the sense that they are concerned with retention intervals measured in weeks, months or years rather than seconds or minutes. There has, however, been a fairly recent development in the study STMM, (see reviews by Schmidt, 1972, Stelmach, 1974 and Marteniuk, 1976). The analogy between verbal and motor STM must be treated with caution. This recent work has been concerned almost exclusively with simple linear positioning responses, usually moving a slider along a rail in a modern version of Thorndike's classic line-drawing experiment. Various kinds and amounts of training may be given, for instance moving the slider up to a mechanical stop or allowing free movement and giving knowledge of results. Retention is then measured not by number of trials to relearn to the same criterion but by some measure of linear accuracy. There has been a prolonged debate about the meaning of various error measures, for example, constant error which reveals under- or over-shooting bias or variable error which may be a better measure of the precision of motor memory. As with verbal STM, interference effects, usually in the form of bias, have been demonstrated. The most interesting current question is whether STMM is conceived as a memory trace of the kinaesthetic sensations arising from the production of a movement or as a record of the motor programme, (i.e. the output instruction which produces the movement) or, indeed, some combination of the two. This makes an interesting contrast with verbal memory where STM is invariably thought of as a trace of earlier sensory activity whilst LTM is variously conceived as a longer lasting trace or as a set of instructions for recreating a version of the original experience.

II. Research Findings

Memory for Different Kinds of Skill

Natural and artificial tasks

Since in this volume our purpose is, if possible, to generalize to real-world situations, the first major division will be between real-life or simulated tasks and artificial laboratory tasks. The two groups probably differ in two major ways, either of which might affect retention; (1) real-life tasks are generally more complex, and (2) the subjects generally have a genuine interest in acquiring and retaining proficiency. One can never be sure of this in laboratory situations with volunteer subjects.

"Natural" tasks appearing in the literature have included typewriting (Hill, 1957, Swift, 1906, Towne, 1922), simulated lunar landing (Cotterman and Wood, 1967), instrument flying (Mengelkoch et al., 1971), a range of military tasks (McDonald, 1967), capstan lathe operating (Henderson, 1974), piano playing (Rubin-Rabson, 1939, 1940a,b, 1941a,b,c,d), and process control (Duncan, 1971). For comparison (albeit rather loose) some studies of the retention of academic skills are mentioned. "Artificial" tasks have included various forms of tracking (Battig et al., 1957, Jahnke, 1958, Melton, 1964, Hammerton,

1963, Trumbo *et al.*, 1965, 1967), combined tracking and procedural tasks (Naylor *et al.*, 1962, 1965, 1968), mazes (McGeoch, 1932, McGeoch and Melton, 1929, Tsai, 1924), lever positioning (Bilodeau *et al.*, 1962, Bilodeau and Levy, 1964, Lavery, 1964), a variety of gymnastic skills such as ball tossing and balancing (Purdy and Lockhart, 1962, Roehrig, 1964, Ryan, 1962, 1965, Meyers, 1967).

The findings from real tasks tend to confirm commonsense observations. Whilst it looks as though skills can be retained without much loss for very long periods there seem to be some differences between tasks, for example, between those requiring perceptual-motor coordination such as the control aspects of flying which are well retained and those requiring memory for procedures or knowledge of facts. However, there is a fundamental difficulty in making comparative assertions such as that tasks of type X are retained better than tasks of type Y. The difficulty is that we lack a common metric for retention and it is this problem that we turn to next.

There have been studies of retention of verbal material of a more meaningful sort such as Watson (1938) and Ansbacher (1940) on introductory psychology and Worcester (1928 in Lahey, 1941), White (1930 in Lahey, 1941), Langton (1932 in Lahey, 1941), on mathematics. These are "real" materials but the objective and multiple choice tests used confine the studies to the retention of factual material. Ansbacher (1940) reviewing the retention of psychology concluded that whilst about 50% was retained after 58 months there would have been opportunities to learn outside the original course. Using a control group to correct the retention scores, retention is reduced to 27%. Lahey (1941) reviewing studies of the retention of algebra found that retention depended very much on the test used. However, within one population, retest retention can be quite high and does not necessarily decrease as the length of the retention interval increases. In some cases due either to additional learning or to maturation of the subjects "retention", scores of over 100% can be found. Lahey's study made use of the long summer vacations to test retention of algebraic operations and problem-solving skill. In the former there was nearly 10% loss between May and September and in the latter a very slight gain. Although it would be unwise to place too much weight on these studies they provide a fairly optimistic picture of the "permanence" of school learning.

The evidence from "natural" tasks, whatever its limitations, justifies the empirical generalization that well-practised motor skills are not readily forgotten. Swift (1906) had previously taught himself typewriting and after 2 years and 35 days without practice, wrote a letter of about 50 words—"The apparent ease with which the few words were written after the lapse of so much time was . . . striking". Hill (1934) after an interval of 25 years was able to type at a rate which had originally taken 27 days' practice to achieve.

Cotterman and Wood (1967) found substantial losses over periods up to 13 weeks in performance on a simulated Apollo Command Module but this was largely ameliorated simply by watching other crews perform. Similarly, Mengelkoch *et al.* (1971) using ROTC volunteers in a Link flight trainer found significant losses after four months without practice, greater for procedural than control aspects of the simulated flying task. McDonald (1967) described the retention of "combat skills" over a one year period. Rifle marksmanship showed a slight but insignificant loss and physical skills such as running, crawling and grenade throwing showed little loss, but scores on a multiple test involving "military courtesy", first aid, guard duty and reporting, showed a 50% loss. Henderson's (1974) capstan lathe operators showed virtually no skill loss over 6–14 weeks of unemployment except for slightly lower ratings of the "finish" of items.

Motor verses verbal tasks

The evidence just cited supports the widely held belief that "motor skills" are better retained than "verbal skills". McGeoch and Melton (1929) and McGeoch (1932) sought to confirm this assertion by comparing maze (motor) and nonsense syllable (verbal) and a maze with a "rational" learning problem. The rational task was a kind of "mental maze" which involves learning a sequence of letter-digit pairs. If subjects notice that each digit is only paired with a single letter the task is less formidable than it seems at first sight. This series of studies brought out, but did little to solve, a number of methodological problems. How can tasks be taken as equivalent in all respects except being "verbal" or "motor"? How can the degree of learning or the amount of forgetting be compared in the absence of a unified scoring system? McGeoch's results were equivocal depending in part on how retention was measured. He found that nonsense syllables were better retained than mazes when both were measured by the number of trials taken to relearn the task to a given criterion but the difference between the two types of task was found to be insignificant if error scores were used. The "rational" task was better retained than the maze when the retention interval was one week, but not when it was three weeks. Freeman and Abernathy (1930 and 1932), taking the point that the verbal and motor tasks ought in some way be made comparable, used as a task the typing of a short passage with the key labels blanked out compared with translating the letter in the same passage into a code, that is, the comparison of a "motor" and a "verbal" coding task. These results favoured "motor" memory. Waters and Poole (1933) taking up McGeoch's finding on the superiority of "rational" learning pointed out that the better retained task might simply have been easier to learn. Their experiment compared the Warden finger maze with the Peterson mental maze (rational learning) in three groups. Group 1 learned both tasks to one errorless trial, Group 2 learned the Warden maze to one errorless trial and the mental maze to three errorless trials and Group 3 learned the mental maze to one errorless trial and the motor maze to three errorless trials. In Groups 2 and 3 ten further "overlearning"

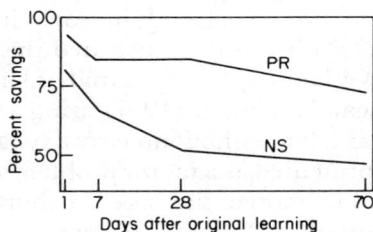

Fig. 3. Percent savings scores on the pursuit rotor (PR) and on nonsense syllables (NS) after 1, 7, 28 and 70 days. Data from Leavitt and Schlosberg, 1944.

trials were given to the mental and motor mazes respectively. The results show that sheer amount of training is a potent variable in retention. Whilst the mental maze was learned in fewer trials, when both types of material were learned to the same degree retention was also equivalent. Van Tilborg (1936) confirmed this finding with "mental" and "motor" mazes, whose initial task difficulty was equated, over 50 days retention interval.

The problem was taken up again by Leavitt and Schlosberg (1944) who compared the retention of pursuit rotor skill with the retention of a nonsense syllable list. Subjects had to learn a 15-item nonsense trigram list by the anticipation method with 2 seconds allowed per item. A learning session consisted of 10 of these 30-second trials. The same subjects were then required to practice on the pursuit rotor for ten 30-second trials. Subjects were divided into four equal groups who were recalled, without warning, to relearn both tasks after 1, 7, 28 or 70 days. ·Figure 3 shows the percent savings scores averaged for individuals in each of these groups. In the full 70 days the nonsense syllable savings score was 51·4% and the pursuit rotor savings score was 75·2%. Even in the one-day retention group pursuit rotor retention was better but the authors felt that some of this difference might be due to reminiscence, a well-known feature of pursuit rotor learning. In the second study by Van Dusen and Schlosberg (1948), the hypotheses that learning an arbitrary list of nonsense syllables provided a less "integrated" task than the pursuit rotor was tested. They used a paired-associate task in which subjects were required to learn pairings between switches label-led with nonsense syllables. The pairings could then be tested either by speaking the syllables or by turning the switches with the syllables concealed. Retention was studied over 1, 7 and 28 days. Although motor responses showed apparently better retention none of the differences whether at 1, 7 or 28 days was statistically significant.

This last experiment points up one of the less obvious difficulties in comparing verbal and motor tasks. Quite early in the study of maze learning (Warden, 1924) it was demonstrated that subjects could use either verbal or non-verbal (e.g. visuo-spatial or kinaesthetic) methods of learning. Newman and Ammons (1957) using a very similar paired-associate switching task, but without nonsense syllable labelling, found that although it was presented as a motor problem 44% of their subjects used a verbal code to memorize the task. In short, although the task may appear to be "verbal" or "motor" the external observer can never be sure (without an additional investigation) what kind of coding the subject is using.

The question of whether verbal or motor tasks are better retained then turns out to be not nearly as sensible as might appear. It is still true that motor tasks have often been shown to be rather resistant to forgetting for long periods. Roehrig (1964) for instance, found virtually perfect recall in a balancing task after an intermission of 50 weeks. The task, known as the stabilometer, was to stand on a see-saw-like plat-form with the feet equidistant from the fulcrum and, by moving the trunk and arms to attempt to keep the platform horizontal. Departures from the horizontal, trigger a switch and for a fixed length of the trial the time in and out of balance is recorded. Ryan (1962, 1965) also using the stabilometer found very little loss over 21 days but in the second study using retention intervals of 3, 6 and 12 months, initial relearning scores were down 50%, 57% and 80% respectively on the final trial of initial training. Nevertheless, four 30-second trials were enough to make good the loss in the 3 months and 6 months delay groups. The discrepancy between this finding and Roehrig's may well be due to the fact that Roehrig's subjects were characterized as highly intelligent and highly motivated and practised daily for a month, whereas Ryan's subjects had only twelve 30-second trials. The apparently high level of retention on balancing may therefore simply be a function of the amount of practice given, a conclusion which receives some support from a study by Carron and Marteniuk (1970).

Continuous versus discrete tasks

A generalization which seems to be clearly supported in the literature is that continuous tasks like tracking are better retained than discrete procedural tasks. Ammons *et al.* (1958), and Brown *et al.* (1963), Adams and Hufford (1962), Mengelkoch *et al.* (1971), have all used flight trainer tasks which combine flight control (i.e. tracking), with procedural tasks, usually a series of push-button responses to signal lights.

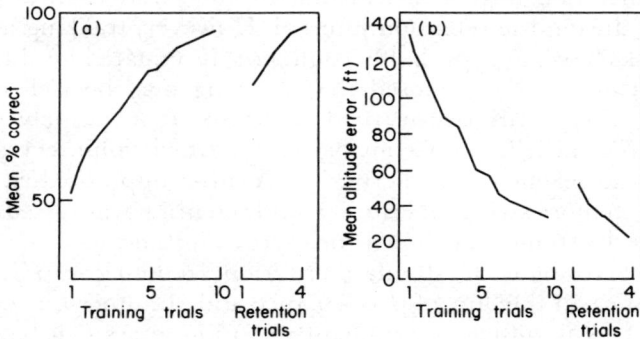

Fig. 4. (a) The learning and retention of a procedural element of a flight simulator exercise. After Mengelkoch et al., 1971. (b) The learning and retention of a control element (altitude control) of a flight simulator exercise. After Mengelkoch et al., 1971.

Adams and Hufford found the procedural aspects of such a task virtually completely forgotten over ten months of no practice but the procedures were relearned in a couple of trials. Ammons *et al.* using separate tracking and procedural tasks and retention intervals ranging from one minute to two years, found retention losses on both types of task related to both the amount of practice and the length of the retention interval. Relearning in both types of task was rapid. Mengelkoch *et al.* found substantial losses of retention of procedures over five months but in flight manoeuvres "statistical significance of retention loss was less frequently found than for procedures". Some of their data are shown in Fig. 4a and b. Unlike Ammons *et al.*, it was found that different amounts of initial training did not affect the retention of the tracking element although this variable did affect the number of trials taken to relearn the procedures.

In these studies we can see the great difficulty in drawing firmly based general conclusions. Even supposing the tracking and procedural elements were roughly comparable other variables in the experiments can be very different. Mengelkoch *et al.*, employed University of Illinois ROTC students who had up to 4 hours' academic training and 15 hours' flight training. Ammons *et al.*, however used 538 subjects (enlisted men) on the procedural tasks and 465 subjects on the aeroplane control task, in the first case using either 5 or 30 training trials and in the second 4 × 1 minute trials. Even supposing these studies were more similar, the comparison between tracking and procedural tasks still presents considerable difficulty. We would expect task difficulty and degree of learning to affect retention as well as experience during the retention interval. However, tracking and procedural tasks have not, (probably could not) be equated for difficulty.

Hammerton (1963) proposed that tracking may be well retained because it is typically overlearned. He took an extremely difficult tracking task (acceleration control) and trained volunteer subjects until they had reached a fixed criterion. A sub-group was then trained up to an even more stringent criterion and retention was tested after 26 weeks. Overlearning was shown to improve initial recall when compared with learning to the standard criterion. In both groups however, there was measurable loss of performance and Hammerton concludes that if the task is sufficiently difficult retention losses can be demonstrated.

We have no way of assuring that the amount of practice is comparable. Whilst we can count the number of steps in a procedure and hence the number of repetitions we have no way of recording the number of repetitions in continuous tracking. There is no way therefore, one could assert that with the degree of difficulty or the amount of learning held constant there are differences in retention between the two types of task.

Task organization: Integrated versus non-integrated tasks

In attempting to account for apparent retention differences between tasks, Van Dusen and Schlosberg (1948) and later, Naylor and Briggs (1961) suggested that more highly "organised" or "integrated" tasks might be better retained. Certainly some of the best retained tasks such as balancing (Roehrig 1964, Ryan, 1962) seem to involve a single highly coordinated activity. Nevertheless, in a fairly extreme case of non-integrated task, simultaneous reading and writing of different materials, Downey and Anderson (1917) found fairly considerable "retention of capacity to maintain two processes" after two years with no practice and rapid relearning of this difficult skill. Naylor and his associates (Naylor *et al.*, 1962, 1968) and Trumbo (Trumbo *et al.*, 1965a; Trumbo *et al.*, 1965b; Trumbo *et al.*, 1967; Swink *et al.*, 1967) have investigated task organization as a factor in retention.

The Naylor task comprised 3-dimensional tracking, that is to say using rudder and stick to keep three dials, indicating pitch, roll and yaw, steady, and combined this with switching procedures to be followed in response to various signal lights. Two degrees of "organization" were obtained by varying the predictability of the signal lights. Amount of training and length of retention were also varied. The coherent procedural task was better retained and also led to better performance and retention than the tracking component of the task. However, amount of training turned out to be the most potent variable and it seems probable that the level of skill attained in the original training task may be sufficient to account for the differences found.

Trumbo's task consisted of pursuit tracking of a target which moved in 1–15 discrete steps or deflections. The task combined some aspects of both tracking and procedures and the sequence of the targets could be made more or less predictable. Using this task Trumbo *et al.* (1965a), and Swink *et al.* (1967) have found retention to be related to the predictability of the stimulus sequence but, with amount of practice and length of retention interval also contributing to retention and speed of relearning.

It is difficult to see "task organisation", as defined in these studies, as anything other than a way of manipulating task difficulty and hence the degree of learning which can be achieved within a fixed practice period or fixed number of trials. All the experiments employed fixed length trials rather than training to a criterion and only if training had been carried out to a common criterion would it have been possible to attribute differential retention to the nature of the task *per se*. Whilst the components of an organized or integrated task would be more predictable the operational definition of "organisation" only in terms of predictability hardly does justice to the concept. However, no-one has yet suggested any more satisfactory way of defining this intriguing but elusive variable. We have to conclude that what at first seemed an interesting idea has not so far been satisfactorily followed up.

Types of Training

The type of training given can affect the efficiency of skill acquisition but it is less clear whether, other factors being equal, the kind of initial training affects retention. In the classical motor skills literature type of training refers to variables such as massed versus spaced practice, part versus whole learning, learning with or without knowledge of results and varied or general versus specific task training. In the applied field "types of training" generally refers to whole philosophies of training, such as Training Within Industry (TWI), Skills Analysis Training, Discovery Learning, Schematic Learning, Programmed Instruction, Computer-aided Learning and so on. Type of training in this sense can seldom be tied down to a limited number of readily manipulable variables and so comparisons in the rigorous scientific sense are virtually impossible.

Naylor and Briggs reviewing massed and distributed learning found only two studies with clear effects. Both used tracking type tasks. Lewis and Lowe (1965) found better retention with distributed practice. Lewis and Lowe had whole week intervals between trials whilst Jahnke and Duncan (1966) compared 20 second and 10 minute rest periods. In the light of these differences and the superficially more equivocal results from Reynolds and Bilodeau (1952), Rubin-Rabson (1940a), and Montgomery (1953) a clear superiority of one method remains to be demonstrated.

Part versus Whole is in not much better state. Rubin-Rabson (1939, 1940b) in a series of studies of piano playing looked at two different methods of part training, one hand at a time and practising short sections of a whole piece, on memory for piano music. In neither case was a significant difference found. Naylor *et al.* (1963) in one of a series of experiments with a combined 3-dimensional tracking and procedural task described in the previous section used part or whole task rehearsal following initial training and followed by retention tests after 5 or 10 days. Rehearsal by part methods was generally less effective than whole methods up to five days but with the longer interval there was no difference between rehearsal methods.

Knowledge of results, (KR) whilst generally agreed to be a *sine qua non* of learning may affect retention in simple positioning skills. Annett (1969) has reviewed a number of studies where knowledge of results so immediate as to be useable as a cue controlling ongoing responses, raised performance levels only temporarily. Removal of this kind of KR, sometimes known as *action feedback*, is like taking away a crutch and performance is affected dramatically. In this limited sense KR can actually militate against retention. However Lavery (1964) in a similar sort of task but interspersing a batch of no-KR trials actually found that more precise knowledge of results gave better retention. In a very different situation, maze learning, Gilbert and Crafts (1935) compared the effects on learning and retention of either a shock or a harmless buzzer as an error signal. Signal and shock were found to be effectively equivalent with a small advantage to the harmless signal on retention.

Bearing in mind that "training methods" as conventionally understood are too loosely defined to permit rigorous generalizations there is scattered evidence that some methods may be more conducive to retention than others. Studies of retention *per se* are, however, rare and the evidence is suggestive rather than conclusive. No studies can be found which permit a conclusion to be drawn about the value of discovery methods but an experiment by Fleishman and Parker (1962) showed some advantage with a 14 month retention interval, for training which began with a "commonsense introduction and demonstration" and included analysis of performance over and above simple knowledge of results. The task was a very difficult joystick and rudder control task with acceleration control on the first and velocity control on the second plus an exponential control lag. It would seem that some degree of understanding of this very difficult task benefits both acquisition and retention. However, the hypothesis that tasks which are better understood are better retained, whilst having some appeal, seems not to have been directly tested.

The many results with programmed learning, most with intellectual rather than motor skills, on the whole indicate that retention is good where acquisition is good. In general, end-of-training performance is the best predictor of performance after an interval of no practice. A study by Goldberg and Dawson (1964) on 47 clerical trainees tested at the end of training and six months later found greater losses with programmed instruction than with classroom teaching but, as in so many of these teacher versus machine "competition" experiments the teacher can usually do better if he analyses and structures the material as carefully as when he is required to write a programme. Kay *et al.* (1963) reviewing some 40 studies found retention in general superior after programmed than conventional instruction. Still in the field of verbal rather than motor learning, but nevertheless highly suggestive, is a recent study by Atkinson (1976) on computer-aided learning. The computer was programmed to use an adaptive teaching strategy for German vocabulary teaching and this was contrasted with a random strategy and a student chosen strategy. The "strategy" simply means the rule governing which items are chosen to rehearse next. The computer strategy was based on a theoretical model which, in brief, suggested that there is greater benefit in practising material which is nearly but not quite fully learned. The effect of this is to give what appears to be relatively poor performance during training but much better performance when tested one week later. Although there have been a number of studies of adaptive control in motor skill acquisition there is no information on retention. It may be that adaptive control strategies are possible which are particularly conducive to retention.

Amount of Training

A major variable is quite simply the amount of training given before the "layoff" or retention period. This can be measured in the number of practice trials, the amount of time spent or in terms of the actual performance level or criterion reached. The latter is often adopted in investigating the amount of overlearning, that is to say the amount of practice given additional to that required to reach a specified criterion. The literature contains examples of the amount of training used which range from a single trial (Bilodeau, 1969) to many hours or weeks of practice, but only those studies which varied amounts of training within the same task and subject population will be considered here.

In general the amount of practice does seem to be relatively potent (sometimes the most potent) variable affecting retention. Early studies by Luh (1923) and Krueger (1929) on nonsense syllables and monosyllabic nouns respectively set the general picture. Subjects learned to a given criterion and then continued with 50%, 100% or 150% more trials. Luh looked at retention over four hours, 1 day and 2 days, and Krueger at 1, 2, 4, 5, 14 and 28 days. Although overlearning was beneficial to retention the returns for effort are diminishing. Luh found that 150% overlearning only improved retention by 17% over a 4 hour retention period and only 10% over 2 days. Krueger too found that the increase in retention was usually proportionally less than the increase in overlearning. Krueger (1930) followed up this experiment in verbal learning with a study of finger maze learning with similar results.

Ammons *et al.* (1958) using a procedural task trained subjects for either 5 or 30 trials and retested them after 1 minute, 1 day, 1 month, 6 months, 1 or 2 years. Retention was found to be a function both of the amount of training and the duration of the retention period. The more training and the shorter the interval, the better the retention. With a pursuit-tracking task however, the absolute loss over a 2 year retention period was the same whether subjects had been originally trained for 1 hour or for 8 hours. Hammerton's (1963) study of a very difficult tracking task in which two groups of subjects learned to two different criteria and were tested after 26 weeks also showed that the more highly trained group retained their skill better, although both groups showed a retention loss. In a series of studies by Naylor and his associates at the Aerospace Medical Centre (Naylor *et al.*, 1962; Buckhout *et al.*, 1963;

Naylor *et al.*, 1968) using a 3-dimensional tracking task combined with a procedural task the amount of initial learning was consistently shown to affect retention, indeed Naylor concluded that it was probably the major factor in retention. In short, the generalization that retention is a positive, but negatively accelerated, function of the amount of original learning in both simple and complex tasks seem justified.

Duration of the Retention Interval

The record for a retention interval must go to Hill (1957) who carried out an experiment on typing skill under Thorndike at Columbia in 1907 and tested his retention 50 years later when he had already been retired ten years. He can be forgiven for having "cheated" by carrying out a relearning test after a mere 25 years! The essential finding was that despite complete absence of actual practice for 25 years the level of performance reached by the end of the first day of relearning had originally not been achieved until 27 days' practice. After the second quarter century of no practice and some decline in physical condition it still took only 8 days to reach the same performance level. Burtt (1941) read three selections in Greek each day for 3 months to a child, starting at 15 months. For the next 3 months three more selections were read daily and this procedure continued until the child had been thus exposed to a total of 21 selections and was 3 years old. At $8\frac{1}{2}$ years the child learned 2 of these plus 3 new selections by the anticipation method and this process was repeated again at 14 years and again at 18 years. Amazingly, an average of 30% saving was found at $8\frac{1}{2}$ years, 8% at 14 years, but none at all at 18, that is 15 years after the original learning. Although these two studies lack controls they do suggest that the retention of both motor and verbal skills is much better than is commonly supposed.

Several studies (Ammons *et al.*, 1958; Bell, 1950) systematically varied retention intervals and retention is probably a negatively accelerated function of the interval duration. However, it is not possible to be precise about a "curve of forgetting" of the sort demonstrated by Ebbinghaus for the special case of nonsense trigram learning. On the basis of a great deal of data on a simple lever positioning task Bilodeau and Levy (1964) proposed the unusual doubly inflected curve. A rather rapid but decelerating curve of forgetting occurred during the first minute and following that is a longer positively accelerated curve. Although this curve *has* a rationale (see Bilodeau, 1969) its value in the present context is limited (a) because it is based on the repetition of a single simple linear movement and (b) because the ordinate unlike most other retention measures we have discussed in this review, is a measure of *consistency*.

Youngling, *et al.* (1968) using a much more complex task, an orbital satellite control situation, found skill loss to vary *linearly* with retention intervals up to 200 days. Bahrick (1964) warns against a variety of measurement artifacts, for example, varying sensitivity of different measures and concludes that it is unwise to base general conclusions on the shape of curves of forgetting.

Interference by Activities in the Retention Interval

Activities occuring during the retention period may interfere with the retention of the original skill. In the field of verbal learning interference of this kind, called retroactive interference because it is assumed to interfere retroactively with the trace of the original learning, can reduce retention. Indeed interference constitutes one of the main hypothetical processes causing forgetting (see e.g. Morris, 1978).

In motor learning studies it is typically very difficult to do more than ensure that subjects do not practise the same task during the retention period. There is no way in which they could be prevented from riding bicycles, driving cars or otherwise exercising skills which might interfere with or enhance the original learning. The problem has been investigated by giving training on a modified form of the original and to-be-remembered task, by Lewis (1947), Lewis and Shephard (1950), Lewis *et al.* (1951), McAllister and Lewis (1951) and McAllister (1952). The task, a modified Mashburn Apparatus, otherwise known as the Complex Co-ordination Test involves using an aeroplane-like joystick and rudder control to illuminate sequences of lights on a display panel. The relationship between the direction of movement and the sequence of lights can be varied. In verbal learning studies similarity of stimulus and response material can be varied, for example, by using homonyms or synonyms in the search for acoustic and semantic interference. In most tasks one can vary the stimuli, responses or stimulus-response connections. The Lewis experiments used the latter. Quite simply the interfering task used involved the opposite stimulus-response (or display/control) connection to that used in the original learning. Lewis *et al.* (1951) compared three degrees of original learning and five different amounts of interpolated practice on the reversed task. The results are quite striking and as Adams (1967) pointed out quite the opposite of what one would have predicted by a simple extrapolation from the results of verbal learning experiments. The so-called interference decrement (that is the retention loss due to interpolated learning) increased, as expected, with the amount of interpolated learning, although the increase was not a simple linear function. However, quite unlike the parallel verbal studies, the greater the amount of original learning the greater the amount of interference. In verbal learning a well-established habit is less susceptible to interference but, if these results are to be believed, the more established the original habit the more will interpolated practice of the reversed task interfere. This finding may conceivably be due to some measurement artifact as suggested by Schmidt (1972) and perhaps ought to be confirmed.

With an eye to generalization to tasks other than the Complex Co-ordinator it must be admitted that there is a very considerable gap in our knowledge. Reversing display-control relationships is only one of a very large number of ways in which interpolated tasks could be related to the criterion task and it is not particularly typical of what is likely to happen in the industrial situation. It will not, for instance, tell us anything about the likely interference or facilitation effects expected by practice with milling interpolated between training and criterion performance on operating a lathe. However, controls on vehicles can sometimes operate in opposite directions in different models. Schmidt (1972) suggests more work is clearly needed to define the nature of the interfering tasks and to determine whether the "laws" of motor and verbal interference are similar. Note that if verbal laws of interference translated to the motor field it would be quite reasonable to suggest that driving a small delivery van could interfere with the skills of driving a juggernaut. Whilst one suspects that this is not the case we do not actually know. A little work has also been done on proactive inhibition. Duncan and Underwood (1953) had their subjects learn a motor paired-associate task, moving a lever in response to coded coloured lights, and then learn a second version, varying in similarity to the first. The degree of original learning was varied and a one day or a one year retention interval was used. The greater the amount of learning on the first task the more forgetting occurred in the second task, that is, proactive interference was demonstrated. Britt (1934) on the other hand, demonstrated positive transfer in learning two different mazes. Having previously learned and then, after 48 days, relearned one maze, facilitated the learning of a second maze. These results on proactive interference and facilitation are somewhat inconclusive. The problem of proactive interference could become important if people typically learned a variety of different skills during the course of their working lives.

Facilitation by Activities in the Retention Interval

Not all intervening activities militate against retention, some facilitating effects have been found. For example, Bunch (1946) found that when a maze is learned and then almost immediately relearned the learning of a different maze between the original learning and relearning was interfering, but with a 120 day interval learning the different maze just before relearning had a facilitating effect on relearning. Although this seems to be an isolated finding which might, perhaps, be attributed to warm-up, various kinds of *rehearsal* have been shown to be effective in warding off skill loss. A series of studies by Naylor's group at the Aerospace Medical Centre (Naylor and Briggs, 1963; Naylor *et al.*, 1963; Brown *et al.*, 1963; Buckhout *et al.*, 1968) looked at various kinds and amounts of rehearsal during the no-practice period on subsequent retention of both procedural and tracking skills. The procedural task resembled an aircraft check-out routine in which lights of various colours are "acknowledged" by push-button responses which have to be made in a particular sequence and with a fixed time delay. The general plan of the first experiment (Naylor and Briggs, 1963) was to give practice on days 1–5, no practice on days 6–14, various kinds of rehearsal on days 15–19 and no further practice until the retention test on day 30. Some subjects rehearsed the timing of the responses, others their spatial location, another group rehearsed both timing and location and a control group had no rehearsal. Rehearsal, even of only one aspect of the task was shown to be helpful to retention. In the second study (Naylor *et al.*, 1963) which combined a 3-dimensional tracking task with a procedural task, rehearsal was found to be more help to the procedural task than the tracking element. Various forms of part-task rehearsal were used and although whole task rehearsal was superior when given in small amounts (5 days' work) part-task rehearsal was equally effective for larger amounts. This finding has the interesting implication that it may be possible to keep a complex skill in "good condition" by rehearsing only selected aspects, if one can identify those aspects of the task most in need of "refresher" treatment. In a third study, Brown *et al.* (1963) using the same basic tracking-cum-procedural task compared nine different conditions including various simplified and generalized versions of both the tracking and procedural aspects of the task. In this case tracking retention was not perfect in the control condition and retention was enhanced by rehearsal, including rehearsal of a simplified version of the tracking task.

In a more recent study by Macek *et al.* (1965) a procedural task, the "star discrimeter" was used. This consists of a lever which can be moved into one of six positions in response to coloured light signals, and is essentially a form of serial association learning. Various forms of rehearsal were used, for example rehearsing the light/lever position combinations presented on a memory drum using various labels or analogues of the star positions. Rehearsal and retention was over a six week period following initial training. The three main findings were that (1) the more similar the rehearsal task to the criterion task the better the retention, (2) the more complex the criterion task the more important was the relevance of the rehearsal task, (3) warm-up, that is, special practice just prior to the retention test proper, was not as effective as rehearsal regularly spaced out over the retention interval.

These results are generally quite promising in that they suggest that skill may be kept at a relatively high level by a relatively small investment in rehearsal, perhaps even only symbolic rehearsal of the criterion task. Whilst Naylor's group consistently emphasize the importance of the degree of original learning, rehearsal even in "impoverished" conditions may be helpful to retention.

Two studies of simulation training by Grimsley (1969a, b) confirm this result. A missile firing control panel simulator was used in three versions, a "hot" (i.e. fully functional) panel, a "cold" (non-functional) panel and a photograph. The task was a 92-step procedure and retention was measured over 4 and 6 week intervals. After 4 weeks there was an average 16% loss in all three simulation conditions. Whilst actual practice gave better retention there was no difference in retention due to simulator fidelity as such. The photograph was as effective as the fully functional panel.

Rather improbably, there is some evidence that "imaginary" practice may aid the retention of motor skills, and it may even show some actual improvement in performance. If this were so, refresher courses might even consist of persuading the trainees to imagine that they are indulging in practice. Sackett (1934 and 1935), used the Miles finger relief maze as the retention task, well aware of the earlier work by Husband and Warden showing that a maze may be interpreted by the subject as a visual, verbal or spatio-motor problem. After having learned the maze, subjects either practised making drawings of the maze, thinking about it, or (hopefully) following the instructions not to think about it. Whereas trials to criterion in original learning had been 20·45, 21·7 and 21·8 trials respectively, relearning scores were 4·3, 5·75 and 8·35. Only the difference between drawing (4·3 trials), and non-rehearsal (8·35 trials) was statistically reliable. In the second study subjects were instructed to think their way through the maze 3 or 5 times for 7 days. The trend in favour of symbolic rehearsal was still present but still failed to reach statistical significance. However, Perry (1939) was able to produce quite clear evidence in favour of "imaginary" practice on five different tasks, a pegboard, mirror drawing, digit-symbol substitution, tapping and card sorting. In Perry's "imaginary" practice the subjects were confronted with equipment on which real practice was carried out and were requested to "think their way through" the task but without moving their hands. The imaginary practice, much more controlled than in Sackett's case, included having the subject report when he had completed the trial and even recording his "imaginary" score! Perry presented his results in terms of equivalence with "real" practice. In each case five imaginary practice trials were given and these were found to be as effective as two actual trials on card sorting, three actual trials on the tapping task, four on mirror drawing, five on digit-symbol substitution and, surprisingly were *more* effective than the five actual trials on the peg-board task. Perry attributes these results to the degree to which each of these rather different tasks is capable of symbolic or verbal representation. Although this explanation is attractive it is clearly *post hoc* and it does not appear to be confirmed by a more recent study by Vandell *et al*. (1943) who used dart throwing and basket ball throwing over 20 days with real practice on days 2–19 or mental practice on days 2–19. A control group simply worked on day 1 and was given the retention test on day 20. The control group showed no improvement whilst the mental practice, as in Perry's study, carried out in the real environment, was almost as effective as active practice.

The implications of these studies, which do not appear to have been followed-up in the intervening years, are considerable, both in terms of the theory of skill acquisition and in terms of the practical possibilities of mental or symbolic rehearsal used to maintain the level of performance of a motor skill during a lay-off period.

Conditions of Recall

Most studies of motor retention have used the relearning or savings method. Relearning is usually fairly rapid. Typical results are those of Braden (1924) whose subjects took ten days to achieve a level of accuracy in ball tossing after a 22 month interval which had originally taken 100 days to achieve and Bell (1950) using the pursuit rotor who found that his subjects took eight 1-minute trials to reach the level they had attained a year earlier after 20 trials.

For the majority of experimental studies the task conditions at recall are physically identical to those obtaining during the original learning. However, in real life, even with physically identical conditions the retention or relearning situation could well be subjectively different. Repetition of responses not only improves performance but can sometimes have detrimental effects attributed to reactive inhibition. Such effects have been found for both verbal learning tasks (Hovland, 1940) and motor tasks such as the pursuit rotor (Ammons, 1947; Irion, 1949) and can give rise to the phenomenon of "reminiscence", that is, better performance after a rest period than on the trials just before rest. Reminiscence as such has not been demonstrated for the rather longer "rest" intervals of retention experiments, but its existence under some conditions draws attention to the fact that the absence of practice is not always deleterious.

Another well known but probably short-lived phenomenon is that of "warm-up". This is often seen in the relatively rapid improvement found during the first few trials of resumed practice. Warm-up trials do improve retention (Macek et al., 1965). The warm-up process is not fully understood but may involve re-orientation to the task and possibly the "recalibration" of responses. Reminscence and warm-up effects can complicate the measurement of retention, particularly where simply pre-rest-post-rest difference measures are used, but they may also be relevant to a condition which probably obtains in all retention in real-life, which we may loosely designate "stress". Starting a new job or resuming work after a lay-off period is likely to be stressful. It is well known that moderate amounts of stress can benefit performance whilst excessive amounts are generally deleterious. Examinees often complain that they recall answers after the examination is over. For a general discussion of stress and memory, see Chapter 7.

Various psychoactive drugs can interact with stress effects. Payne and Hauty (1955) have reviewed evidence showing that work decrements in tasks such as multi-dimensional tracking can be mitigated by drugs such as dextro-amphetamine sulphate and methyl caffeine. It is by no means impossible that long-term retention and stress interact and that this interaction might be affected by pharmacological agents but the relevant research is yet to be carried out.

Individual Differences

As with much of the psychological literature on almost any topic, students constitute the main subject populations, with a few, but sometimes extensive, studies in which American servicemen were used. As far as motor memory is concerned there has been no systematic examination of the relationships between individual difference variables, for example age, or ability and retention variables. There are some hints that performance at the end of original learning, which will generally be positively correlated with ability, is a good predictor of retention. Fleishman and Parker (1962) in a realistic flying task for example, found correlations of between 0·84 and 0·98 between original performance and retention and moreover these correlations were unaffected by the duration of the no-practice period. Roehrig (1964) who found almost perfect retention on the balancing test remarked on the high ability and motivation of his subjects and Carron and Marteniuk (1970) found differential retention on the same balancing task with different ability subjects. So, by and large, one would expect that level of attainment, which may in part depend on underlying ability, and motivation is effective in retention.

With regard to age and the notorious failing of memory of the aged Welford (1958) and his associates have found two main effects. One could be described as a progressive reduction in information processing capacity as age increases and this can show up in tasks which rely heavily on short-term memory (STM). Second, older subjects tend to introduce compensatory strategies if their performance is being limited by any significant loss in processing capacity—that is they tend to alter their approach to the task in order to make the best use of whatever capacities they retain. Welford's researchers produced no evidence to show poorer long-term retention with increasing age. There have been hints, but little more, that the effects of stress become more severe with increasing age (Hauty et al., 1965) and to the extent that stress may adversely affect retention some effect of increasing age might be expected. However, the older worker is also likely to be more experienced and one of the more reliable generalizations is that retention is closely related to the level of skill attained. Thus, although there is a possibility that age may handicap retention, the greater experience of the older workers may more than compensate for this disadvantage. Once again it must be stressed that the absence of any thorough investigation of relationships between retention and individual differences makes generalization hazardous.

III. Summary and Conclusions

Well-learned motor skills are generally well retained in the sense that they are rapidly relearned in only a few trials even after extensive periods without practice. Verbal nonsense material often appears to show much poorer retention but attempts to establish the relative permanence of verbal and motor learning which have run into methodological difficulties, most especially the problem of establishing task equivalence in all relevant variables except the verbal/motor distinctions.

Establishing the comparability of degrees of initial learning in two different tasks provides another problem not confined to comparing verbal and motor memory. The literature appears to provide some support for generalizations such as that continuous tasks are better retained than discrete tasks, that the more meaningful, organized, coherent or integrated the task the better is it retained. Difficulties in making these comparisons arise largely from the lack of a method of performance scoring which is independent of the nature of the task. Even the use of the savings method does not enable us to escape the problem if either of the tasks being compared cannot be divided into meaningful trials or repetitions. The problem of comparing tasks and making useful generalizations to practical situations is further exacerbated by the lack of a generally agreed taxonomy of tasks. Thus it would be unwise to make predictions about the retention of driving skills on the basis of results in tracking experiments, even if the two have a superficial similarity, since the full extent of the similarities and differences is unknown.

One of the more reliable generalizations seems to be that retention is heavily dependent on the degree of skill at the end of the original learning. So far, no one training variable or training method has been thrown up as being particularly conducive to retention and it may be that the best form of training for retention is that which gives the best "end of training" performance level. The function relating retention and degree of initial learning is probably negatively accelerated, that is, overlearning gives progressively smaller returns in retention. Although most empirical retention curves will be exponential, suggesting a gradual decay process, the shape of the retention curve probably depends on the nature of the task and is strongly influenced by the specific measure of retention which is employed.

As in other forms of learning, activities in the retention interval are capable of interfering with or enhancing retention. Not much is known about interference, but display-control reversal, as one might expect, interferes with retention. Paradoxically, however, interference appears to be greater when the original skill is overlearned. This finding, if confirmed, is the opposite of what one might expect from comparable studies of verbal learning.

Rehearsal of various kinds helps retention, even if it is rehearsal of a simplified form of the task and there is evidence to suggest that even purely "mental" rehearsal can have worthwhile effects in retention.

As a matter of practical importance, for instance in carrying out emergency procedures, little is known, except anecdotally, about the effects of stress on the retention of skills. Individual differences is another area where there is little reliable information and further research could have useful consequences in relation to the training of groups of workers likely to be unemployed for extended periods or, indeed, for any group who cannot immediately put their training to use, for instance on a long space voyage.

Adams' comment on the lack of a satisfactory theory of memory for skills seems amply justified. Most researchers have been content with empirical generalizations about the effects of major variables on gross performance measures. Although it may at first sight appear to be a strange question, no-one seems to have asked what exactly is forgotten when performance has deteriorated after a long period without practice. Even simplified laboratory skills like tracking represent complex patterns of behaviour, and whatever happens when a skill is not practiced may not have a uniform effect on all aspects of skill. It may be that some skills, perhaps those which involve very fine discriminations or exact timing can only be maintained by constant practice where coarser skills remain unaffected. In forgetting verbal material, sometimes whole chunks, such as a line of verse, may be forgotten and it may well be that something similar happens in memory for skill.

Modern theories of memory are concerned with the problem of coding. In the field of STMM several possible ways in which memory for movement might be coded have been suggested. In more complex skills retained over longer periods we should, perhaps, be asking how the information needed to perform is coded. As in verbal memory interference effects could provide some clues and others might come from the study of facilitation effects such as those found in various types of rehearsal.

Finally, let us turn to practicalities. Industrial society is entering a period in which any individual's store of skills may not be needed all the time. As this chapter is being written government agencies are preparing plans for the training of young people and it is expected that many may not find jobs for some time after training. Expert knowledge of how to provide training that is retained and how to provide appropriate rehearsal and retraining to revive valuable skills when they are required provides a challenge for applied psychologists.

Acknowledgement

The author acknowledges the support of the Training Services Division of the Manpower Services Commission in the preparation of this chapter.

References

Adams, J. A. (1967). "Human Memory." McGraw Hill, New York.

Adams, J. A. and Hufford, L. E. (1962). Contribution of a part-task trainer to the learning and relearning of a time-shared flight maneuver. *Human Factors* **4**, 159–170.

Ammons, R. B. (1947). Acquisition of Motor Skill II: rotary pursuit performance with continuous practice before and after a single rest. *J. exp. Psychol.* **37**, 393–411.

Ammons, R. B., Farr, R. G., Bloch, E., Neumann, E., Dey, M., Marion, R. and Ammons, C. H. (1958). Long term retention of perceptual-motor skills. *J. exp. Psychol.* **55**, 318–328.

Annett, J. (1969). "Feedback and Human Behaviour." Penguin, Harmondsworth.

Ansbacher, H. L. (1940). On the permanence of college learning. *J. educ. Psychol.* **XXXI**, 622–624.

Atkinson, R. C. (1976). Adaptive Instructional Systems: some attempts to optimise the learning process. *In* "Cognition and Instruction" (D. Klahr, Ed.). Wiley, New York.

Bahrick, H. (1964). Retention Curves: facts or artifacts? *Psychol. Bull.* **61**, 188–194.

Bahrick, H. (1965). The ebb of retention. *Psychol. Rev.* **76**, 60–73.

Battig, W. F., Nagel, E. H., Voss, J. F. and Brogden, W. F. (1957). Transfer and retention of bi-dimensional tracking after extended practice. *Am. J. Psychol.* **70**, 75–80.

Bell, H. M. (1950). Retention of pursuit rotor skill after one year. *J. exp. Psychol.* **40**, 648–649.

Bilodeau, E. A. (1969). Retention under free and Stimulated Conditions. *In* "Principles of Skill Acquisition" (Bilodeau, E. A. and Bilodeau, I. McD., Eds). Academic Press, New York and London.

Bilodeau, E. A. and Levy, C. M. (1964). Long term memory as a function of retention time and the conditions of training and recall. *Psychol. Rev.* **71**, 27–41.

Bilodeau, E. A., Sulzer, J. L. and Levy, C. M. (1962). Theory and data on the interrelationships of three factors of memory. *Psychol. Monogr.* **76**, No. 20, No. 539.

Bourdin, E. (1901). *L'Année Psychologique* **VIII**, 327.

Braden, S. R. (1924). An extensive experiment in motor learning and relearning. *J. educ. Psychol.* **15**, 313–315.

Britt, S. H. (1934). The relationship between transfer of training and age of previous associations. *Am. J. Psychol.* **46**, 113–116.

Broadbent, D. E. (1971). "Decision and Stress." Academic Press, London and New York.

Brown, D. R., Briggs, G. E. and Naylor, J. C. (1963). "The retention of discrete and continuous tasks as a function of interim practice with modified tasks." AMRL–TDR–63–35. Aerospace Medical Laboratories, Wright-Patterson Air-force Base, Ohio.

Bryan, W. L. and Harter, N. (1897). Studies in the physiology and psychology of the telegraphic language. *Psychol. Rev.* **4**, 27–53.

Bryan, W. L. and Harter, N. (1899). Studies in the telegraphic language. The acquisition of a hierarchy of habits. *Psychol. Rev.* **6**, 345–375.

Buckhout, R., Naylor, J. C. and Briggs, G. E. (1963). "Effects of modified task feedback during training on performance of a simulated attitude control task after 30 days." AMRL–TDR–63–125, Aerospace Medical Research Laboratories, Wright-Patterson Air-force Base, Ohio.

Bunch, M. E. (1946). Retroactive inhibition or facilitation from interpolated learning as a function of Time. *J. comp. Psychol.* **39**, 287–291.

Burtt, H. E. (1941). An experimental study of early childhood memory. *J. genet. Psychol.* **58**, 435–439.

Carron, A. V. and Marteniuk, R. G. (1970). Retention of a balance skill as a function of initial ability level. *Res. Q.* **41**, 478–483.

Cotterman, T. E. and Wood, M. E. (1967). "Retention of simulated lunar landing mission skill: a test of pilot reliability." AMRL–TR–66–222. Aerospace Medical Laboratories, Wright-Patterson Air-force Base, Ohio.

Downey, J. E. and Anderson, J. E. (1917). Retention of skill after lapse of practice; simultaneous reading and writing. *Am. J. Psychol.* **28**, 396–408.

Duncan, C. P. and Underwood, B. J. (1953). Retention of transfer in motor learning after 24 hours and after 14 months. *J. exp. Psychol.* **46**, 445–452.

Duncan, K. D. (1971). Long-term retention and transfer of an industrial search skill. *Br. J. Psychol.* **62**, 439–448.

Ebbinghaus, H. (1885). "Uber das Gedächtnis." Leipzig. (Original translation in *Memory*, 1913, Teacher's College, New York.)

Fleishman, E. A. (1960). Abilities at different stages of practice in rotary pursuit performance. *J. exp. Psychol.* **60**, 162–171.

Fleishman, E. A. and Parker, J. F. (1962). Factors in the retention and relearning of perceptual-motor skill. *J. exp. Psychol.* **64**, 215–226.

Freeman, F. F. and Abernethy, E. M. (1930). Comparative retention of typewriting and of substitution with analogous mate. *J. educ. Psychol.* **21**, 639–647.

Freeman, F. N. and Abernethy, E. M. (1932). New evidence of the superior retention of typewriting to that of substitution. *J. educ. Psychol.* **23**, 331–334.

Gardlin, G. R. and Sitterley, T. E. (1972). Degradation of learned skills: a review and annotated bibliography. The Boeing Co., Seattle, Washington. D180–15080–1. Contract NAS9–10962.

Gilbert, R. W. and Crafts, L. W. (1935). The effect of signal for error upon maze learning and retention. *J. exp. Psychol.* **18**, 121–132.

Goldberg, M. H. and Dawson, R. I. (1964). Comparison of programmed and conventional instructional methods. *J. appl. Psychol.* **48**, 110–114.

Grimsley, D. L. (1969). "Acquisition, retention and retraining: effects of high and low fidelity in training devices." HUMRRO Tech. Rep. 69–1; 69–4.

Hauty, G. T., Trites, D. K. and Berkley, W. J. (1965). "Biomedical survey of ATC facilities: experience and age." Federal Aviation Agency, Office of Aviation Medicine, Report AM 65–6.

Hammerton, M. (1963). Retention of learning in a difficult tracking task. *J. exp. Psychol.* **66**, 108–110.

Henderson, P. (1974). Unpublished report of the Applied Psychology Advisory Service, Queen's University, Belfast.

Hill, D. S. (1914). Minor Studies in learning and relearning. *J. educ. Psychol.* **5**, 375–386.

Hill, L. B. (1934). A quarter century of delayed recall. *Ped. Sem. J. gen. Psychol.* **44**, 231–238.

Hill, L. B. (1957). A second quarter century of delayed recall, or relearning at eighty. *J. educ. Psychol.* **48**, 65–69.

Hovland, C. I. (1940). Experimental studies of rote-learning theory: VI comparisons of retention following learning to same criterion by massed and distributed practice. *J. exp. Psychol.* **26**, 568–587.

Hovland, C. I. (1951). Human learning and retention. *In* "Handbook of Experimental Psychology" (S. S. Stevens, Ed.). Wiley, New York.

Irion, A. L. (1949). Reminiscence in pursuit-rotor learning as a function of length of rest and amount of pre-rest practice. *J. exp. Psychol.* **39**, 492–499.

Irion, A. L. (1969). Historical introduction. *In* "Principles of Skill Acquisition" (Bilodeau, E. A. and Bilodeau I. McD., Eds). Academic Press, New York and London.

Jahnke, J. C. (1958). Retention in motor learning as a function of amount of practice and rest. *J. exp. Psychol.* **55**, 270–273.

Jahnke, J. C. and Duncan, C. P. (1956). Reminiscence and forgetting in motor learning after extended rest intervals. *J. exp. Psychol.* **52**, 273–282.

Kay, H., Annett, J. and Sime, M. (1963). "Teaching Machines and Their Use in Industry." HMSO, London.

Krueger, W. C. F. (1929). The effect of overlearning on retention. *J. exp. Psychol.* **12**, 71–78.

Krueger, W. C. F. (1930). Further studies in overlearning. *J. exp. Psychol.* **13**, 152–163.

Lahey, Sister M. F. L. (1941). Permanence of retention of first year algebra. *J. educ. Psychol.* **XXXII**, 401–403.

Lavery, J. J. (1964). Retention of a skill as a function of display/hand movement ratio during training. *Percept. Mot. Skills* **19**, 626.

Leavitt, H. J. and Schlosberg, H. (1944). The retention of verbal and motor skills. *J. exp. Psychol.* **34**, 404–417.

Lewis, D. (1947). Positive and negative transfer in motor learning. *Am. Psychol.* **2**, 423.

Lewis, D. and Lowe, W. (1956). Retention of skill on the SAM Complex Coordinator. *Proc. Iowa Acad. Sci.* **63**, 591–599.

Lewis, D. and Shephard, A. H. (1950). Devices for studying associative interference in psychomotor performances. I the modified Mashburn Apparatus. *J. Psychol.* **29**, 35–46.

Lewis, D., McAllister, D. E. and Adams, J. A. (1951). Facilitation and interference in performance on the modified Mashburn Apparatus. I. The effect of varying amounts of original learning. *J. exp. Psychol.* **41**, 247–260.

Luh, C. W. (1923). The conditions of retention. *Psychol. Monogr.* **31**, No. 142.

McAllister, D. E. (1952). Retroactive facilitation and interference as a function of level of learning. *Am. J. Psychol.* **65**, 218–232.

McAllister, D. E. and Lewis, D. (1951). Facilitation and interference in performance on the modified Mashburn Apparatus: II. The effects of varying amounts of interpolated learning. *J. exp. Psychol.* **41**, 356–363.

McDonald, R. D. (1967). "Retention of military skill acquired in basic combat training." HUMRRO Tech. Rep. 67–13.

McGeoch, J. A. (1932). The comparative retention values of a maze habit, of nonsense syllables and of rational learning. *J. exp. Psychol.* **15**, 662–680.

McGeoch, J. A. and Melton, A. W. (1929). The comparative retention values of maze habits and nonsense syllables. *J. exp. Psychol.* **12**, 392–414.

Macek, A. J., Vilter, P. F. and Stubbs, D. W. (1965). "Rehearsal and warm-up in skill retention: final report." Honeywell Report 20153–FR–1 to NASA.

R. G. Marteniuk (1976). Cognitive Information Processes in Short-Term Memory and movement production. *In* "Motor Control: Issues & Trends" (G. E. Stelmach, Ed.). Academic Press, New York and London.

Melton, A. W. (1964). "Retention of tracking skill: final report." Department of Psychology, University of Michigan, ORA Project 02855.

Mengelkoch, R, F., Adams, J. A. and Gainer, G. A. (1971). The forgetting of instrument flying skills as a function of initial proficiency. *Human Factors* **13**, 397–405.

Meyers, J. L. (1967). Retention value of balance learning as influenced by extended layoffs. *Res. Q.* **38**, 72–78.

Montgomery, V. E. (1953). Transfer in motor learning as a function of distribution of practice. *J. exp. Psychol.* **46**, 440–445.

Morris, P. E. (1978). Encoding and Retrieval. *In* "Aspects of Memory" (M. M. Gruneberg and Morris, P. E., Eds). Methuen and Co., London.

Naylor, J. C. (1962). "Parameters affecting the relative efficiency of part and whole practice methods: a review of the literature." NATRADEVCEN. 9512–1.

Naylor, J. C. and Briggs, G. E. (1961). Long-term retention of learned skills: a review of the literature. ASD Tech. Rep. 61–390.

Naylor, J. C. and Briggs, G. E. (1963). Effects of rehearsal of temporal and spatial aspects of the long-term retention of a procedural skill. *J. appl. Psychol.* **47**, 120–126.

Naylor, J. C., Briggs, G. E. and Reed, W. G. (1962). "The effects of task organisation, training time and retention intervals on the retention of skill." Aerospace Medical Research Laboratories, Wright-Patterson Air-force Base, Ohio. AMRL–TDR–62–107.

Naylor, J. C., Briggs, G. E., Brown, E. R. and Reed, W. G. (1963). "The effect of rehearsal on the retention of a time-shared task." Aerospace Medical Research Laboratories, Wright-Patterson Air-force Base, Ohio. AMRL–TDR–63–33.

Naylor, J. C., Briggs, G. E. and Reed, W. G. (1968). Task coherence, training time and retention interval effects on skill retention. *J. appl. Psychol.* **52**, 386–393.

Neumann, E. and Ammons, R. B. (1957). Acquisition and long-term retention of a simple serial perceptual-motor task. *J. exp. Psychol.* **53**, 159–161.

Payne, R. B. and Hauty, G. T. (1955). Factors affecting the endurance of psychomotor skills. *J. aviation Medicine* **26**, 382–389.

Perry, H. M. (1939). The relative efficiency of actual and "imaginary" practice in five selected tasks. *Archiv. Psychol.* **34**, (243).

Purdy, B. J. and Lockhart, A. (1962). Retention and relearning of gross motor skills after long periods of no practice. *Res. Q.* **33**, 265–272.

Reynolds, B. and Bilodeau, I. McD. (1952). Acquisition and retention of psychomotor tests as a function of practice during acquisition. *J. exp. Psychol.* **44**, 19–26.

Roehrig, W. C. (1964). Psychomotor task with perfect recall after 50 weeks of no practice. *Percept. Mot. Skills* **19**, 547–550.

Rubin-Rabson, G. (1939). Studies in the psychology of memorising piano music: I a comparison of the unilateral and coordinated approaches. *J. educ. Psychol.* **30**, 321–345.

Rubin-Rabson, G. (1940a). Studies in the psychology of memorising piano music: II a comparison of massed and distributed practice. *J. educ. Psychol.* **31**, 270–284.

Rubin-Rabson, G. (1940b). Studies in the psychology of memorising piano music: III a comparison of the whole and part approaches. *J. educ. Psychol.* **31**, 460–476.

Rubin-Rabson, G. (1941a). Studies in the psychology of memorising of piano music: IV the effect of incentive. *J. educ. Psychol.* **32**, 45–54.

Rubin-Rabson, G. (1941b). Studies in the psychology of memorising of piano music: V a comparison of pre-study periods of various lengths. *J. educ. Psychol.* **32**, 101–112.

Rubin-Rabson, G. (1941c). Studies in the psychology of memorising piano music: VI a comparison of two forms of mental rehearsal and keyboard overlearning. *J. educ. Psychol.* **32**, 593–602.

Rubin-Rabson, G. (1941d). Studies in the psychology of memorising piano music: VII a comparison of three degrees of overlearning. *J. educ. Psychol.* **32**, 688–696.

Ryan, E. D. (1962). Retention of stabilometer and pursuit motor skills. *Res. Q.* **33**, 593–598.

Ryan, E. D. (1965). Retention of stabilometer performance over extended periods of time. *Res. Q.* **36**, 46–51.

Sackett, R. S. (1934). The influence of symbolic rehearsal upon the retention of a maze habit. *J. gen. Psychol.* **10**, 376–398.

Sackett, R. S. (1935). The relationship between amount of symbolic rehearsal and retention of a maze habit. *J. gen. Psychol.* **13**, 113–128.

Schmidt, R. A. (1972). Experimental Psychology. *In* "The Psychomotor Domain: Movement Behaviors" (Singer, R. N. Ed.). Lea and Feiberger, Philadelphia.

Stelmach, G. E. (1974). Retention of motor skills. *In* "Exercise and Sport Sciences Review" (Wilmore, J. H., Ed.). Vol. 2. Academic Press, New York and London.

Swift, E. J. (1905). Memory of a complex skillful act. *Am. J. Psychol.* **16**, 131–133.

Swift, E. J. (1906). Memory of skillful movements. *Psychol. Bull.* **3**, 185–187.

Swift, E. J. (1910). Relearning a skillful act: an experimental study of neuromuscular memory. *Psychol. Bull.* **7**, 17–19.

Swink, J., Trumbo, D. and Noble, M. (1967). On the length-difficulty relation in skill performance. *J. exp. Psychol.* **74**, 356–362.

Towne, B. M. (1922). An individual curve of learning: a study in typewriting. *J. exp. Psychol.* **5**, 79–92.

Trumbo, D., Noble, M., Cross, K. and Ulrich, L. (1965a). Task predictability in the organisation, acquisition and retention of tracking skill. *J. exp. Psychol.* **70**, 252–263.

Trumbo, D., Ulrich, L. and Noble, M. (1965b). Verbal coding and display coding in the acquisition and retention of tracking skill. *J. exp. Psychol.* **49**, 368–375.

Trumbo, D., Noble, M. and Swink, J. (1967). Secondary task interference in the performance of tracking tasks. *J. exp. Psychol.* **73**, 232–240.

Tsai, C. (1924). A comparative study of retention curves for motor habits. *Comp. Psychol. Monogr.* **2**, Whole No. 11.

Vandell, R. A., Davis, R. A. and Clugston, H. A. (1943). The function of mental practice in the acquisition of motor skills. *J. gen. Psychol.* **29**, 243–250.

Van Dusen, F. and Schlosberg, H. (1948). Further study of the retention of verbal and motor skills. *J. exp. Psychol.* **38**, 526–534.

Van Tilborg, P. W. (1936). The retention of mental and finger maze habits. *J. exp. Psychol.* **19**, 334–341.

Warden, J. C. (1924). The relative economy of various modes of attack in the mastery of a stylus maze. *J. exp. Psychol.* **7**, 243–275.

Waters, R. H. and Poole, G. B. (1933). The relative retention values of stylus and mental maze habits. *J. exp. Psychol.* **16**, 429–434.

Watson, R. I. (1938). An experimental study of the permanence of course material in Introductory Psychology. *Arch. Psychol.* No. 222.

Welford, A. T. (1958). "Ageing and Human Skill." Oxford University Press, Oxford.

Woodworth, R. S. (1899). The accuracy of voluntary movement. *Psych. Rev. Mongr. Suppl.* **3**, No. 3.

Youngling, E. W., Sharpe, E. N., Ricketson, B. S. and McGee, D. W. (1968). "Crew skill retention for space missions up to 200 days." McDonnel-Douglas Astronautics Co., Eastern Division. Report F.7666.

9. Disorders of Language and Memory

J. C. MARSHALL

Interfakultaire Werkgroep Taal- en Spraakgedrag,
University of Nijmegen, The Netherlands

I. Introduction

Textbooks of normal psychology not infrequently contain a chapter on language and a chapter on memory; textbooks of neurology and neuropsychology often contain a chapter on disorders of language (the aphasias) and a chapter on disorders of memory (the amnesias). It is not my intention here to write two such chapters. Psychologists have postulated so many varieties of "memory" that the topic has become virtually co-extensive with studies of the whole of human and animal behaviour, or even co-extensive with physics:

> Is it as plainly in our living shown,
> By slant and twist, which way the wind hath blown?
> That is memory in trees . . . (Gerard, 1963.)

Similarly, for a language-using animal, such as man, the number of tasks that can be performed with significant linguistic involvement is horrendously large, and the number of tasks that are typically so performed is only slightly less. In order to render the discussion (almost) manageable I intend the conjunction of the title to signify a more intimate bond than is customarily formed between the two topics. That is, my theme is indeed "disorders of language and memory", not "disorders of language and disorders of memory". One somewhat regettable consequence of this attempt at unification is that I have been forced into inventing yet more terminology for the different types of memory that I consider. Given the already massive proliferation of terms over the last twenty years, one might suppose that the field needs this like fish need bicycles. I shall try to reduce the confusion by indicating the areas of overlap between my terminology and the traditional labels.

II. On-Line Memory

One of the most obvious yet nonetheless striking aspects of language perception (and production) is the rapidity with which "high-level" information may be assigned to the physical signal. For example, Chistovich *et al.* (1960) have demonstrated that some subjects can "shadow" continuous speech at latencies of the order of 150–250 ms, and with an extremely low error-rate. Although these subjects said that "they repeated before they had managed to understand", later work suggests that these intuitions may not be veridical. In a comparison of "normal" and close shadowers, Marslen-Wilson (1973) could find no significant relationship between shadowing latency and memory for content even when subjects were not told in advance that they would be given a comprehension test; even more critically, the vast proportion of the errors that were made by the close shadowers were both syntactically and semantically appropriate to the preceding context.

What this suggests is that the duration of primary memory in the sense of William James (1890) can be very brief indeed. That is, it is often not necessary to "preserve" (remember) long segments of an incoming signal in a relatively "pure" (sensory) form before beginning the work of high-level analysis. The idea of speech-perception as a fast, "interactive parallel process" (Marslen-Wilson, 1975) that is driven both by the signal and by internally-generated predictions is most appealing (Miller, 1962). However, the present whilst short cannot be vanishingly so. The nature of the "speech-code" is such that in many instances information relevant to the identification of the phonemes in a CVC syllable accrues simultaneously (Remington, 1977); the phonological variation characteristic of natural fluent speech combined with the short-range ambiguity of many linguistic units also suggests that it would be rational for nature to have devised sensory stores as "windows" onto the input signal. As Chomsky and Miller (1963) point out, it may be some time before one can decide whether the acoustic signal is to be interpreted as "Gal, amant de la Reine, alla (tour magnanime)" or as "Galamment de l'arène à la Tour Magne, à Nîmes". One expects, then, to find a "holding" mechanism that permits delayed decisions, or a re-check if an earlier decision turns out to be incompatible with subsequent context. The existence of "pre-categorial" stores for both visual stimuli (Averbach and Sperling, 1961) and acoustic stimuli (Crowder and Morton, 1969) is now fairly well-established. Such systems in which a signal may persist for a second or two would not, of course, provide an "all-purpose" memory-store but they would enable a more informative message to reach other components of comprehension procedures.

There are very few studies that have explicitly contemplated the possible behavioural implications of brain damage that might impair the functioning of these peripheral stores; and indeed Crowder and Morton (in the legend to figure 1, 1969) issue the stern injunction that "No reference whatever to locations or pathways in the nervous system is implied". I shall accordingly put forward a few speculations in the hope of persuading others to investigate the relationships between normal and impaired performance in these input mechanisms that are on the boundary of perceptual and memorial processes.

We know that the peripheral stores ("iconic" and "echoic") are highly susceptible to various masking effects; in one sense one might say that such stores were postulated just in order to interpret the phenomena of masking (Turvey, 1973; Crowder, 1978). Crowder (1978) has suggested that the *type* of masking that is involved within pre-categorial acoustic storage is analogous to Hartline-Ratcliff lateral inhibition; and Bridgeman (1978) has proposed a model of lateral inhibition that provides for the brief storage of information as a neces-sary property of the system. Could it be that *some* of the effects of rate of presentation on discrimination and comprehension in aphasia (Albert and Bear, 1974; Lasky *et al.*, 1976; Tallal and Newcombe, 1978) are due to excessive inhibition within pre-categorial acoustic storage (PAS) at normal presentation rates? It might also be suggested that part at least of the reading deficit shown by the patient with simultanagnosia (War-rington and Rabin, 1971; Levine and Calvanio, 1978) could be due to similarly increased lateral inhibition within an iconic store. In this condition, patients can identify single visual elements (letters, for example) with reasonable accuracy, but performance deteriorates dramatically when a spatial array of such elements is presented (Luria, 1959). In a comparison of dyslexic children and normal readers, Bouma and Legein (1977) have shown that the two groups did not differ in recognizing individual letters, but the dyslexic subjects were impaired when reporting "embedded" letters, that is, letters flanked on either side by other letters. Could such results be interpreted as a developmental analogue of simultanagnosia?

III. Control Memory

By "control memory" I intend to refer to at least some aspects of what other workers have discussed under the names "short-term memory" (STM) (Broadbent, 1970) and "working memory" (Baddeley and Hitch, 1974). I use the term "control memory" in order to emphasize that the system (or systems) is (are) implicated in rehearsal (Morton, 1970), and in the distinction between incidental and intentional recall. In part, then, the system is under the strategic control of the subject and (or) the experimenter (Shiffrin, 1975). This component is the first system that is fairly unambiguously memorial rather than perceptual; it is also clearly a "store" in terms of the distinction that Bruner (1969) draws between memory with- and without- record. Neuropsychological research has, however, rather effectively disposed of the idea that STM is the sole, obligatory input channel to long-term memory (LTM). It would seem that we must invoke parallel input from perceptual processes to both LTM and STM, or in some cases postulate that short-term storage is subsequent to higher-level analysis that draws upon long-term ("structural") memory without record.

The evidence that this is so involves the assumption that certain span tasks (ordered immediate recall of digit or word sequences) draw upon an auditory STM system. There are well-documented cases where patients with left parietal injuries (Warrington *et al.*, 1971) are found to have dramatically reduced digit spans but essentially normal performance on a variety of LTM tasks, including paired-associate learning, short story retention and free recall learning to criterion (Shallice, 1979). Some of these patients have quite adequate spontaneous speech and their comprehension of simple sentences is fairly well preserved; they certainly do not have perceptual or articulatory impairments that could account for their poor span performance. This being so, the question naturally arises as to the *normal* function of the system that is involved in span (and some superspan) tasks; to use a somewhat hackneyed expression, the ecological validity of a store that is only useful for remembering telephone numbers would be a little suspect. Many scholars have accordingly conjectured that the system may function as a "back-up" store that is implicated in the parsing and interpretation of complex sentences, a system that allows a longer-lasting and more flexible representation than that provided by an "echoic" store. Let us consider the evidence.

Schuell *et al.* (1964) have noted that for many aphasic subjects "difficulty in perceiving and structuring messages appear to be secondary to reduced vocabulary and verbal retention span". If this is so, one

would expect to find that immediate sentence recall was disproportionately impaired in aphasic subjects when semantic constraints are
reduced. This result was found by Newcombe and Marshall (1967).
Men with left hemisphere lesions consequent upon gunshot injury (and
with mild residual aphasic symptoms) performed as well as a control
group in the immediate verbatim repetition of such sentences as
"Wasn't the stone wall built by the kind husband?", where selection
restrictions serve to code the order of noun phrases and the appropriate
pairing of adjectives with nouns. Repetition was dramatically
impaired, however, with syntactically equivalent sentences without
such constraint, for example "Wasn't the rich uncle advised by the nice
manager?". A similar point is made in Newcombe and Marshall
(1972). Two control groups, one with right hemisphere injuries and one
with left hemisphere injuries but without clinically detectable aphasia,
showed little difference in their accuracy of recall for "Healthy young
babies eat frequently" versus "Colourless green ideas sleep furiously".
The semantically anomalous sentence provoked great difficulty for a
group of aphasic subjects. The error patterns were highly informative.
When the material was well formed the errors made by the aphasic
subjects reflected and preserved much of the syntactic and semantic
structure of the sentences. For example, "The burglar that the police
found escaped easily" would be "repeated" as "the burglar escaped
from the policeman". When the material was deviant, either syntactically or semantically, the aphasic subjects would tend to "normalize"
it. Thus "She has washed plastic red small cups" would be recalled as
"She has washed small red plastic cups", or "Wasn't the fat ceiling
robbed by the tired pen?" would be recalled as "Wasn't the red ceiling
robbed by the felon?".

Similar results have been reported in an elegant single-case study by
Saffran and Marin (1975). Their patient had only mild expressive
difficulties in the context of a gross span impairment and many qualitative departures from normal performance on a variety of tasks that
contain a STM component. For example, the patient showed no
recency effect in the serial recall of auditory lists, although the recency
effect was of normal magnitude with visually-presented lists. Immediate recall of sentences showed the following kinds of error:

The residence was located in a peaceful neighbourhood →
The residence was situated in a quiet district
The man the child hit carried the box →
The man hit the child who carried the box
The soldiers knew that pleasing women can be fun →
the soldiers knew that going with charming women can be fun.

The overall pattern of the patient's performance suggests to Saffran and Marin (1975) that "short-term" performance is being mediated by a more or less intact LTM store. They conclude with the conjecture that "auditory short-term memory is not essential for long-term retention, or for the understanding of plain English, at least when it comes in loud and clear. Having the phonemic record around for a while does seem useful, however, when there is need to reconsider the first or ongoing interpretation: when syntax is tortuous . . . and when messages are garbled or otherwise noisy". This conclusion is fully consistent with the report of Shallice and Buttersworth (1977). Their patient (J.B.) showed normal spontaneous speech and no primary defect of acoustic perception. Her digit span was, however, more than two standard deviations below the norm. Although the patient's comprehension was adequate for most ordinary conversational purposes, she made frequent ". . . mistakes in understanding relatively short sentences which contained much nonredundant information . . ., sentences which were syntactically complex or which could not easily be disambiguated". Much the same point is made by Heilman et al. (1976) who have shown that in aphasic subjects there is a significant correlation between comprehension of spoken language and digit span scores. The evidence, then, from both normal and aphasic subjects shows fairly conclusively that heuristic, predictive parsing (Morton, 1964; Caramazza and Zurif, 1976) is peculiarly error-prone unless supplemented by a veridical phonological record. The above discussion has concentrated on the functions of acoustic verbal STM, but it is worth noting that neuropsychological evidence supports the existence of a separate visual STM (Warrington and Shallice, 1972), and of a short-term storage system for non-verbal sounds that is functionally (and perhaps anatomically) distinct from the acoustic verbal store (Shallice and Warrington, 1974).

We have considered cases of aphasia where relatively intact long-term ("semantic") processing co-exists with a severe impairment in STM functions. Can the reverse dissociation be found in aphasia? To some extent this is indeed seen in subjects with "transcortical aphasia" and in the so-called "isolation syndrome". In the transcortical aphasias, immediate repetition is remarkably well preserved despite a severe impairment of either spontaneous speech or comprehension (or both). The preserved repetition, however, cannot reflect the "pure" operation of a veridical acoustic memory for Davis et al. (1978) have shown that these patients, like the ones we have previously considered, tend to "normalize" sentences containing "minor" syntactic violations. For example, "The maids sweeps the floor" will be repeated as

"The maids sweep the floor", or "The boy gave she a present" will be reproduced as "The boy gave her a present". Sentences that contravened semantic selection restrictions (e.g. "The milk drank the cat") are, however, repeated verbatim. Somewhat analogous results have been reported by Whitaker (1976) for a case of "isolation syndrome". This woman had virtually no spontaneous speech or comprehension of language; but she had pronounced echolalia in the sense that she would repeat back what the examiner said *without* being instructed to do so. These "echolalic" responses, however, also frequently showed the phenomenon of syntactic "correction". Thus "Have you dinner?" would be "echoed" as "Have you had dinner?", and "Can you told me your name?" as "Can you tell me your name?" Word-order deviations were also "corrected" ("I have hair gray" → "I have gray gray hair"). As in the previously mentioned report, semantic anomalies ("The pencil can't see very well") were often repeated verbatim (and certainly were not "normalized").

It would seem that the above patterns of impairment (and preservation) of acoustic STM must be firmly distinguished from another type of "repetition" problem that has often been regarded as a cardinal feature of "conduction" aphasia (Benson *et al.*, 1973). These latter patients frequently experience great difficulty in "repeating" a single word upon command. The variables of length, familiarity and syntactic and semantic class may influence the adequacy of performance (Brown, 1975; Goldstein, 1948). Goldstein (1948), who discusses the phenomenon as a component of "central" aphasia, regarded voluntary repetition as under the control of the "abstract attitude", an attitude that he suggests can be impaired by brain damage. We can see something of the distinction between voluntary "repetition" and spontaneous speech in the familiar story of the aphasic patient, who, asked to say "No" struggles valiantly and unsuccessfully to do so before finally bursting out with "No, no, I can't say 'no'".

Finally, one should note that the STM system that is implicated in speech comprehension appears to be quite distinct from the "response buffer" (Morton, 1970) that plays a role in speech production. Many of the properties of this store which is concerned with the "chunking" and serial ordering of speech can be deduced from the work of Garrett (1975) and Ellis (1979). The store provides a crucial interface between a partially parallel process (the elaboration of structural descriptions) and a largely left-to-right process (the motor programming of speech). The phonological paraphasias that characterize the speech of so many aphasic patients are, in large part, interpretable as impairments of this response buffer. However, the existence of patients with perfectly normal spontaneous speech, a severe STM deficit, and comprehension problems for complex sentences (Shallice and Butterworth, 1977) establishes the functional independence of the input and the output buffers.

IV. Structural and Procedural Memory

If we were to interpret the notion of "memory" as broadly as some authors have done, we would be forced into reviewing *all* of the varied disorders of language production and comprehension that are consequent upon brain injury. Some idea of the extent of applications of the term can be gained by recalling that Broca (1866) described his patients with severe expressive aphasia as having lost "the memory of the procedure that one must follow in order to articulate words". And Wernicke (1874) believed that the comprehension deficits of his patients was due to loss of the acoustic "memory images" for words.

I shall restrict the domain by considering only certain "anomic" conditions in which disorders of word-production or comprehension are the most striking feature. What I am calling "structural and procedural memory" thus has considerable overlap with what others have referred to as "access, storage, and retrieval processes in semantic memory". There is also overlap with the expression "memory without record" whereby Bruner (1969) refers to experiences that are "converted into some process that changes the nature of the organism, changes his skills, or changes the rules by which he operates but which are virtually inaccessible in memory as specific encounters". Learning the vocabulary of a language (as a child) clearly changes the nature of the organism, but the specific learning experiences are not, as a rule, time-tagged into a conscious record of events.

By the time he is a young, educated adult a native speaker will have a (sight) vocabulary in the order of 75 000 words (Oldfield, 1966); in only a little over a half-second, a subject can perceive a character string, decide whether or not it is an item in the vocabulary of his language, and respond appropriately by pressing a "Yes" or a "No" key (Forster, 1976). In spontaneous speech, a subset of elements from this vocabulary will be produced at a rate of two to three items per second. What form of organization allows the normal adult such ready and (relatively) error-free access to the pattern of interconnection of our vocabulary and its appropriate deployment in the expression of utterances? Although this achievement is impressive, performance is not, of course, totally without error even in normal subjects. "Tips of the slung" do occur (Fromkin, 1973); spoonerisms (Potter, 1976) and malapropisms (Fay and Cutler, 1977) are not proprietary to Dr. Spooner and Mrs. Malaprop. Similarly, "tip-of-the tongue" states (Rubin, 1975) are far from unknown in all of us. The frequency of "word-finding problems" is, however, much greater in the brain-injured patient where these difficulties are seen after a wide variety of focal (Geschwind, 1967) and diffuse (Schilder and Curran, 1935) lesions. Relatively mild word-finding deficits are a common residual symptom in the evolution of many aphasic syndromes. There is, however, a specific syndrome in which such difficulties are disproportionately severe relative to the fluent articulation, normal syntax, good repetition and fair-to-good comprehension shown by the patient. The syndrome—anomic or amnestic aphasia—is usually found with lesions of the left parietotemporal area; word-finding deficits are apparent in spontaneous speech and in "confrontation naming" irrespective of the modality of presentation of the stimulus (visual or tactile). To some extent the term "anomia" is inappropriate for the disorder of spontaneous speech may involve abstract nouns, adjectives and verbs as well as concrete nouns.

It is tempting to assume that normal "tip-of-the tongue" states are an analogous, albeit milder, form of the aphasic anomic deficit. As with the normal subject, the aphasic patient seems in some sense to "know" the word he is searching for and can often demonstrate this by pantomime or circumlocution; if the "missing" word is given by the examiner he will recognize that it is the required response. He will also be able to pick out the "missing" word from a list that the examiner offers. All of this suggests that it is only the phonology (and "graphology") of the response that is temporarily unavailable. If so, one might expect that, as with the normal subject, an anomic patient would have access to some of the phonological features of the item that has provoked a "tip-of-the tongue" state. Goodglass et al. (1976) have, however, shown that subjects with anomic aphasia (and those with Wernicke's aphasia) perform essentially at chance level when required to "guess" the first letter and the number of syllables in words that they failed to produce in a confrontation object-naming task. Contrariwise, subjects with conduction aphasia performed rather well on the "partial recall" task despite showing a level of naming failures that was strictly comparable with that of the anomic subjects. Marshall (1977) contains some speculations on a possible mechanism for naming failure at a stage preceding that of phonological retrieval. In a particularly interesting paper, Cohn (1970) has reported on some amnestic patients who "forget" object-names immediately after the examiner has prompted them with the name and they have correctly repeated it.

What can be said concerning the overall structure of lexical access, storage and retrieval? Psychologists who work with normal subjects have traditionally studied the properties of the "mental dictionary" via such techniques as free and constrained association, tachistoscopic (or noise-masked) recognition, word- and object-naming, and, most recently, by collecting lexical decision latencies. We assume that the qualitative pattern of response and the quantitative analysis of error-rates and response latencies in such tasks will enable us to work out (1) The basic architecture of lexical organization (Treisman, 1978); (2) The dynamics of accessing and retrieval procedures (Coltheart, 1978); and (3) The range of control processes and "strategy" variations (Carr et al., 1978).

The foundations and pre-suppositions of experimental studies in psycholinguistics are rarely stated explicitly. Nonetheless, I think that the following "reconstruction" is an accurate statement of the implicit viewpoint adopted by many students of mental lexicography:

(1) There is (are) one (or at most two) "central", modality-free semantic system(s). With minor idealization the semantic system(s) is (are) common to all (native) speakers of the language in question.

(2) There are a variety of input and output mechanisms, some of which may reasonably be regarded as parts of the lexical system. Many of these "peripheral" devices are modality-specific, but they all lead either to or from the modality-free semantic system(s).

(3) Different tasks will draw upon different input and output mechanisms; different subjects will adopt different control and strategy procedures involving these peripheral devices. *Variation* in behaviour from task to task will accordingly not be interpreted in terms of the mode of operation of the semantic system(s).

The existence of two semantic systems was, of course, first postulated in order to interpret individual differences in behaviour following "similar" cerebral lesions and made special reference to differential rates and extents of recovery from aphasia (Schilder, 1924); more recently, studies of commissurotomy (Zaidel, 1978) and hemispherec-tomy (Dennis, 1979) have renewed interest in the idea of left and right hemisphere lexicons.

We now ask the question: To what extent is such a framework consistent with the neuropsychological evidence? In principle, the "disconnectionist" interpretation of deficits (Geschwind, 1965) that is implied by the above approach need have no difficulty in interpreting differential performance as a function of output mode. Lhermitte and

Derouesné (1974) have reported on two cases of fluent aphasia in which the disorder of spontaneous speech was disproportionately severe relative to the patients' rather well-preserved written expression. The primary abnormalities of spoken language consisted, however, of phonemic paraphasias and frank neologisms; postulation of a disorder of a speech-specific response buffer would accordingly serve to characterize the deficit. Hier and Mohr (1977) have studied a related case of Wernicke's aphasia. Their patient too had fluent paraphasic speech. On a picture-naming test the man's performance was greatly superior with written responding than with oral responding. With the exception, however, of one correct vocal response, his performance in oral-naming consisted of failures to respond—the paradigm case for disconnectionist interpretations. Although dissociated disorders of speaking and writing in aphasia are undoubtedly rare (Basso et al., 1978) they certainly do exist. However, the available published cases do not appear to embarrass the framework I have outlined; clamour for a paradigm-shift would only occur if cases were described with preservation of, say, object-naming in one output modality and *semantic* errors in another output modality.

Let us turn now to naming-disorders that are specific to a particular *input* modality. Once again, dissociations of naming performance to visual and tactile presentation can, albeit rarely, be found (Spreen *et al.*, 1966); in the best-studied cases a primary "sensory" loss or higher-level perceptual deficit is ruled out by showing, for example, that the patient can copy the visual stimulus quite adequately or can discriminate between closely similar stimuli on tactile presentation.

We will first consider an example that is fairly unproblematic. Mack and Boller (1977) describe a patient whose object-naming to tactile presentation is considerably superior to his performance with pictures and visually-presented objects. This latter failure is not to be accounted for perceptually as the patient can copy the pictures (that he fails to identify) sufficiently well that others can recognize the identity of his copies, but in addition to total failures to name to visual confrontation, the errors were typically similar in *form* to the stimulus item. Thus an apple was called a "ball", a cigar was called a "screwdriver". This pattern, then, is consistent with a (partial) disconnectionist approach in which information is degraded *en route* from perceptual analysis to lexical access.

One of the cases reported by Spreen *et al.* (1966) is a little more disturbing. This patient also showed good naming to palpatation (with either hand) and a severe disturbance of naming with objects presented in the visual modality. Perceptual processes were intact to the extent that the patient could recognize in a multiple-choice matching task the objects that had been presented for naming. The conceptual problem arises from the fact that the patient would frequently indicate the *use* of the visually-presented objects that he was unable to name. *Ex hypothesi*, the modality-free semantic system is intact, and appropriate verbal output is possible (as witness performance with tactile naming); with visual presentation the information that reaches the semantic system is specific enough to permit descriptions of the use of objects. Why then is naming so poor with visual presentation?

A similar puzzle is raised by the report of Lhermitte and Beauvois (1973). In their patient, naming to tactile presentation is again remarkably well preserved but numerous errors are made when the patient is required to name visually-presented objects or pictures. Once again, "when objects were misnamed, the patient very clearly showed by pantomime that he had correctly recognized them". In a substantial proportion of instances, the errors in visual naming bore a semantic or associative relationship to the stimulus (e.g. SHOE → "hat"; HELMET → "cassock"; CAP → "jockey"). Although Lhermitte and Beauvois (1973) do interpret their case as a "visual-speech disconnection syndrome" it is far from clear that such an explication is consistent with the traditional model. One can, of course, attempt to save the appearances by invoking two modality-free semantic systems, one in the left hemisphere (from whence come the correct responses in tactile naming) and one in the right hemisphere (from whence come the semantic errors in visual naming). An argument of this type becomes, however, a little tortuous when one notices that a case displaying precisely the inverse syndrome has been reported from the same laboratory. The patient of Beauvois *et al.* (1978) showed excellent naming to visual confrontation but made numerous semantic errors when objects were presented to either hand.

The possibility therefore arises that there may be distinct modality-specific semantic systems (Warrington, 1975), and that within these systems brain injury may result in differential loss of features and categories(McKenna and Warrington, 1978).

V. Autobiographical Memory

The primary deficit that characterizes the "amnesic" syndromes is a disorder of autobiographical memory in the sense that knowledge of a (variable) proportion and time-slice of the events in his past (i.e. prior to the onset of his illness) life is unavailable to the patient ("retrograde" amnesia); similarly, a (variable) proportion and time-slice of post-illness events may be unavailable almost immediately after they have passed ("anterograde" amnesia). In some cases, the patient lives in a permanent specious present (Scoville, 1968). One traditional interpretation of the retrograde amnesia claims that memories that have not been "consolidated" are wiped from the record; one traditional interpretation of the anterograde amnesia is in terms of a "learning" deficit associated with transfer from short- to long-term storage. New information fails to consolidate, just as old but unconsolidated information is removed (Milner, 1966). The amnestic patient does not lose previously acquired skills, including verbal skills; in terms of the distinction drawn by Tulving (1972) one would accordingly regard the disorder as one of episodic not semantic memory. In "pure" cases, the learning deficit extends similarly across a wide variety of different tasks. Thus Scoville and Milner (1957) report that the mother of H.M. "still has to tell him where to find the lawn mower, even though he may have been using it only the day before. She also states that he will do the same jigsaw puzzles day after day without showing any practice effect and that he will read the same magazines over and over again without finding their contents familiar".

To a first approximation, amnestic patients do not show disorders of language; they can hold perfectly rational conversations with good understanding and without showing any easily detectable expressive deficit. The above remarks are, of course, subject to the qualification that the patients will break certain rules of discourse structure as a consequence of, for example, "forgetting" the name of their partner in conversation or indeed the topic of the conversation if they are momentarily distracted. The point is simply that the amnestic patient's language behaviour seems to have nothing in common with that shown in any of the aphasic syndromes. The combination of preserved semantic memory and good STM, as assessed by span tasks at least (Drachman and Arbit, 1966), appears to guarantee the effective operation of the language-system *per se*. (Controversy about the intactness or otherwise of STM in amnesia has centered around the Peterson paradigm, not span phenomena: Baddeley and Warrington, 1970; Butters and Cermak, 1974).

Why, then, do we include mention of the amnesias when reviewing disorders of language and memory?

The reason is that one of the many interpretations of amnesia is to the effect that patients typically fail to employ a *semantic* code for input to (or "tagging" in) long-term storage. Thus the results of Cermak *et al.* (1973) suggest that in a cued recall paradigm amnesic patients (suffering from Korsakov syndrome) may benefit less from "category" cues than they do from rhyming cues, whereas this pattern is reversed for an (alcoholic) control group. Similarly, in a task involving the detection of repeated items in visually-presented word-lists, the Korsakov patients made significantly more false positive responses to homonyms (bear–bare) and to associates (table–chair) than did the control group whilst not differing from the controls on false positives to synonyms (robber–thief). In a related experiment, Cermak and Moreines (1976) compared the detection of rhyming words and words from the same semantic category during the reading of a list by the experimenter. At slow rates of presentation and with only between 0 and 2 items intervening, the Korsakov patients were differentially impaired on the detection of "same category" words.

Cermak (1976) has reported some results from a patient with amnesia due to encephalitis which, while very strange, are compatible with the notion of severe semantic deficit. It is well known that amnesic patients *can* learn new motor skills and new verbal responses (although they take an inordinately large number of trials to do so), Cermak's patient (with a verbal I.Q. of 130) was labouriously taught some useful responses to questions; for example, "Put on my sweater" as a response to "What do you do when you enter your house?", or "Take a Shower" as a response to "What should you do first thing in the morning?" However, "When he went home he never put on a sweater. If his wife said to him 'What do you do when you enter the house?', he would reply 'Put on my sweater' and then would stand there. If his wife said 'Why don't you'? he was likely to reply 'Do what?' (Cermak, 1976). In terms of new "verbal learning" then, this patient does seem to have speech without access to the semantic and cognitive systems that transmute structured noises into language.

It is unlikely, however, that such semantic impairments could provide the necessary and sufficient cause for the full range of deficits shown in amnesic states (Baddeley, 1975). Future work will, no doubt, investigate more closely the putative differences between amnesia consequent upon bilateral temporal lobe and hippocampal removal, upon vitamin deficiency (as in the Korsakov syndrome), and upon encephalitis (Lhermitte and Signoret, 1972; Mattis *et al.*, 1978). It is also possible that current accounts of the neuroanatomy of the lesions responsible for severe amnesia may need to be drastically revised (Horel, 1978). Be that as it may, it would be interesting if Freud's speculation that memories (as opposed to learning skills) are only possible in a creature with language should turn out to possess more than a grain of truth (Freud, 1895).

References

Albert, M. L. and Bear, D. (1974). Time to understand: A case study of word deafness with reference to the role of time in auditory comprehension. *Brain* **97**, 373–384.

Averbach, E. and Sperling, G. (1961). Short-term storage of information in vision. *In* "Information Theory: Proceedings of the Fourth London Symposium." (C. Cherry, Ed.). Butterworth, London.

Baddeley, A. D. (1975). Theories of Amnesia. *In* "Studies in Long Term Memory." (A. Kennedy and A. Wilkes, Eds). Wiley, London.

Baddeley, A. D. and Hitch, G. (1974). Working Memory. *In* "The Psychology of Learning and Motivation." (G. H. Bower, Ed.). Vol. 8. Academic Press, New York and London.

Baddeley, A. D. and Warrington, E. K. (1970). Amnesia and the distinction between long- and short-term memory. *J. Verb. Learn. Verb. Behav.* **9**, 176–189.

Basso, A., Taborelli, A. and Vignolo, L. A. (1978). Dissociated disorders of speaking and writing in aphasia. *J. Neurol. Neurosurg. Psychiat.* **41**, 556–563.

Beauvois, M.-F., Saillant, B., Meininger, V. and Lhermitte, F. (1978). Bilateral tactile aphasia: A tacto-verbal dysfunction. *Brain* **101**, 381–401.

Benson, D. F., Sheremata, W. A., Bouchard, R., Segarra, J. M., Price, D. and Geschwind, N. (1973). Conduction Aphasia: A Clinopathological study. *Archiv. Neurol.* **28**, 339–346.

Bouma, H. and Legein, C. P. (1977). Foveal and parafoveal recognition of letters and words by dyslexics and by average readers. *Neuropsychol.* **15**, 69–80.

Bridgeman, B. (1978). Distributed sensory coding applied to simulations of iconic storage and metacontrast. *Bull. math. Biol.* **40**, 605–623.

Broadbent, D. E. (1970). Psychological aspects of short-term and long-term memory. *Proc. R. Soc. L.* B, **175**, 333–350.

Broca, P. (1866). Sur la faculté générale du langage, dans ses rapports avec la faculté du langage articulé. *Bull. Soc. d'Anth.* **2**, 396–399.

Brown, J. W. (1975). The problem of repetition: A study of "conduction" aphasia and the "isolation" syndrome. *Cortex* **11**, 37–52.

Bruner, J. S. (1969). Modalities of memory. *In* "The Pathology of Memory." (G. A. Talland and N. C. Waugh, Eds). Academic Press, London and New York.

Butters, N. and Cermak, L. S. (1974). Some comments on Warrington and Baddeley's report on normal short-term memory in amnesic patients. *Neuropsychol.* **12**, 283–285.

Caramazza, A. and Zurif, E. (1976). Dissociation of algorithmic and heuristic processes in language comprehension: Evidence from aphasia. *Brain and Language* **3**, 572–582.

Carr, T. H., Davidson, B. J. and Hawkins, H. L. (1978). Perceptual flexibility in word recognition: Strategies affect orthographic computation but not lexical access. *J. exp. Psychol: Hum. Percept. Perform.* **4**, 674–690.

Cermak, L. S. (1976). The encoding capacity of a patient with amnesia due to encephalitis. *Neuropsychol.* **14**, 311–326.

Cermak, L. S. and Moreines, J. (1976). Verbal retention deficits in aphasic and amnesic patients. *Brain and Language* **3**, 16–27.

Cermak, L. S., Butters, N. and Gerrein, J. (1973). The extent of the verbal encoding ability of Korsakov patients. *Neuropsychol.* **11**, 85–94.

Chistovich, L. A., Aliakrinskii, V. V. and Abul'ian, V. A. (1960). Time delays in speech repetition. *Vopr. psikhol.* **1**, 114–119.

Chomsky, N. and Miller, G. A. (1963). Introduction to the formal analysis of natural languages. *In* "Handbook of Mathematical Psychology." (R. D. Luce, R. R. Bush and E. Galanter, Eds). Vol. 2. Wiley, New York.

Cohn, R. (1970). Amnestic aphasia and other disturbances in naming. *Archiv. Neurol.* **22**, 515–520.

Coltheart, M. (1978). Lexical access in simple reading tasks. *In* "Strategies of Information Processing." (G. Underwood, Ed.). Academic Press, London and New York.

Crowder, R. G. (1978). Mechanisms of auditory backward masking in the stimulus suffix effect. *Psychol. Rev.* **85**, 502–524.

Crowder, R. G. and Morton, J. (1969). Precategorial acoustic storage (PAS). *Percept. Psychophysics* **5**, 365–373.

Davis, L., Foldi, N. S. Gardner, H. and Zurif, E. B. (1978). Repetition in the transcortical aphasias. *Brain and Language* **6**, 226–238.

Dennis, M. (1979). Language acquisition in a single hemisphere: Semantic organization. *In* "Biological Studies of Mental Processes." (D. Caplan, Ed.). MIT Press, Cambridge, Massachusetts.

Drachman, D. A. and Arbit, J. (1966). Memory and the hippocampal complex II. *Archiv. Neurol.* **15**, 52–61.

Ellis, A. W. (1979). Speech production and short-term memory. *In* "Psycholinguistics Series." (J. Morton and J. C. Marshall, Eds). Vol. 2. Elek, London.

Fay, D. and Cutler, A. (1977). Malapropisms and the structure of the mental lexicon. *Linguistic Inquiry* **8**, 505–520.

Forster, K. (1976). Accessing the mental lexicon. *In* "New Approaches to Language Mechanisms." (R. J. Wales and E. Walker, Eds). North-Holland, Amsterdam.

Freud, S. (Ed.) (1895). Project for a scientific psychology. *In* "Standard Edition". Vol. 1. Hogarth Press, London.

Fromkin, V. (Ed.) (1973). "Speech Errors as Linguistic Evidence." Mouton, The Hague.

Garrett, M. (1975). The analysis of sentence production. *In* "The Psychology of Learning and Motivation." (G. H. Bower, Ed.). Vol. 9. Academic Press, New York and London.

Gerard, R. W. (1963). The material basis of memory. *J. Verb. Learn. Verb. Behav.* **2**, 22–33.

Geschwind, N. (1965). Disconnexion syndromes in animals and man. *Brain* **88**, 237–294; 585–644.

Geschwind, N. (1967). The varieties of naming errors. *Cortex* **3**, 97–112.

Goldstein, K. (1948). "Language and Language Disturbances." Grune and Stratton, New York.

Goodglass, H., Kaplan, E., Weintraub, S. and Ackerman, N. (1976). The "tip-of-the-tongue" phenomenon in aphasia. *Cortex* **12**, 145–153.

Heilman, K. M., Scholes, R. and Watson, R. T. (1976). Defects of immediate memory in Broca's and Conduction aphasia. *Brain and Language* **3**, 201–208.

Hier, D. B. and Mohr, J. P. (1977). Incongruous oral and written naming: Evidence for a subdivision of the syndrome of Wernicke's aphasia. *Brain and Language* **4**, 115–126.

Horel, J. A. (1978). The neuroanatomy of amnesia: A critique of the hippocampal memory hypothesis. *Brain* **101**, 403–445.

James, W. (1890). "The Principles of Psychology." Macmillan, London.

Lasky, E. Z., Weidner, W. E. and Johnson, J. P. (1976). Influence of linguistic complexity, rate of presentation, and interphrase pause time on auditory-verbal comprehension of adult aphasic patients. *Brain and Language* **3**, 386–395.

Levine, D. N. and Calvanio, R. (1978). A study of the visual defect in verbal alexia—simultanagnosia. *Brain* **101**, 65–81.

Lhermitte, F. and Beauvois, M. F. (1973). A visual-speech disconnection syndrome. *Brain* **96**, 695–714.

Lhermitte, F. and Derouesné, J. (1974). Paraphasies et jargonaphasie dans le langage oral avec conservation du langage écrit. *Revue Neurologique* **130**, 21–38.

Lhermitte, F. and Signoret, J-L. (1972). Analyse neuropsychologique et differenciation des syndromes amnésiques. *Revue Neurologique* **129**, 161–178.

Luria, A. R. (1959). Disorders of "simultaneous perception" in a case of bilateral occipito-parietal brain injury. *Brain* **82**, 437–449.

Mack, J. L. and Boller, F. (1977). Associative visual agnosia and its related deficits: The role of the minor hemisphere in assigning meaning to visual perceptions. *Neuropsychol.* **15**, 345–349.

McKenna, P. and Warrington, E. K. (1978). Category-specific naming preservation: A single case study. *J. Neurol. Neurosurg. Psychiat.* **41**, 571–574.

Marshall, J. C. (1977). Disorders in the expression of language. *In* "Psycholinguistics Series." (J. Morton and J. C. Marshall, Eds)." Vol. 1. Elek, London.

Marslen-Wilson, W. (1973). Linguistic structure and speech shadowing at very short latencies. *Nature* **244**, 522–523.

Marslen-Wilson, W. (1975). Speech perception as an interactive parallel process. *Science* **189**, 226–228.

Mattis, S., Kovner, R. and Goldmeier, E. (1978). Different patterns of mnemonic deficits in two organic amnestic syndromes. *Brain and Language* **6**, 179–191.

Miller, G. A. (1962). Decision units in the perception of speech. *IRE Transact. Inform. Theory* **IT–8**, 81–83.

Milner, B. (1966). Amnesia following operation on the temporal lobes. *In* "Amnesia." (C. W. M. Whitty and O. L. Zangwill, Eds). Butterworth, London.

Morton, J. (1964). A model for continuous language behaviour. *Lang. Speech* **7**, 40–70.

Morton, J. (1970). A functional model of memory. *In* "Models of Human Memory." (D. A. Norman, Ed.). Academic Press, New York and London.

Newcombe, F. and Marshall, J. C. (1967). Immediate recall of "sentences" by subjects with unilateral cerebral lesions. *Neuropsychol.* **5**, 329–334.

Newcombe, F. and Marshall, J. C. (1972). Word retrieval in aphasia. *Int. J. ment. Health* **1**, 38–45.

Oldfield, R. C. (1966). Things, words and the brain. *Q. J. exp. Psychol.* **18**, 340–353.

Potter, J. M. (1976). Dr. Spooner and his dysgraphia. *Proc. R. Soc. Med.* **69**, 639–648.

Remington, R. (1977). Processing of phonemes in speech: A speed-accuracy study. *J. Acoustic. Soc. Amer.* **62**, 1279–1290.

Rubin, D. C. (1975). Within word structure in the tip-of-the-tongue phenomenon. *J. Verb. Learn. Verb. Behav.* **14**, 392–397.

Saffran, E. M. and Marin, O. S. M. (1975). Immediate memory for word lists and sentences in a patient with deficient auditory short-term memory. *Brain and Language* **2**, 420–433.

Schilder, P. (1924). "Medizinische Psychologie." Springer, Berlin.

Schilder, P. and Curran, F. (1935). Paraphasic signs in diffuse lesions of the brain. *J. nerv. ment. Dis.* **82**, 613–636.

Schuell, H., Jenkins, J. J. and Jimenez-Pabon, E. (1964). "Aphasia in Adults." Harper and Row, New York.

Scoville, W. B. (1968). Amnesia after bilateral mesial temporal-lobe excision: Introduction to case H.M. *Neuropsychol.* **6**, 211–213.

Scoville, W. B. and Milner, B. (1957). Loss of recent memory after bilateral hippocampal lesions. *J. Neurol. Neurosurg. Psychiat.* **20**, 11–21.

Shallice, T. (1979). Neuropsychological research and the fractionation of memory systems. *In* "Perspectives in Memory Research." (L-G. Nilsson, Ed.). Erlbaum, Hillsdale.

Shallice, T. and Butterworth, B. (1977). Short-term memory impairment and spontaneous speech. *Neuropsychol.* **15**, 729–735.

Shallice, T. and Warrington, E. K. (1974). The dissociation between short term retention of meaningful sounds and verbal material. *Neuropsychol.* **12**, 553–555.

Shiffrin, R. M. (1975). Short-term store: The basis for a memory system. *In* "Cognitive Theory." (F. Restle, R. M. Shiffrin, N. J. Castellan, H. R. Lindman and D. B. Pisoni, Eds). Vol. 1. Erlbaum, Hillsdale.

Spreen, O., Benton, A. L. and Van Allen, M. W. (1966). Dissociation of visual and tactile naming in amnesic aphasia. *Neurol.* **16**, 807–814.

Tallal, P. and Newcombe, F. (1978). Impairment of auditory perception and language comprehension in dysphasia. *Brain and Language* **5**, 13–24.

Treisman, M. (1978). A theory of the identification of complex stimuli with an application to word recognition. *Psychol. Rev.* **85**, 525–570.

Turvey, M. T. (1973). On peripheral and central processes in vision. *Psychol. Rev.* **80**, 1–52.

Warrington, E. K. (1975). The selective impairment of semantic memory. *Q. J. exp. Psychol.* **27**, 635–657.

Warrington, E. K. and Rabin, P. (1971). Visual span of apprehension in patients with unilateral cerebral lesions. *Q. J. exp. Psychol.* **23**, 423–431.

Warrington, E. K. and Shallice, T. (1972). Neuropsychological evidence of visual storage in short-term memory tasks. *Q. J. exp. Psychol.* **24**, 30–40.

Warrington, E. K., Logue, V. and Pratt, R. C. T. (1971). The anatomical localisation of selective impairment of auditory-verbal short-term memory. *Neuropsychol.* **9**, 377–387.

Wernicke, C. (1874). "Der aphasische Symptomenkomplex." Cohn and Weigert, Breslau.

Whitaker, H. (1976). A case of the isolation of the language function. *In* "Studies in Neurolinguistics." (H. and H. A. Whitaker, Eds). Vol. 2. Academic Press, New York and London.

Zaidel, E. (1978). Lexical organization in the right hemisphere. *In* "Cerebral correlates of conscious experience." (P. A. Buser and A. Rougeul-Buser, Eds). North-Holland, Amsterdam.

Author Index

Q

R

S

Subject Index